PENGUIN BOOKS

ADDICTIVE DRINKING

Clark Vaughan is a former teacher of foreign languages and the original designer of School Year Abroad. A recovered addictive drinker himself, he has spent years counseling in the field. Mr. Vaughan lives on and sails his own boat in the Caribbean and off the Florida coast.

CLARK VAUGHAN

ADDICTIVE

The Road to Recovery for Those Who

DRINKING

Problem Drinkers and
Love Them

PENGUIN BOOKS

Penguin Books Ltd, Harmondsworth,
Middlesex, England
Penguin Books, 40 West 23rd Street,
New York, New York 10010, U.S.A.
Penguin Books Australia Ltd, Ringwood,
Victoria, Australia
Penguin Books Canada Limited, 2801 John Street,
Markham, Ontario, Canada L3R 1B4
Penguin Books (N.Z.) Ltd, 182–190 Wairau Road,
Auckland 10, New Zealand

First published in the United States of America by
The Viking Press 1982
Published in Penguin Books 1984
Reprinted 1984, 1985

LIBRARY OF CONGRESS CATALOGING IN PUBLICATION DATA
Vaughan, Clark.
Addictive drinking.
Bibliography: p.
Includes index.
1. Alcoholism—United States. 2. Alcoholism—
Treatment—United States. 3. Alcoholics—United States—
Family relationships. I. Title.
[HV5292.V38 1984] 616.86'106 83-25090
ISBN 0 14 00.6969 0

Printed in the United States of America by
Fairfield Graphics, Fairfield, Pennsylvania
Set in Video Baskerville

Grateful acknowledgment is made to the following for permission to reprint copyrighted material. Crown Publishers, Inc.: Selections from *Dr. Atkins' Superenergy Diet* by Robert C. Atkins, M.D., and Shirley Linde, copyright © Robert C. Atkins, M.D., and Shirley Linde, 1977. The Dial Press: A selection from *When I Say No, I Feel Guilty* by Manuel J. Smith, copyright © Manuel J. Smith, 1975. Hazelden Foundation: "The Lady," from a Hazelden copyrighted cassette entitled *The Liberated Woman* by Patricia McGuire.

TO PEGGY

First Mate extraordinary, top foredeck hand,
navigator, seacook, editing consultant,
and woman—among other things

AND TO ADDICTIVE DRINKERS DOWN THE AGES

So badly misunderstood by others,
so sadly misunderstood by themselves

PREFACE

This book has been written out of pure frustration. As a recovered addictive drinker, I remember vividly the years of trying to find answers to my questions as to how to get well. Always the answer was the same, in different words: "Just keep coming back to us and you will get better." When I asked how and why I would get better, so that I could have some faith in the process, the answers were also much the same. The authorities implied that their Olympian knowledge was too much for me to be able to understand in a few words, and the amateurs told me that it was too dangerous for me to try to understand. The fact was that neither group knew or was sure enough about any of the real answers to tell me what they really thought, although a few of the amateurs, at least, tried to be honest about it.

The psychiatrists said it might take years at forty dollars an hour to dredge up out of my childhood the original traumas that had made me a drunk, but I needed answers today (yesterday), with my life falling to pieces around me, and also, I was hurting like hell all the time I wasn't blind drunk. They and other doctors gave me tranquilizers, which turned me into a kind of zombie who didn't drink some of the time. The amateurs (Alcoholics Anonymous) at least gave me love and understanding, for which I shall be eternally grateful, and a lot of very practical help; but they kept talking about how belief in a Higher Power was going to do it for me. While I could accept the idea that such a belief might work for them, I knew that it wouldn't for me, because I had been looking for belief in a Higher Power for over forty years and saw no good reason for it to come suddenly, like a special-delivery package, in A.A. It didn't.

The truth is that, after wandering around this world for nearly fifty years, I had learned to accept very little on faith from authorities of any kind, whether they were auto mechanics or doctors of psychiatry. I had seen too many authorities make too many irreparable mistakes in the areas of their own "expertise," and too many who were obviously incompetent. So, when the psychiatrists were still stroking their beards knowingly and still asking me to tell them more about my childhood, while I got sicker by the day, I got out of that. At least that improved my financial situation, since at that time I still had my job as a teacher. The amateurs said, "Don't analyze." Well, they had belief in a Higher Power, but I didn't, so I decided it was analyze and figure out what was really helping them to get sober, or go down the tube. I thought that maybe belief in a Higher Power was a help, but I didn't think that was the whole story. I found out that it wasn't.

I got sober, mainly, by staying away from psychiatrists, doctors, and tranquilizers, by going to A.A., which helped at that time in some inexplicable way (even without God), and by analyzing anything and everything I could find about addictive drinking, psychology and recovery. I was a receptive audience for anybody who seemed to have a piece of the truth. What I learned was that all these sources usually had bits and pieces of common-sense truth that sounded reasonable enough to be worth a try. I looked especially carefully at anybody or any therapy that seemed to be actually helping people to get well. To hell with the high-flown theories of "experts," medical or otherwise; when you're on the sauce and want desperately to get off, you tend to be pretty pragmatic. If it works, I'll buy it, but it better make sense to me. Answers, that's what I wanted, and sensible-sounding answers were the only thing I could or would buy.

I didn't know what I was doing at first, but by trial and error I finally learned how to stay dry long enough for my thinking to begin to function better with more complicated ideas. I began to understand what had really happened to me to turn me into a drunk, and I began to see what I had to work at to get myself sorted out and really well. To do this, I found I could take advantage of a great variety of specialized facilities and therapies I hadn't even known were there, as long as *I* was able to figure out what it was that I needed from each, so that *I* could use it at a *time* when it made sense to *me* and in a *way* that made sense. Nobody could tell me this. I was the only person in a position to do it, because I was the only person who knew exactly how I felt and what I could accept at any particular stage in my recovery.

It worked. And so, in due time, I went into recovery counseling work, taking college courses in the evenings, continuing my reading in the field, and always trying to observe and evaluate every new idea that came along. Then, finally, out of all this there began to emerge a pattern of cause for addictive drinking—not "the cause," or "the final combination of causes," but a pattern of causal factors that distinguish the addictive drinker from the ordinary heavy drinker—even before he has become a drunk.

As an alcohol addiction counselor I saw people come for help, find hope, make a tremendous effort to get well, and then fall back into drinking again, not because they failed, but because the treatment system failed. Several things now seem certain to me: Getting well is a process of individually chosen progressive actions—specific things you can do to change your situation or yourself for the better, each leading to the next logical step. Each must be taken in a sensible order, without skipping around indiscriminately, as most people tend to do in their desperation, because they don't understand the process and because there is almost nobody around to tell them. Only you can know what you feel and what you can accept at any given time, so only you can intelligently diagnose and prescribe for your own recovery—but for that, you need answers. There are many charlatans in the recovery treatment field for the money alone, a fair number of sincere fools offering far-out instant cures that don't work, and many competent people who have parts of the answers. It is possible—in fact, absolutely necessary—for each individual to use one or more of the various good treatment facilities and/or therapies if he wants to have the best possible assurance of getting well. *Nobody does it by himself.* But how do you choose?

I have become convinced that no single therapy is broad enough to assure or even offer almost total freedom from dependence of any kind, but judicious use of a variety of facilities, therapies, and certain ideas can.

This is not a book full of generalized stuff about "alcoholism" and theories of possible ways to recover, as most of the some three hundred books I have read on the subject are. It is a practical do-it-yourself kit, with step-by-step instructions, an all-in-one recovery program planning guide based on what people who are truly getting well are doing and what others who got well did. As with all kits, you furnish the batteries. As an ex-drunk, who before that was a social drinker who never expected to become a drunk, I know how frightened, isolated, confused, and lost you may be feeling at this moment. At that time in my life there was no book to tell me where to turn. No professional has dared to write such a book, because he could not claim to offer his answers on the basis of a provable cause or combination of causes. No amateur, however successful in helping addictive drinkers to recover, has dared to write such a comprehensive guide, because he felt he didn't know enough answers. I do not know all the causal factors either, and I certainly don't know all the answers, but I do know the major ones, and I do know how the people who get well do it. That is what this book is about, and I believe that you can use it to chart your own way out of the valley of fear and confusion that is addictive drinking. I believe that, because I have been there and found my own way out. Since then, I have worked with a lot of others and helped them to do the same. Those who succeeded used these principles, actually chose their own recovery program once they had the information they needed. Recovery is just a matter of making intelligent choices, as you will see.

CONTENTS

PART TWO: HOW TO GET DRY AND STAY THAT WAY, THE SHORT-TERM GOAL

PART THREE: CHOOSING YOUR OWN SITUATION, THE LONG-TERM GOAL

PART FOUR: CHOOSING YOUR OWN SELF, THE ULTIMATE GOAL

PART ONE

THE ADDICTIVE DRINKER IS DIFFERENT

HEAVY DRINKER VS. ADDICTIVE DRINKER

There are two kinds of people who habitually or frequently drink very heavily and are often drunk, the *heavy drinker* and the *addictive drinker*. When they first begin drinking, the two are indistinguishable. Both appear to enjoy drinking heavily and the associations and feelings that go with it, and neither is addicted. For a long time, often for many years, there is no noticeable difference between them; they just choose to drink more heavily than other people. But at some point, a subtle difference comes into play, a difference that will ultimately make their major reasons for drinking as different as Scotch and beer. So if your drinking is causing problems, the first thing to do is to isolate the kind of drinking problem you have. If you want to do something about the problem, one kind is simple to deal with. The other is not simple at all.

A heavy drinker is a person who likes to drink for the feelings and associations that go with heavy drinking. He* may be drinking much more than his family wishes; but as far as he is concerned, no matter what his family may say, the pleasure he

*Throughout this book, I have generally employed the masculine pronoun. Except where noted, the feminine pronoun is interchangeable.

finds in heavy drinking outweighs whatever disadvantages he is aware of. In other words, he chooses to drink heavily because he enjoys it, and he is willing to pay the price, whatever that may be, for the pleasure. That is why he drinks that way, and that is all there is to it, unless he goes over the line into addictive drinking at some point, which many do.

Assuming that he does not become an addictive drinker, he will continue to drink heavily until the disadvantages outweigh the pleasures he gets from alcohol. If that happens, he can and will quit entirely, or cut down as much as he feels necessary to restore a happy balance. To do this, he can either taper off and avoid almost all discomfort, or quit "cold turkey," in which case he may have some uncomfortable physical withdrawal symptoms. Neither method requires a tremendous effort of will.

In my opinion, it is the heavy drinker who finally cuts back to more or less normal social drinking who has given support to the belief, even among some professional treatment people, that an addictive drinker can sometimes return to social drinking. Unable to distinguish between the drinking of the heavy drinker and that of the addictive drinker—in fact, usually unaware that there are two different kinds of excessive drinkers—some people assume that both are addictive. Since one can stop and the other can't, it is assumed that one has strength of character and willpower and the other is a weakling. Prejudice is always based on false assumptions.

An addictive drinker is a person who likes to drink for the feelings and associations that go with heavy drinking—but with an added and significant difference. He has lost control over where, when, and how much he drinks (under certain circumstances). He can never be sure. Sometimes he can control his drinking, either not drinking at all or severely limiting his consumption; at other times, and in spite of the best intentions and the use of considerable willpower not to drink, he drinks—often to "drunk." *The heavy drinker never loses control.* That is why he can quit or cut down whenever he chooses to. Because he *has* lost control, the addictive drinker frequently drinks too much when he knows beforehand that to do so is completely inappropriate in that social situation: when invited to his boss's home for dinner or before giving a very important speech, for example. The heavy drinker rarely makes such an error. Since he always has a choice, he can and usually does control his drinking under such circumstances. The significant difference is that of control or the loss of it.

Once a person clearly begins to lose control, he has become an addictive drinker. It is essential to be absolutely honest with yourself. Have you begun to lose control? Do you sometimes get drunk when you don't intend to, even planned very seriously not to, and may even have promised someone you wouldn't? Yes, anyone can get drunk by mistake when he planned to drink sensibly—*once or maybe even twice*—but we're not talking about once or twice. If there is any doubt in your mind, we can nail it down easily with the self-test in the following section.

DO I REALLY HAVE AN ADDICTIVE DRINKING PROBLEM?

If you think you may have an addictive drinking problem; if your husband, wife, or friends have been making veiled comments or complaining about your drinking; if you have "gone on the wagon" (decided to give up all drinking for a while) even once; if your doctor has ever told you to cut down on your drinking and you didn't; if you have had more than one drunk-driving ticket or more than one car accident after drinking—it is almost certain that you have a problem. If you usually have a glass of wine or three with certain unpleasant or boring housekeeping tasks, such as ironing or mopping the floor; if you are drinking more, more often than five years ago; if you tend to pick up a drink when you're feeling "down"; then you probably have an addictive drinking problem. If there is any question in your mind, read a bit further and you will know for sure. If you are afraid to find out for sure, by the way, you already have the answer—but don't let it frighten you. We now know why people have addictive drinking problems and how to deal with them.

Take the following test, but remember that it is of no value whatsoever unless you are completely honest in your answers. For this reason, I suggest you write the answers on a piece of paper so that there will be no evidence left on the page. This should be an entirely private matter between you and the test.

Twenty Questions

1. Can you or could you at any time in your life drink more than other people without showing it?
2. Do you often have a drink before going to a party where you know that drinks will be served?
3. Do you sometimes drink enough to get high when you are alone?
4. Do you ever have arguments (or "discussions") with any members of your family about your drinking or the money it costs?
5. Do you ever decide to limit yourself to a certain number of drinks at a party and then sometimes go over that limit?
6. Do you usually want a drink when you're angry, frustrated, or otherwise uptight?
7. Do you need a drink at a specific hour daily?
8. Have you ever decided to stop drinking entirely for a specific period of time and then not kept your promise (to yourself or others)?
9. Do you ever sneak an extra drink at a party or make yours stronger, so the others won't know?
10. Do you sometimes drink to build up your self-confidence?

11. Are you drinking more, more *often* than you did five years ago?
12. Do you ever lie about how much you've had to drink?
13. Do you ever wake up in the morning and find that you can't remember some of what you did and said the night before when you were drinking?
14. Have things you did or said while drinking embarrassed you or members of your family on a number of occasions?
15. Do you tend to think of people who do not drink at all as stuffy and boring?
16. Do you find that you tend to finish your first drink faster than most other people?
17. Do you think it would be difficult to enjoy life if you could never have another drink?
18. Do you often have drinks after dinner, as well as before, when you're at home?
19. Would it be very unlikely that you would leave a drink half full on the bar or table because you just didn't want any more?
20. Do you ever drink because you just can't stop worrying?

Turn to page 55 for the key to this test.

If you have just found out that you have an addictive drinking problem, or a potential problem, is it really any surprise to you? You have probably been mulling "you" over in your mind and suspected it for some time. Don't panic. Have a drink if you want one. Now is not the time to stop drinking. That comes later, if you choose to do it. Drinking is not your problem anyway, as you will soon see.

Let's get into what else you know about yourself—deep down. And let's get into some things that you and "they," the professionals in this business, have never talked about at all. After the next hundred pages or so, you will know not only what you want to do about your drinking and how to go about it but also why you had the problem in the first place. And you will have identified your particular version of the Real Problem—which is worldwide, from slum to suburb to the seats of great power.

WHERE ARE YOU ON THE SLIPPERY SLIDE?

At this point it may be helpful for you to look at "the slippery slide," the down elevator of alcohol addiction.* Here you will see where you are at the moment and where the always progressive nature of alcohol addiction will take you unless you choose to arrest it. Very few addictive drinkers touch every point on the slippery slide, but everyone will find himself somewhere.†

Since people's drinking patterns are highly individual, especially before the chronic stage is reached, you will find yourself on the slide by locating that section at which a cluster of symptoms most nearly fits you at this moment. Also, it should be understood that the order of events is highly variable for any one individual. Some people drink addictively almost from their first drinking experience. The first blackout (an experience of amnesia, a hole in the memory, not becoming unconscious) may occur early or late, as can the first car accident, drunk-driving ticket, loss of a job because of drinking, etc.

---

*"From the Road Back to the High Road," the up elevator to recovery, is in Part Four, pages 265–75.

†The first such progression was drawn by Professor E. M. Jellinek in 1951, *The Phases of Alcohol Addiction in Males*, and represents a summary of lectures delivered by him at the European Seminar on Alcoholism, Copenhagen, and copyrighted by the World Health Organization, Geneva. It was later updated and broadened in scope in 1973 by Dr. N. M. Glatt in the *British Journal of Addiction*, Volume 54, No. 2: "A Chart of Alcohol Addiction and Recovery." I have used these as a guide to my own updated equivalents, entitled "The Slippery Slide" and "The Road Back."

The Slippery Slide

HEAVY DRINKER OR EARLY STAGE OF ADDICTIVE DRINKING

—Social drinking
—Gets very high (drunk*) occasionally for fun and excitement
—Increasing ability to drink more than other people without showing it (tolerance)
—Drinking after work or before dinner becomes a custom
—Occasionally drinks for relief of pressure
—Often drinks more than most at parties
—Drinks faster than others

CRUCIAL STAGE OF ADDICTIVE DRINKING

—Begins to lose control over where, when, and how much to drink
—Drinking for relief of pressure becomes more frequent
—Sneaks drinks or drinks secretly
—Decrease of ability to stop drinking when others stop
—Feelings of guilt about things done or said while drinking become frequent
—Memory blackouts begin or increase in frequency
—Drinking too much always blamed on other people and circumstances
—Grandiose and aggressive feelings and behavior while drinking
—Reproofs by family and/or friends
—Persistent remorse

---

*The word "drunk" is almost meaningless today, because it is so amorphous, so different in meaning from one person to another. I would say that a person is drunk when he suffers clearly notable motor impairment (staggering, slurred speech), irrational or obviously inappropriate behavior (uncharacteristically crude, silly, or highly repetitive speech). However, an experienced addictive drinker can learn to mask and control these symptoms with practice and great willpower to such an amazing extent that he can be very drunk indeed with no one in the room aware of it.

CRUCIAL STAGE OF ADDICTIVE DRINKING

—Drinking for relief of emotional pain becomes common
—Loss of control over where, when, and how much to drink occurs more and more
—Automobile accidents and drunk-driving tickets become more likely
—Promises and resolutions to quit or cut down fail
—Feels more and more different, misunderstood, and alone
—Unreasonable resentments achieve serious proportions
—Tries going on the wagon, changing drinking pattern, and geographic cure—to no avail
—Problems caused by drinking increase exponentially
—Unable to discuss the problem with others
—Rejects friends who drink normally
—Family fights begin or increase
—Serious loss of self-respect has occurred
—Work suffers as result of poor judgment, mistakes, accidents, and lost work time
—Begins to neglect eating
—Begins to drink in morning to control shakes and to be able to function
—Begins to drink with inferiors
—Drinking alone and blackouts now common
—Indefinable fears, bitter resentments, and insoluble problems are constant

CHRONIC STAGE OF ADDICTIVE DRINKING

—Bitter arguments and fights with family have become common
—Loss of or resignation from job
—Loss of all interests that do not include drinking
—Loss of family
—Binge drinking for days around the clock now common
—Decrease in alcohol tolerance is notable
—Malnutrition and serious physical problems

CHRONIC STAGE OF ADDICTIVE DRINKING

—Frequent jailing for public drunkenness
—Hospitals or asylums
—Almost total loss of self-respect
—Moral deterioration (stealing, begging, anything for a drink; loss of concern about physical appearance and personal hygiene)
—Totally lost, hopeless, and miserable except when drunk, and often even then
—Serious physical conditions advanced (brain damage, cirrhosis of the liver, etc.)
—Death from accident or progressive physical deterioration, with the likelihood of insanity as a way station

If none of the really bad things listed on the slide have happened to you yet, the always progressive nature of the illness guarantees that they will, if you are an addictive drinker and continue drinking. This is so invariably true that these things are commonly called the "yets" by counselors and others in the field. The first day of counseling a man who had never had a "yet," I told him that he certainly would suffer the "yets" in due time if he kept on. Three days later he came to see me again, and his first words were, "You bastard! You said it would happen, but did you have to make it happen so soon? I left you on Friday, had a few *last* drinks in a bar, and started to drive up to that recovery home you recommended. On the way I got lost, had an accident, socked a cop, spent the night in jail, and now I'm going to court on charges of drunk driving and assaulting an officer—" The "yets" can come that fast.

According to the extent of the varying physical, psychological and environmental factors in each case, the whole process from the first drink to the chronic stage usually occurs in seven to twenty-five years. The average is fifteen years. For women this period is often shorter.

The text which accompanies the Jellinek chart (see footnote, page 8) states the following, with which I wholeheartedly agree:

A BLACKOUT is a partial amnesia without loss of consciousness; intoxication may not be apparent. If it happens frequently after medium amounts of alcohol, the blackout foreshadows alcohol addiction.

When the drinker begins to have drinks of which others do not know (sneaking drinks) and when he is preoccupied with whether there will be enough liquor at any occasion, he gives evidence that drinking means something else to him than to the average drinker. [I prefer the words "normal drinker" to "average drinker" here.] For others it is a custom or part of their diet, but for him it has become a necessity. It has passed from beverage to drug.

The slippery slide applies equally to the periodic drinker, except when he does not drink or sticks to social drinking for an extended time. These dry or completely controlled periods may be long, many months in some cases. However, the progressive nature of alcohol addiction still applies. Binges and periods of loss of control tend to become longer with the passage of time, and the periods between become shorter, until the periodic drinker is indistinguishable from the daily addictive drinker in the final stage.

Probably the most common pattern in France (relatively uncommon in the United States) is that of the addictive drinker who is rarely or never drunk, but also rarely or never sober. These people do not exhibit the extremes of behavior seen in those who frequently get thoroughly drunk. For this reason, in a drinking society such as that of the United States, they may appear to be controlling their drinking, thus not addicted. Nevertheless, they have, in fact, lost control, because they can no more stop drinking than the more obvious addictive drinker, except for essentially meaningless periods of time to prove a point, if the motivation to do so is sufficient. The only advantages to this type of drinking are the decreased likelihood of serious accidents and the lesser amount of physical damage caused by alcohol, since the greatest bodily damage is a result of high blood alcohol concentration, such as occurs when an executive comes home sober and drinks four big martinis in an hour. The typical skid-row bum tends to drink more or less constantly, like the French type mentioned. Also, he has usually lost his tolerance by then, so it takes far less to get him drunk. As a result, he never reaches very high concentrations of alcohol in his blood and can frequently go on for years with relatively little physical damage.

The beginning of loss of control is very hard to identify at first, because normal people drink too much once in a great while. Maybe they have not yet learned to recognize their normal limits. Perhaps they are drinking a powerful unfamiliar cocktail that tastes innocuous; perhaps they are drinking on an empty stomach or when very tired; or perhaps there has been a particularly stressful event in their lives, which signals a sudden unusual need for relief of stress. The key to the difference is the five words "once in a great while." A normal adult (heavy drinkers excluded) drinks to the point of drunkenness no more than one to three times a year for all reasons. An addictive drinker will do so much more often than that, even though he may not drink at all for long periods.

Loss of control in the early and crucial stages is not a constant, but it is always progressive. Control is lost at first only on rare occasions. Then, with time, the occasions occur more and more often, as drinking occurs more and more often. It comes on so subtly that before you even begin to think you're "that kind of girl," you are.

PROFESSIONAL FAILURE TO IDENTIFY THE REAL PROBLEM

Failure to identify the Real Problem has, for a long time, made a proper understanding of addictive drinking impossible. As a result, recovery occurred in a very small proportion of cases.

An example of this failure of understanding is the continued use, even to this day, by professionals and laymen alike, of two labels that cause further misunderstanding and confusion in the minds of all but a very few: *alcoholism* and *alcoholic*.

Here are their definitions (from *The American Heritage Dictionary of the English Language*): "Alcoholism" is "a chronic, pathological condition, chiefly of the nervous and gastroenteric systems, caused by habitual and excessive alcoholic consumption." Clearly, this word as defined is limited to the purely physical effects of habitual alcohol abuse on the nervous system and other parts of the body. The word "alcoholic" is defined as "suffering from alcoholism." The trouble is that these two words—as used by "friends," people on the street, partygoers, and many professional medical people—do not have the dictionary's severely limited and highly specific meaning.

Society's present definition would sound more like this: "Alcoholism is a terrible physical and mental condition a person gets into because he does not have the strength of character and sense of personal responsibility to control his drinking." What we've got here is prejudice and social stigma—not a definition at all. And as you might or might not expect, this social stigma is usually accepted by the addicted person about himself.

One person uses Tylenol for his headache. Another uses Demerol, and a third takes aspirin. Would any reasonable person use the terms Tylenolic, Demerolic, or aspirinolic to describe a person suffering from a headache?

The concern of society and of the addicted person should be with the reason for the addiction, not with the pain killer the individual uses to find relief. In the mind of the addictive drinker his choice of analgesic—alcohol—offers at least the illusion of solving the problem and at least temporary relief from the "pain." However, he realizes after a while that it does not solve the problem most of the time. The real reason he keeps drinking is that it *does* relieve the pain. He may realize that his drinking usually makes the problem much worse and creates new ones, yet he continues because he knows no other effective way to relieve the pain. (Of course, sometimes he may drink for the same reasons other people do.)

The rest of this book is concerned with the almost too simple answer to this. So simple we have been walking all over it and around it for several hundred years, looking in vain for complicated answers to a worldwide problem. Today it is possible for any person addicted to alcohol to learn how to break that addiction and turn his life into an exciting and challenging adventure. The problem is that it has been almost impossible to find out how to go about it. If that sounds strange, consider the situation today:

1. The medical profession today is highly specialized. It takes far too much of a doctor's free time just to keep up with developments in the field of medicine in general, and in his field of specialization in particular, to allow time also for in-depth study of addictive drinking, which is both subtle and complicated. Add to that the fact that the subject of addictive drinking was not even taken up in American medical schools until very recently. And even now the information taught is usually inadequate, inaccurate, or both. As a result, doctors have had so little success in treating addictive drinking that many do not even try, or simply prescribe tranquilizers or recommend joining A.A. (Alcoholics Anonymous).

2. The psychiatric profession is still dominated by the ideas of Freud and some of his followers, and this profession, most counselors agree, has the lowest batting average of all in treating addictive drinkers. Only in recent years has a growing number of psychiatrists begun to break away from those useful but sorely out-of-date ideas which necessitated deep psychoanalytical search for childhood traumas. This modern group works with the patient as he is at the time of entering therapy, using modern methods to help him deal with his problems as they exist today, without too much concern for the early causes, and they often achieve marked success. The important question for this modern school is not "Was this forest fire (of abnormal behavior) caused by a

match or a bolt of lightning?" but rather, "Do we know how to put out forest fires?" However, very few of these excellent specialists understand addictive drinking sufficiently to make their modern expertise effective for the addictive drinker.

Since psychiatrists, like other doctors, have to go through medical school, and are indoctrinated there with the wonders of pills and a myriad of marvelous nostrums, they are all too ready to prescribe tranquilizing drugs to addictive drinkers for a variety of apparently sound reasons. (See "Tranquilizers," page 115.) The trouble is that since they generally know very little about addiction to alcohol, they are quite unaware of the fact that an addictive drinker cannot overcome his addiction while on tranquilizers, even when taking only prescription doses. In addition, the addictive drinker often combines the prescribed tranquilizer with booze, an action that brings higher and faster kicks, but is also frequently fatal.

3. The psychologists know a great deal about how the human animal functions mentally and emotionally, but they rarely understand addictive drinking, which is a highly specialized problem for which their training has not prepared them. In addition, they usually come across as the professional trying to help the poor addict, and addictive drinkers, with their damaged egos, cannot stand authority figures. They often feel that the psychologist is playing games with their head, and this they cannot bear.

4. Neither the medical nor any other profession has been able to agree on The Cause of addictive drinking. So any charlatan who wants to make money, any fool with a theory, any well-meaning person with a part of the truth in his hands, is free to offer treatment for addictive drinking, simply because nobody can prove that he is wrong. Much confusion and harm are the result.

5. The vast majority of good people working in the field today, many of them recovered addictive drinkers, are also highly specialized, working in detoxification centers, recovery homes, or hospitals. However dedicated and totally in-

volved in their work they may be, they are in no position to see or help with the big picture, the long-term process of recovery appropriate for each individual. They see a person in trouble whom they can help in their particular area of knowledge and treatment. This they usually do well. But each sees him for only a short period before he moves on to someone and something else. There is no continuity of treatment, and continuity is essential.

6. There is another large group working in the field. These are the members of Alcoholics Anonymous. As recovering addictive drinkers, they have a unique practical and emotional understanding of the condition, which is virtually impossible to attain for anyone who has not gone through it. And they have the principles and long practical experience of A.A. to guide them. As a result of this understanding, knowledge, and experience, they are able to identify with and communicate with the addictive drinker who wants to get well, and they have good advice to offer. These men and women, some of them working professionally in the field, have had far more success in helping addicts to recover than all other professional people combined, and this is readily admitted by most professionals. However, these people usually have a limited professional expertise and are, in fact, amateurs—remarkably successful as far as they are able to help, but amateurs nevertheless. As such, they, too, are unable to see the big picture, and thus are limited in their knowledge of what has to be done if the drinker is to get truly well.

Add to all this the fact that most groups and individuals in the field of alcohol addiction treatment disagree with one another about "causes" and methods of treatment. In most cases, they don't even know or understand exactly what the other people are doing, because they are totally involved in their own work and blind to everything else. The result is very little referral of individuals from one group to another, with the outstanding single exception of A.A., which is recommended by almost everyone in the field. (There is one responsible agency, whose business is not primarily treatment but information and referral. This is the National Council on Alcoholism. It is discussed on page 68.)

To sum up: The entire field of alcohol addiction treatment is a mess.

Now consider the fact, which most good professionals will verify, that the process of recovering from addictive drinking is one of moving by logical stages of personal growth from the moment the individual first thinks seriously about solving a drinking problem to final freedom from dependency on any drug, institution, or person—and each person's needs are different. This is perhaps the most basic problem in recovery, especially because individual counseling to help each person choose a logical growth program is virtually nonexistent.

CHOOSING YOUR OWN RECOVERY PROGRAM

Given the above situation, where do you turn for help? How much help do *you* need? What kinds of treatment from all the kinds available? The answer is, I don't know; you have to do it yourself. That is why I have written this book, to try to give you the information *you* will need to understand your own particular problem and to make the intelligent choices *you* must make in order to plan a sensible, logical program of recovery. At present, no one else can do it for you.

As you will soon see, the addictive drinker is faced with one major obstacle in trying to do the planning job himself. Because of certain effects that occur in all addictive drinkers, to some degree at least, the drinker cannot trust his own judgment, because he cannot see the full reality of his own condition, especially at first. And this will continue to be true for a considerable length of time. (Explained in "Assault on Denial," page 44.) However, it will be less and less true as progress toward recovery is made; and if he hangs in there, the recovering addictive drinker will see many signs of progress even in the earliest stages.

It is simply a matter of choosing to do much more than seems necessary to you at first. If you don't do so, you will get drunk again. Thus you have an automatic warning system. Getting drunk again means you didn't choose to do enough. So you sober up again, if you're still alive, and choose more the next go-round. It took eighteen months and three drunks, including one that lasted three weeks, to teach me that lesson. And thousands have the same experience; so don't be surprised or discouraged if it happens to you.

As I said, drinking is not your real problem—it's only a medicine, the aspirin for the headache. So let's begin to look at the Real Problem.

If you become exasperated with all this explanation and delay, it is understandable. It is typical of the addicted person to become exasperated whenever he does not find instant satisfaction. However, the simple answers are not simple to understand if we do not proceed by sensible stages. Those who are recovering completely, by whatever method or combination of methods, are all doing it in essentially the same ways, ways that experience has proven work. It is these ways that I have attempted to describe and explain in this book, but it's a complex business and we can only go at it one step at a time.

STRESS—THE SURFACE MANIFESTATION OF THE REAL PROBLEM

Is the makeup of an addictive drinker different? I think so. After long observation in the recovery field of hundreds of persons, extensive questioning (using a controlled questionnaire) of A.A. members in several cities, and an exhaustive reading of published works in the field, including those written by both professional authorities and former drunks, I have come to the conclusion that the addictive drinker is different in four fundamental ways. The first involves his body chemistry; the second his inability to deal appropriately with stress; the third his faulty perception of reality; and the last, but not least, his genius for denial of his real situation.

I have found also that starting with an explanation of the stress problem in any discussion with an addictive drinker gets us further faster.

Every person on earth is under some degree of stress, as a result of physical, mental, and emotional factors, twenty-four hours a day, every day. First, physical stress. The degree of complex interaction among nerves, muscles, and bones required to bring about even apparently simple body movements is truly incredible, even for such an apparently simple action as writing your name. This was brought home to me with great force near the end of my drinking days, when I found that, stone-cold sober and not suffering from the shakes, I could not write my signature in a form that could be identified as definitely mine. Too much alcohol had thrown my whole delicate muscle control system just a little out of whack—temporarily—and the result was shocking to me. Yet, under normal circumstances, we write our signature automatically, without thought or awareness of effort.

Our mental and emotional equipment runs in a similar manner, the operational units of each interacting together with amazing precision to achieve organized conscious thought and emotional balance. And here also we have become so accustomed to controlling these equally delicate systems that we operate them almost entirely *unconsciously* and *automatically*. Example: While crossing a street, my mental computer automatically measures the speed and distance of oncoming cars. In the emotional area: I feel pleased when my son brings home an "A" paper, or I bark at him for playing his rock music too loud, but I don't think about my emotional state when I do this. I am on full automatic. We are usually unaware of stress in such cases.

On the other hand, when we call upon ourselves to perform above and beyond the level of our normal everyday activities, we become immediately conscious of stress. Physical stress: If I want to load a hundred-pound bag of corn into a truck, I must consciously think about where to place my hand to get a good hold and remember to bend my knees and lift with my legs, and I will be conscious of the effort needed to perform the lift. Emotional stress: Here stress above and beyond the everyday level gets a whole lot stickier. When my wife took our children to visit her parents for two weeks, leaving me suddenly alone with four walls, I became so miserable that I was conscious of my loneliness, my inability to function well by myself, and my emotional distress (stress). Since I was an addictive drinker at the time, my "solution" was 86-proof.

It takes a long time and considerable suffering to reach a normal adult level of adaptation to even the usual stresses of life—all the years from babyhood to adulthood, in fact. When a baby becomes conscious of the world around him, he takes a rather dim view of it a good part of the time, to judge by the amount of crying and yelling that goes on. He wants what he wants when he wants it. And he yells. From the moment he first gets the message that the world and other people do not exist exclusively for his entire satisfaction and pleasure until the day he dies, he is going to spend a lot of time worrying and suffering in order to adjust to that nasty fact. This is actually what a large part of growing up and maturing is all about.

It isn't easy, but most people manage to bumble through well enough, so that they can get along in life without coming apart at the seams when the going gets tough.

Every person's level of stress is constantly rising and falling. In well-adjusted people, this process is easily kept within comfortable limits, because they have learned—without conscious thought—a whole array of attitudes and simple methods of reducing stress whenever it rises above a comfortable level. Occasionally, when really provoked, the usual attitudes and methods are inadequate and the well-adjusted person's stress level rises to "blowing point." When that happens, these people scream, swear, throw things, smash something, or hit out at someone or something. Others use more sophisticated techniques (take a walk, visit a friend, construct a model, paint a picture, bake a cake, write in a diary). But of whatever kind, these actions function to reduce the pressure to a manageable level. These are healthy safety valves. The heavy stress is over, gone, done with.

The bumbling-through method of growing up and maturing, resulting from the unconscious learning of attitudes and stress-reducing mechanisms used to deal automatically with each problem, resolving each, one by one, produces adaptation to this world and appropriate response to stress in some people better than in others. We who become addicted to alcohol or other substances or behaviors did not learn how to use these mechanisms well. ("Learn" is hardly the right word here, as the process is a sort of osmosis—entirely unconscious. There are no schools or courses to teach "emotional fitness" as there are for "physical fitness.") As a result, many of these stresses, even those of normal daily living, are not resolved. For us they are not "over, gone, done with."

Consequently, the addictive drinker operates differently. While sober, he may blow up like other people on rare occasions, but usually it is impossible for him to blow up unless he has been drinking. For years he has felt that such behavior was stupid and unacceptable, because he was conditioned to feel that way by his parents, or because he came to the conclusion long ago that people would not like him for it and that it did not get him what he wanted. So he has become conditioned to maintain iron control, jamming every hurt, insult, frustration, and anger down inside where it won't show—but where it can simmer and boil into deep and bitter resentments against what he believes to be uncaring, stupid, vicious people, an impossible chain of inimical circumstances, and bad luck. These resentments then grow, fester, and compound into a massive *generalized* resentment.

If we drink addictively long enough, we become certifiably *paranoid.*

We addictive drinkers have all fought back with great courage and tremendous effort, frequently achieving spectacular successes along the way, but however much we may succeed in the eyes of other people—and even temporarily in our own—we cannot seem to win, to find the contentment and peace we need so badly. We can go along quite well for varying periods of time, actually feeling remarkably happy and even beginning to think that perhaps we are finally on the verge of finding that elusive comfort, but it always seems to fall apart. And back come the depressions, the fears, the sense of being different from other people, and the sense of failure as a person. No one who has not experienced it can possibly appreciate how terrible, how desperate that feeling is. It is an exquisite form of torture, which, at times, becomes literally unbearable. *Here is maximum compulsion.* It is not compulsion to *drink,* however. It is, rather, compulsion to find relief from unbearable pain.

However, when we speak of compulsion, we are not always talking about maximum compulsion; we are usually talking about *abnormally* high levels of unrelievable stress at some point below that level. Compulsion begins when a person's level of stress reaches the point of causing conscious discomfort (pain) which the individual cannot relieve by using whatever healthy, normal, stress-relieving techniques and attitudes he has learned in the process of growing up. The non-addicted person does not suffer compulsion—under normal circumstances—because his arsenal of such attitudes and techniques is sufficient for dealing with all his daily problems. (However, such people often get drunk, or are sedated, when faced with a traumatic event of major proportions, as the death of a spouse or child, because even their well-developed stress-relieving techniques and attitudes are inadequate at these times. Here the compulsion to drink is just as real as it is for the addictive drinker. The only difference is that the normal person does not do it habitually, because he does not suffer compulsion habitually.)

As the level of unrelievable pain (stress) rises, the level of compulsion rises, until the individual person's "stress threshold" is reached, the level of maximum compulsion. This is the point beyond which he can bear no more without finding relief or going insane. We addictive drinkers find relief with alcohol; other compulsion-driven people with other substances (tranquilizers, food, whatever) and other behaviors (workaholics, sportaholics, you know). Others do go insane, and that, too, is a form of stress relief.

After release of a high level of abnormal stress by means of a drunk (the safety valve), the drinker's total stress level may be very low. When it is, compulsion for relief is minimal, and the addictive drinker can easily refrain from drinking and, frequently, even control his drinking, if he wants to badly enough. However, when the level of compulsion (unrelievable stress) approaches too close to the "stress threshold" or actually reaches it, the concept of willpower becomes meaningless. This is the reason for the apparent unpredictability of the stress drinker's drinking.

People who have never had a serious addiction problem have wondered for centuries how an intelligent addictive drinker who has managed to stop drinking for a period of time can choose to go back to drinking, knowing full well that it is ruining his life and will kill him eventually. Maximum stress level, compulsion, is the answer. At that point *he has no choice*. It's about as reasonable to expect a person to use willpower to refrain from going to the bathroom at the level of maximum compulsion in a case of diarrhea.

At this point you may be saying, "Well, it sounds reasonable, but I'm not suffering abnormal stress. Oh, sometimes, yes, but I have to drink lots of times when I'm not feeling any stress at all, so I guess this doesn't really apply in my case." Fact: The medical profession has not yet found any reliable way to measure emotional stress. Actually, if you are an addictive drinker, you can assume that you have slowly learned to adapt to more and more stress over a period of years so gradually that you may be living under abnormal stress—relatively low levels of it, at least—most of the time and be almost completely unaware of it. How can you compare your normal stress level with that of other people in order to know whether your stress level is abnormal or not? In fact, you can't.

I used to comment from time to time, when I was drinking, that I ran hot like a good diesel engine. I thought it was beneficial to be that way, to be keyed up to produce at my best. Now I know that I was dimly recognizing the fact that I was living under abnormal stress most of the time, and drinking more and more to relieve the pressure. I must have said a thousand times to my wife, "I need a drink. I've got to get off the dime."

Over and over, in counseling, addictive drinkers have said to me, "Yes, but I wasn't under any abnormal stress when my alcoholic drinking began." Then I ask them to tell me what was going on in their lives at the time, and it always comes out: the concealed shyness and fear of failure in the professional comedian; the sense of being different of the Mafia "hit" man, who told me he really believed that he felt "nothing at all" when he killed a man on contract but knew that a "normal" person would; the housewife who was a pillar of society and supermother "happily married" to a very successful businessman (the "American Dream for Women"), who later admitted she got through the winter by planning the summer, through the weekdays by planning the weekend, and saw no alternative for years to come. Then there was Louise, in and out of A.A. for ten years, who swore to me that she was under no particular stress when she started drinking addictively. Later, in a completely different context, she mentioned that at that time she had had a hysterectomy, and was allergic to pain killers, so she had to drink for the relief of the physical pain. This may be true, but it is equally clear that the emotional pain of the operation was at least as great, if not greater, and that she drank more for that reason than for the physical pain. If you're an addictive drinker and you believe you're not living under abnormal stress, think about it.

As a child, I remember that I was often having such a good time playing that I would put off going into the house to go to the bathroom, until I sometimes wet my pants. I outgrew that, but the principle continued to have a lot to do with my way of living—right up to sobriety. We addictive drinkers tend to be people of great energy, drive, and enthusiasm. We are so engrossed in what we are doing, and so determined, that we pay no attention to the state of our bodies and minds, certainly never to anything like preventive maintenance. We tend to wear ourselves out physically and emotionally, drinking for energy and lift when we belatedly feel the need, and still pushing to do more in a day than most sensible people would dream of. Then, worn out and full of booze, we finally go to bed, where, because of the booze and our state of almost permanent nervous tension, we sleep poorly, often waking feeling almost as tired as when we went to bed. Or we stay up all night if we're having fun or meeting a work deadline, and then go right on to work at the office, school, or shop, along with the normies who slept all night. We skip meals or grab a junk-food sandwich instead of having a proper meal, so we can get right back to the fun or the job.

As stress illness progresses, addictive drinkers tend to let up on the physical excesses gradually, because the constantly increasing emotional and nervous strain drains more and more energy. In fact, all fun activities slowly drop away, given up for work, worry, and booze. Still, the drinker pays no attention to the needs of the body and mind for regular balanced meals, rest, and relaxation. Work, work, work, and worry, worry, worry, and drink, drink, drink—more and more. That is the pattern to such an extent that by the time an addictive drinker goes for help, he has usually lost the ability to listen to his body and recognize the frantic messages it is sending. About all he is aware of is that he is terribly uptight most of the time, and tired, and we all know what the answer is for that—hoist a few to "get off the dime." This is unrelieved stress in spades.

The unconscious learning or not learning of stress-relieving mechanisms is particularly subtle in the emotional area. When people cry, scream, throw things, or suddenly bark harshly at someone, they are venting (relieving) emotional stress. When someone in a violent argument suddenly storms out of the house and walks for hours, going nowhere, he often doesn't realize that he was under heavy stress and so unconsciously set two stress-relieving mechanisms into operation: (1) He removed himself from the stress-creating situation (what the stress drinker is doing when he drinks for oblivion). (2) He used a long, tiring walk to remove the muscular tension created by the emotional tension.

We talk about physical and emotional stress as though they were entirely separate areas, but we do this only as a means of simplifying the problem, for purposes of understanding more easily. Actually, both these stress-creating areas are interdependent and interrelated. When the walk relieves the muscle tension, the emotional tension is relieved too, sympathetically. Tension headache is caused by emotional tension, an abnormal level of emotional stress, but the muscles at the back of the neck tighten up like iron rods, responding "sympathetically" (and becoming part of the problem).

The emotional area creates the most difficult problem for the addictive drinker, because it *is* so subtle. It is an art to be accurately aware of one's actual emotional state at any particular time with any degree of precision. What are the elements involved (anger, hurt, frustration, worry, fear, sorrow, envy, etc.) and how much stress is each responsible for? This is the art of self-awareness, knowing one's own emotional self intimately enough to discriminate, and it is difficult to learn. The rest of it, learning to assess the levels of physical stress (tiredness and physical strain), is far easier, because it is far more obvious.

When we consider that the learning of emotional stress-relieving techniques is primarily done unconsciously and that their use is usually both automatic and unconscious, it is easy to see how anyone might not learn some of them, or fail to learn how to use them correctly. This is the failure of the person *who is to become addicted*, if the word "failure" can be used with no implication of personal responsibility, as it should be in this case.

Over and above this "failure" is another vital factor which further compounds the problem. Society and even many parents have blamed the addicted person for his drinking behavior, and in almost all cases punished him unmercifully in untold numbers of ways on the false assumption that he had a choice—when compulsion made no choice possible. Yet society, and even more, the parents, had, and have today, a heavy responsibility for the addiction, a responsibility of which they have always been totally unaware. Society and parents spend a lot of time, money, and effort to train or condition young people to behave properly according to a complex system of rules designed to make it possible for large numbers of people to live closely together. This all adds up to our "social education."

A large part of that social education involves building into the individual a complex of attitudes and rules of behavior to cover every imaginable social situation, but often these attitudes and rules are too rigid, or become so in the individual. "A man does not cry," for example. Yet crying is one of the greatest stress-relieving mechanisms there is.

How many of these stress-relieving mechanisms are totally blocked out, conditioned out, of children by parents, teachers, churches, clubs, whatever, because the actions involved are considered to be inappropriate. *How often does the child misinterpret these injunctions as absolute, when in the mind of parents and society exceptions are considered a matter of course but not necessary to mention?* For example, most people would agree that it is all right for a man to cry in private for relief, but the typical addicted man can't cry at all unless drunk.

Trying to live up to the expectations of others in childhood becomes a way of life, *the* way of life to the person who knows no other, and is one of the greatest stress-makers there is. Consider a woman's attempt to live up to the expectations of "being a lady":

> The perfect woman, according to American middle- and upper-middle-class standards, should be a "lady," poised, serene, unruffled, competent. If she is married, she should have children, and she should be a wise and loving mother. As a result, she should have children who are well-adjusted, smart, successful, popular and handsome. She should be an excellent cook and housekeeper, a gracious hostess, and a warm and understanding companion. She should never look as though she has ever done any hard physical work, yet her home should always be immaculate. [Mr. Clean-clean.] She should be perpetually young and beautiful, slender and sleek, but plump in the right places. Her voice should be sweet, low, and seldom used. She should be clever in certain things, but never too bright. Too much education is not good for her. She should be faithful and devoted. She will always be offended by language which has a strong, negative emotional overtone, particularly if the language has a sexual connotation. This is because she is virginally pure and her ears are delicate.
>
> On the other hand, in the privacy of the bedroom she should be both compliant and aggressive, something of an athlete, and as knowing as Lolita or Fanny Hill—but only when her husband desires it to be so. She should be free from unsightly blemishes, soft, fragrant, and as obedient and responsive as a well-trained horse. She should never be angry, never rebellious, and always extremely patient. She may occasionally indulge in some kind of activity outside of the home with others of her sex, provided it is trivial and silly enough. In fact, it makes her amusing and she should be amusing. [Like Mary Tyler Moore's TV character.] She should be independent enough to find her own amusement when her mate is busy with more important business. But she should not have any more important business than her husband, home, and offspring. She should spend some

> time in church—it keeps her satisfied with her lot and helps with the family socialization. She should be a knock-out when her husband decides to share his social life with her. She must be beautifully groomed and dressed, very discreet in her conversation, and she should be able and willing to hold her liquor—at least well enough to be pleasant and relaxed, and to demonstrate that she is sophisticated and not too straitlaced.
>
> If she is not middle or upper class, she must still be cool, hip, and capable. If she has children, she must keep them out of sight and hearing range. Her man expects her to have beer and food ready for his friends at a moment's notice. She should remain quiet and in the background. She should be provocatively attractive, but aloof to all but her own man. She should be always faithful to him, though very tolerant of his roving eye. Whether she wants to or not, she had better hold his interest through sexual aggression. But she must not assert herself anywhere but in the bedroom. She should be able to hold quantities of liquor, but if she fails to hold it well she will provide entertainment and be encouraged to amuse others. However, when she returns home, she had better be prepared for her man's extreme disapproval.

Trying to live up to the expectations of others as to what is correct behavior for a woman libber can be just as stressful, and more so if such a woman still has one foot in society's "lady" and the other foot in society's "libber."

The total effect of early conditioning, the social-educating process, can lead not only to trying to measure up for the rest of your life, but also often results in blocking out *entirely*, inhibiting, some of the unconsciously learned stress-relieving mechanisms which might have made it possible for the potential addict to deal with his stress in normal ways, instead of being forced to find bottled relief as the only alternative.

When a person has failed to acquire some of the unconsciously learned stress-relieving methods and has had others blocked out by inhibitions, he doesn't have much left to work with. Then comes his first introduction to alcohol—instant stress relief. For a person who doesn't know any condition other than living twenty-four hours a day with an abnormal level of stress, though unaware that it is abnormal, is it any wonder that alcohol appears to be the magic elixir of life? Is it any wonder that he is soon drinking more, and more often, than other people?

As this person drinks more and more, and as his problems and frustrations become larger and more complex, the pressures created become much greater. So that now when he drinks, the floodgates open and the repressed emotions are suddenly released: he may actually try to live fantasies of revenge or heroic action; angry word battles with anyone close at hand, fights, high-speed driving (down the wrong side of the street), destruction of property are a few of the common results. Is it any wonder that "alcohol causes more violence than any other drug"? However, those who make this statement are wrong in one respect. Alcohol does not cause the violence. The potential for violence was there before the liquor, but it was completely locked in by inhibitions. Alcohol released the inhibitional dam, and the violence poured out.

People often comment on the unreasonable anger and the apparently illogical destructive acts of the drunk, when there seems little or no reason for them. In reality he is not reacting to a particular provocation, in most cases. He is simply suddenly venting the repressed rage of days or years. Violence and crying are only two of the expressions of emotion the addictive drinker can usually release only while drinking. Often he is hilariously happy, maudlin, foul-mouthed, or absurdly amorous. All this because he can't express his emotions when sober and so represses them to the point of explosion. The compulsion to drink is really the compulsion to release emotional pressure.

The addictive drinker does not always seek relief of emotional pressure only at the threshold level of stress (maximum compulsion). He also "chooses" to drink at any level (of compulsion) below that. Thousands of addictive drinkers (or those on the way) need a few drinks to release their sexual inhibitions. And it should be noted that one of the problems most commonly faced by recovering drinkers is the difficulty of making love sober. (See "Sober Isn't Sexy—At First, page 193.) Others drink to feel comfortable in social situations, to relax before a speech—in fact, whenever they feel uptight (any special stress). Drinking relieves every stress problem, and the addictive drinker soon sees booze as the answer, not only to special stress situations, but to any kind of discomfort. So he drinks to feel better when he has a cold or flu, when he is bored, or for the same reason that non-addicted people do—just to relax and feel better. When the individual begins to use alcohol as medicine to relieve the conscious pain of abnormal stress (compulsion), he has moved over the line from social drinking to addictive drinking.

Is it surprising, then, how everyday drinking becomes a way of life in the high-pressure middle years and leads to out-of-control addictive drinking in the late forties and early fifties, as is so often the case? It is not only effective where other techniques are inadequate, it is almost *instantly* effective, where the addictive drinker's limited store of other techniques is usually slow to act.

At some point, abnormal levels of stress become the addicted person's "normal." As times passes, the individual attempts to adapt and invariably achieves some degree of success, thus managing to push upward both his stress threshold and the maximum level at which he can *feel* normal. This is why he can function well at levels of stress that would cause many other people to scream and throw things for relief. This is perhaps admirable, but it also means that he may be the last person to realize that he is suffering a *stress illness*. This is also why the addictive drinker *enjoys drinking* more than other people. He feels no special stress, and so assumes he is as normal as the next guy; but when he drinks, he relieves far more stress than the next guy, and at the same time often releases more and deeper inhibitions, so his sense of relief and well-being are proportionately that much greater. He also has to drink *more alcohol* than the other person, because he has more stress to relieve and because he has developed "tolerance" (the ability to drink more than others before feeling or showing the same effects).

It is emotional stress raging out of control that is the major cause of addiction. That must be dealt with first. I know about bending my legs to lift a heavy weight safely and more easily. I know how to assemble all the elements of a problem, examine their interrelationship, and come up with a reasonably satisfactory answer. But I remember thinking so many times, "What a silly thing for someone to say," when he said to someone else, "Cheer up" or "Calm down." People don't just cheer up or calm down by choice, I used to think. Then when I started getting well, I discovered that a great many people actually know how to do just that, to "handle" their emotions. *They know how!* In fact, I have since learned *how* myself, to such an extent that I can control my own emotional climate almost as well as a thermostat controls room temperature. For me, this has been a revelation. I suspect it may be for you.

I am not saying that I can always keep all my feelings under perfect control. What I am saying is that I have learned a collection of attitudes and techniques—tricks, if you will—with which I can deal with my stress-created feelings (anger, guilt, resentment, etc.) to such a point, at least, that they can never run away with me the way they used to.

If you are addicted to *anything* and still don't think that stress is your problem, then tell me why every method of treatment which man has so far devised, by which addicted people are getting well, is almost entirely concentrated on helping them to learn new attitudes, actions, and techniques whereby they can avoid, reduce, deal effectively with, or compensate for the factors in their lives that are causing abnormal stress.

Stress is the surface manifestation of the Real Problem; "surface manifestation" because, in fact, it is necessary to understand that stress is only the top part of the iceberg. Later on we will examine what lies below the water. Unaware of the real causes of his emotional pain, the addictive drinker reduces or relieves the pain, not the causes of it, with alcohol. This is why I said alcohol is not the Real Problem. It is only the analgesic that the addictive drinker uses, because he knows no other way to relieve the pain.

What really happens in recovery and getting well is that you start out working to recover, and if you go at it right, you end up learning how to live and be happy in a way that very few people in the world ever know. The reason why is that most people learn how to live more or less by chance. To get well from addiction, you learn how to live by design.

There is also a beautiful corollary. After you have learned these new attitudes and techniques for reducing stress, and practiced using them for a while, you will find yourself using them automatically and unconsciously, just as other people do—but with an outstanding difference. Since you have learned to control your emotional climate consciously and rationally, rather than by pure chance, your control system is far more effective, and you are in a better position to deal with all kinds of stress-creating problems than are other people. And this is particularly true for the really traumatic stresses of life, such as the death of a loved one or sudden financial ruin. Most normal people are not prepared to handle those very well, but you can be.

Learning to live, not by chance, but by design, is the major focus in recovery from addictive drinking.

ACCEPTING, AND ACCOMMODATING TO, THE WORLD AS IT REALLY IS

In addition to an incomplete learning of healthy techniques and attitudes for dealing with emotional stress and the acquisition of damaging inhibitions, there is a second large problem area that creates massive stress in people who suffer from behavioral problems, such as addiction to alcohol.

This broad area—a faulty perception of reality—marks a second clear difference between the addicted person and so-called normal people.

Sometime, usually in early childhood and long before his first drink, something went wrong for the addicted-person-to-be. For some reason or complex of reasons, the normal growth process of adaptation was never completed, or, at least, not as well as it is in most people—the adaptation from the totally self-centered and highly imaginative world of the young child to full recognition and accommodation to the world as it really is; and this complete adaptation fails to occur even in full adulthood. As a result, the person retains such a vivid picture of the ideal world, the world as he would like it to be, as it *should be*, that he never manages to reconcile himself to the real world—the world as it is. A simple example is the expectation that the world and people should treat him fairly. They should, but they won't, and don't, a good part of the time. This is a fact, and nothing that a person can say or do will change it very much. It's fine to work for fairness and equality in the world and to try to treat others fairly yourself, if it pleases you to do so. It may even do some good; but to *expect* to be treated fairly in this world is to suffer constant hurts, frustrations, angers, and resentments. It just doesn't pay. But addicted people do it all the time, and most have been doing it since childhood. Failure to accept and accommodate to reality in this one area alone creates constant emotional stress, and so is a specific direct cause of addiction.

Until you have learned to accept the world as it is (rainy and snowy, often unfair, sometimes mad, and always demanding) and made a satisfactory adaptation to it, you will be recurrently and too often furious, sad, hopeless, disappointed, discouraged, depressed, frustrated, lonely, and afraid. Sound familiar? And every one of those feelings is a direct cause of heavy stress. They are felt by everyone at various times in their lives, but the addicted person, or the one heading that way, feels them much more often and far more deeply, because he has never learned to avoid, deal with, reduce, and compensate for stress to the degree that other people have.

The realist is in no way surprised when he is treated unfairly or when he has had a run of bad luck. Things happen that way; but he also knows that some people *will* treat him fairly, that there are ways to protect himself, and that there are runs of good luck, too. He knows that, if he is equipped with the right knowledge and attitudes, he will be able to minimize the effects of the bad things in his life and take full advantage of the good ones. Of course, he is not pleased when the bad things happen, but he balances that by being very pleased about the good ones.

If you are an addicted person, the idea that you could actually be—and react—this way may sound absurd, impossible. In a sense you are right. I doubt if anyone ever achieves perfect accommodation to the world as it is, but people do succeed in coming remarkably close sometimes. You may even know one or two and wonder how they manage to be so happy. What I am saying is that it's all a matter of degree, that an addicted person is so loaded down with unrealistic expectations that he is miserable much of the time, but that he can learn to have realistic expectations of the world to such a degree that his life becomes much more efficient and a joy to live most of the time. Then the residue of bad things is not a heavy load to bear. It all depends on your attitude, your point of view. The difference is incredible.

If you call yourself an idealist, as many addicted people do, if only to themselves, then an imperfect perception of reality is almost certainly an important part of your problem—although it is entirely possible to work for idealistic goals while being a complete realist. In fact, when a realist works for idealistic goals, he has by far the best chance of achieving them, as he does of achieving any goal; because, being a realist, he only works to achieve the possible and does so by working in sensible, practical ways.

Two amateur organic gardeners I know exemplify the difference beautifully. Both set out to have organic gardens for the same idealistic reasons. One was a realist, while the other had his head in the clouds. Apparently the latter assumed that since what he was trying to do was pure and good, it would naturally work out well. That assumption was unrealistic. He did not discover until much too late that while pesticide-free vegetables are better for you and taste better, too, all the "vegetarian" bugs take the same point of view. His beautiful, idealistic garden became a banquet for bugs, known affectionately as Don's Disaster by his friends.

My other idealistic friend was a realist. He didn't use pesticides either, but he knew he had to do *something* about bugs if he was to grow any crop worth having, so he found out how professional organic gardeners deal with bugs and achieved both his idealistic and practical goals.

Learning to cope with any and all kinds of factors that can create abnormal stress, either individually or in combination with others, is the first stage in recovery—after finding the means to stay dry long enough to make it possible for this learning to take place. This is like putting your finger in a small hole in a dike to prevent its getting bigger, and then putting in better and better patches (stress-relieving techniques) for the different kinds of holes. But this is not the way to solve the whole problem. You can't do that with patches. Patching the holes is a necessary emergency measure to buy more time—time to change old destructive, negative attitudes into new realistic, positive ones. Such attitudes can be acquired only over an extended period of time—six months to a year for a good beginning—and they are fundamental to recovery; building these new attitudes is analogous to the major reconstruction work of widening, heightening, and strengthening the dike so that holes (requiring patches) are unlikely to appear in the first place.

When a typical addicted person, late for an appointment, steps out the door and discovers he has a flat tire, he usually becomes frustrated, angry, and miserable, a condition not conducive to efficiency, either in changing a tire or in functioning well at the appointment. He responds in this way because of his unrealistic attitude, which makes him see the event as an insult and a frustration of his desire directed against him personally by fate, when, in fact, it is nothing more than a flat tire, which can and does happen to everybody. On the other hand, a person who has made a reasonable adjustment to reality, first, has allowed a time margin to cover such things as flat tires and traffic jams, and, second, sees the flat tire for exactly what it is, an occurrence that will delay him. He changes the tire and goes on to the appointment, with no added stress to affect his functioning there adversely. If the event has, nevertheless, made him late, he calls ahead to explain the situation and perhaps changes the appointment, so that the other person will not be inconvenienced. This is the only sensible and realistic way to deal with a small setback.

The addicted person's dike was never built wide, high, or strong enough to begin with, which is why the holes keep opening up. The well-adapted person's dike is wide, high, and strong. As a result, he has only an occasional trickle to deal with. When a leak does occur, he knows how to handle it, does so quickly, and goes on tending the garden of his life behind the protection of his safe and solid dike. He doesn't get furious, terribly frustrated, terrified of failure, suicidally depressed, or desperately lonely in the first place. His ups are not manic, and his downs are not depressive. Normally he is not "terrified" or "infuriated." For him the potential setback is a necessary symptom to let him know that some sort of action is required to deal with a threat to his well-being. It is for him, then, a useful thing. Instead of running around in circles wondering what to do, worrying himself into a state in which he can no longer think clearly, and getting drunk while the situation grows and compounds itself, he takes appropriate action (as in the previous example) to avert, deal with, or minimize the setback when it first appears. He deals with the trickles.

Building new, positive attitudes takes time. It is major reconstruction work. So, learning and using the more obvious stress-reducing techniques, in order to get through the emergency and buy time for the solid construction work to take place, is vital. The basic attitudes, however, are the long-term building blocks which are absolutely necessary if you are ever to have real self-confidence, peace of mind, and a reasonable modicum of happiness. It is the sum of these positive attitudes, working in concert, which results in acceptance of the world as it really is, practical accommodation to it, and joy in living. Recovery starts with hope and action, and continues with more and more hope and more and more efficient action as it chugs along, until—like a good diesel engine—there's almost no way to stop it once it gets going properly.

How does a faulty perception of reality occur in the development of an addictive person? Typically, it begins with the overprotection of the young child, so that he does not become aware of the unpleasant realities which surround him. Mother drives him to school, so that he does not have to cope with "bad" children or "bad" weather. He is not punished realistically for infractions of rules because of possible damage to his delicate psyche. When he tells his parents of his problems in getting along with other children at school, he is supported and they are blamed. And so it goes. He is filled with slogans in the guise of fundamental truths to such an extent that he comes to believe them absolutely: "Fighting is bad." "If it's wrong, it's wrong, no matter what other people do." "Act like a lady." "Don't make a spectacle of yourself." "Do unto others . . . [implying that they will treat him the same way]." The sum total of the child's absolute belief in such slogans (platitudes) guarantees a faulty perception of reality. Parents know, don't they?

By the onset of his teenage years, a child with such a faulty perception of reality is already set up for addiction. In a drinking society like ours, nearly everyone is introduced to alcohol by or before the age of sixteen. For most young people the first-time high is an exciting adventure, which may be repeated from time to time throughout their lives for fun and relaxation with relatively little danger. That is all it amounts to for them. For the young person who is to become an addictive drinker, however, the situation is often very different, not in kind, but in degree. Nearly all young people are insecure and suffer a good deal from shyness, although these feelings are often concealed behind a façade of pretended confidence and social ease. Our preaddictive boy or girl is feeling far more insecure and shy than the others and is more nervous about acceptance by his peers.* And, of course, his faulty perception of reality makes it impossible for him to make the appropriate adaptation. He expects everyone to like him. Why don't they? As a result, he usually tries two or three times as hard to win acceptance and popularity and, more often than not, succeeds only in coming on too strong and alienating the very people he wants most to impress. Now he feels more different and more shy and insecure than before. Consequently, he lives in constant fear and expectation of the next unkind remark, the next stupid blunder he will make, the next social failure. This is a low level of paranoia, which creates even more such incidents, either real or imagined—a perfect example of the negative, destructive attitudes which lead to addictive drinking. If he is a poor student or a very bright one, comes from a poor family or a rich one; in short, if he is in any way further set apart from the peer group, the whole problem is intensified. For such a person, the first-time high is usually more in the nature of a revelation, a miracle.

His abnormally high level of emotional stress, which he considers normal if he is aware of it at all, is suddenly washed away, and the resulting senses of perfect freedom, total well-being, and instant complete acceptance by his peers are pure joy. The experience is truly euphoric in a way that others cannot even begin to understand. Everyone around him becomes nicer and more friendly. Suddenly the world is as it should be. This is the true meaning of euphoria and the first step to addiction. The moment of discovery is so indescribably wonderful that he never forgets it for the

---

*For an excellent inside look at shyness and this period of youth, read *Shyness* by Philip Zimbardo, Ph.D. You will almost certainly find yourself in these pages if you are an addictive drinker.

rest of his life. Whenever he is uncomfortable, under strain or tension of any kind, he remembers the magic elixir that is always available and turns to it with gratitude.

People often say that the addictive drinker is a loner who withdraws from other people and the world itself more and more as the illness progresses. Of course he does. For years, usually, the hope and optimism of youth buoy him up. No matter how shy, insecure, and frightened he may feel in his teens, things will be better when he becomes an adult. Then at twenty-one, when he still feels the same way, still somehow different from other people, he finally decides that some people just *are* different and he must be one of them. After all, the great men and women throughout history were different, so what's so bad about that? It's harder, yes, but maybe that's the price of greatness. (The beginnings of grandiosity and false pride?) With this driving motivation, he works longer hours with greater intensity than others on the same job and spends extra time thinking about his work and looking for ways to do it better and faster. As a result, he is often the best welder in the shop, the best student in the class, the salesman with the monthly sales record. Promotions come, and it looks as though he was right after all. Of course he is drinking more now, but so is everyone else. It's normal to hoist a few with the boys after work: "You have to drink with your customers," "What's a party if you don't loosen up a little so you can all have fun?" Then, too: "You have to tie one on every so often just for a healthy break from the routine," and "A few drinks in the right atmosphere are just what the doctor ordered to make everything just right for lovemaking." And everyone else agrees.

During this period, while he is drinking more and more often and getting drunk, sometimes on purpose and sometimes by mistake, it all seems perfectly normal, and in fact, he can hold his liquor better than most people. He's the guy who takes the others home or drinks them under the table. (This, of course, is because he has developed a tolerance for alcohol, a sure proof according to many professionals in the field of alcohol addiction that he is already addicted.) Still, he has not lost all control. He finds it easy to mesh his drinking with his overall schedule, so that it rarely interferes seriously with his job, family, and other responsibilities. "Life is good." He is successful in his work. He's "got a great wife and family," and he's generally "having a ball." At this time in his life, it is probably even true to say that his drinking actually improves his efficiency to function well in most areas by relieving his abnormally high stress level at irregular intervals.

It might seem that, with things going so well for him, there would be no reason for abnormally high stress levels, but let's look below the surface. This is a driving young man for whom perfection is the goal. A fine American image, but a stressful reality. He is spending untold amounts of energy, time, and worry to fulfill that ideal image and reach his goal (or "their" goal) of affluence, prestige, power, and perfection. He also plays very hard. In fact, he is a person who tends to do everything to excess; well, but to excess. When he is young and healthy, he can drive himself to the limit—physically, mentally, and emotionally—for years with no apparent ill effect and be admired for his energy. He can push toward a high goal with tremendous singleness of purpose, however long it takes; but then a strange thing happens. Once the goal has been achieved, it doesn't really mean much to him. It's not that he isn't pleased with his success. He is—but it doesn't bring the satisfaction he expected. There's a feeling of letdown, of disappointment, even. Is that all there is? So he sets a higher goal and starts off again.

What is wrong with this picture?

What's wrong is that our young hero in search of the American Dream is not acting very sensibly, because he is not enough of a realist to see that he is setting himself up to fail. He has lost perspective and looks only at the goal, a goal which is far too limited to offer any real expectation of happiness. What good will it all be to him or to his family if he reaches the top, only to die of a heart attack, to find that he is hopelessly addicted to alcohol, or to discover that he doesn't know how to enjoy his money and power once he has them? How happy can he hope to be if he has sacrificed time to relax with his family and enjoy his life along the way? If he has allowed himself no time to develop outside hobbies and interests over forty years, how can he expect to do that suddenly at sixty-five when he retires? Addiction to alcohol pulls down a high proportion of these people long before they reach the top, and when it does, all that driving effort comes to worse than nothing—to loss of wife and family, material possessions, self-respect, and everything he holds dear. Such a man is just as much an idealistic fool as the worst ivory-tower dreamer. In fact, the latter is often better off.

To achieve goals and to be a happy person, one needs a balance of work and rest and play. For that he needs a realistic perception of all the elements in the equation of his life, and for that he needs to be sober and take a very careful look at what is real and what is illusion.

A client asked me straight out a while ago, "What is reality? How do you tell the difference between what is real and what is illusion?" That stopped me cold, but I have given the question a lot of thought. I have come to the conclusion that there is no final answer, because each person's perception of reality is different and constantly changing with mood, age, and circumstances. However, I believe that one's ability to see reality and cope with it effectively is directly proportional to his knowledge, understanding, and self-confidence. For example, the stormy sea was a terrifying reality to the seamen of the ancient world. In order to lessen that terror, they went to their oracles and priests for favorable sailing dates and arranged for special prayers, rituals, and amulets to protect them on the voyage. Today how different is the attitude of a member of the Seamen's Union about to ship out on a modern merchantman. He knows about lightning, he understands the power of the storm, but he has full faith and confidence in his modern, superbly designed ship, in his well-trained and experienced officers, and in himself.

How different is his reality from that of the Norseman or early Phoenician sailor. His knowledge, understanding, and self-confidence leave little room for fear.

The addictive drinker's life is out of balance, and he lives much of the time in a should-be world. Unable to see the reality of his situation, he constantly makes poor judgments and finds his world more and more inimical, more and more unfair. Then he drinks for relief and compounds his problems by adding more. As a result, he slowly becomes convinced, as failures and problems increase, that there is no hope for him, and he is absolutely right. There is no hope for him until he isolates the destructive elements in his life and destroys them one by one.

ASSAULT ON DENIAL OR TURN ON THE NIGHT LIGHT

Less than 5 percent of the addictive drinkers in the United States are skid-row bums. The vast majority of the other 95 percent are married, with children, homes, and steady jobs. They include surgeons, lawyers, priests, teachers, business executives, social and political leaders, and people in skilled trades. Men and women. A person who is an addictive drinker is by no means necessarily a bum, but anyone will finally become one if he allows his addictive drinking to follow its inevitable progression to its logical end. As a friend of mine put it, "Just before I found help, I was living on skid row; my skid row was a $95,000 house in a fashionable suburb, but I qualified as a skid-row bum in all but two respects, my address and the labels on my bottles."

Nor do the majority of addictive drinkers have to go on to the depths of human degradation before recognizing their situation and taking action to stop the process. As they say in recovery circles, "It's like an elevator going down. You can get off at any floor on the way to the basement." By the way, it is far easier to get off and to get back on an up elevator if you get off early. The problem is *denial.**

Every addictive drinker is in a state of constant denial until he dies or has made good progress in a recovery program. The word "every" here means including *you. You are in a state of denial,* and unless you recognize that and deal with it intelligently, it is highly unlikely that you will succeed in stopping drinking and getting well.

Denial is caused by addictive drinking itself and by the social stigma against it. As the compulsion and the drinking increase, accompanied by ever-increasing loss of control, the individual is faced with an insoluble dilemma. The thought that he might be an "alcoholic," a person too weak-willed to control his drinking and, therefore, deserving of the terrible stigma of society, is completely unacceptable to him. He couldn't be one of those. So there must be other explanations, other reasons for his drinking so much.

This is the stage at which three very interesting psychological defense mechanisms come into operation. These defense mechanisms develop in everyone in early childhood and are absolutely essential for survival as a sane, effective person. Man learns primarily by making mistakes, which hurt the body, the pride, or both, but he learns very young from adults that while "to err is human," he is not expected to err nearly so often as he does. This situation is serious, because a sense of constant failure could easily destroy his self-confidence and his pride, both of which are essential to his sanity and his success as a functioning person. Clearly something has to happen to protect the developing ego, and fortunately it does, very early in childhood. What happens is that he learns to play games with his own mind and with the minds of other people. The three basic games, each with its own rules, are called projection, rationalization, and repression.

---

*The American Heritage Dictionary defines denial as the "refusal to grant the truth of a fact, statement, or allegation." In this case, refusal to grant the truth of one's own addiction to alcohol and all that that implies.

Projection: removal of the blame for any inappropriate behavior from oneself by placing it on another person, in order to reduce or avoid feelings of guilt or failure. "I was being very careful not to get dirty, but Johnny pushed me down in a mud puddle." Nothing is said (or thought) about what the child did beforehand to cause Johnny to push him down. Instantly Johnny is the guilty party and not he, both to his mother and probably to himself, since he can effectively choose to forget what he did beforehand if it suits his need. "I drank too much last night because Frank loaded my drinks."

Rationalization: removal of the blame for any inappropriate behavior from oneself by placing it on circumstances, either external or internal, to reduce or avoid feelings of guilt or failure. "I couldn't do the homework, because I was too tired after football practice and fell asleep." "I didn't have the accident because I had been drinking. The guy's headlights coming over the hill blinded me."

Repression: removal of the blame for any inappropriate behavior from oneself by forgetting entirely that the behavior ever occurred, to avoid feelings of guilt or failure. For over a year after I got off alcohol, I was telling people quite honestly that alcohol had never caused me any serious problems when I was a young man. Later, as I began to lose my fear of being an "alcoholic," I remembered the fact, which I had managed to "forget" for years, that I had lost two jobs because of drinking before I was twenty-two.

It is interesting to see that these three defense mechanisms, which exist to protect the individual from ego damage, actually cause terrible harm in the case of addictive drinking by making it possible for the individual to hide his addiction from himself and, for a long time, from many other people. This can be done so successfully that the illness can progress to insanity and death in some cases without his ever really accepting the reality of it. This seems downright incredible, but it is true.

I was talking with a man one day who had totaled two cars after drinking and was in a detoxification facility after his third drunk-driving arrest. He still staunchly maintained that he was not an "alcoholic." I mentioned these things and asked him why they did not convince him that he was an addictive drinker. He explained that he often would get so angry in arguments with his wife that he could stand no more and would storm out the door and drive off. Then he would decide to "let her stew in her own juice for a while until she calmed down," as he put it. Since this required time and he had no place to go, he would go to a bar to "have a place to sit and someone to talk to." Since it was necessary to wait some four or five hours for the cooling effect to occur, and since he couldn't very well sit that long in a bar without giving the place some business, he often had a little too much, and that was how the accidents and the tickets came about. They were all his wife's fault, she started the fights, she was the one who wouldn't stop, forcing him to leave his own home. What was he supposed to do, sit in his car for four hours with nothing to do? This is denial in action.

On the basis of what you have read so far, you may have grudgingly admitted to yourself that you may be an addictive drinker. You may even have decided that there is no question about it. That is only intellectual acceptance. You have not truly achieved recognition of the reality of your illness until you have accepted it emotionally as well—in your gut, as they say—and can feel comfortable about it. That means getting rid of a lot of fear. Until full acceptance is achieved, until you can begin to feel comfortable about the fact that you are or have been an addict, the denial system continues to operate, becoming weaker and weaker as final acceptance is approached—but still there, still doing serious damage.

One person sees the handwriting on the wall, and his imagination is so vivid that he needs no further proof of the progressive nature of the illness. He goes for help immediately, accepts it easily and rapidly, because denial is not yet fully developed, and proceeds to recover faster than most others, because he has caught the illness at an early stage. At the other end of the spectrum is the person who, for reasons which we cannot adequately explain, fails to see the handwriting on the wall early enough, slips into deeper and deeper denial, and progressively loses everything—jobs, home, family, all self-respect. He then spends ten years as a bum on skid row before being motivated to seek help. Everyone else falls somewhere along that spectrum.

If you happen to be one of those in the first category, consider yourself luckier, but not better, than someone in the second. The illness is so complex and so subtle that, had a few factors in your life been different, you, too, might just as well have been in the second category. You may choose not to believe this, because we are always looking for opportunities to think of ourselves as more clever, better than other people, to buttress our self-esteem and build self-confidence. Maybe you are cleverer, but don't allow yourself to pay little or no attention to the parts of this book that don't *seem* to apply to you. They usually do.

Addictive drinking is invariably progressive. However early you catch it, there is always the danger that you will underestimate its seriousness because of denial, fail to do enough to guarantee recovery, and start drinking again. If you do, the second time around you may well see skid row before you come back to recovery; that is, if you ever come back at all. Such cases are common.

If you know that you are an addictive drinker or a good "candidate," be advised of one thing from my long observation: you are in some phase of denial. Every professional in the field will support that statement. You are in no position to evaluate your situation and make a good judgment as to how much treatment you need. But you do know—whatever your phase of denial—that you are suffering from an illness which will ruin your life and kill you if you don't arrest it. That being the case, is it not more reasonable to decide on more treatment than you think you need, if only to be sure? When a doctor gives you penicillin for a serious infection, he doesn't give you what he considers to be the absolute minimum dose that will do the job. He gives you a dose that will act beyond any question of a doubt. In prescribing the amount of treatment you're going to take for addictive drinking, you could do much worse than to follow the penicillin plan.

As long as the denial system is operating to any extent, the individual will find it difficult to decide to take enough treatment to ensure success and to keep up enough treatment once it is begun, and he will not get the full return from the treatment that he does take until acceptance is finally achieved. While the denial system is still functioning, the individual hears the words in treatment but, most of the time, has great difficulty applying the meaning to his own life, which is the only way he can hope to get the results he is after.

Denial was set in motion in the first place, and is maintained, by the most basic human emotion of all: fear—fear of social stigma and fear of addiction itself, fear that one may not be able to find the way and the strength to overcome it. So it is that fear we must attack, and the best way to attack fear is to see it clearly for exactly what it is, so that you can understand just what it is that has to be dealt with—that is, what is real and what is imaginary. The real we can handle. It is the unknown, the imaginary, that causes fear.

My major concern has been to convince you that addictive drinking is no longer a mystery, and that anyone can get well if he really wants to, if he is not immobilized by fear. Everyone has the necessary strength of character to do the job. Strength of character is not like a bank account which can be overdrawn. If it were, skid-row addicts I know who had lost absolutely everything, including all self-respect, would not have been able to get well after ten years of total degradation, as I have seen them do. The point is that compulsion makes strength of character meaningless, and that strength has very little to do with addiction, though it is a factor in recovery.

As to the "social stigma" in your own mind, we have seen that it is simply another form of prejudice. As such, it is based on false assumptions, and is not worthy of consideration as a basis for applying any of those dumb ideas to yourself. This being the case, if willpower and strength of character don't have anything to do with addictive drinking, it is clearly absurd to go on punishing yourself with the belief that you're some kind of failure in life because you didn't have enough to stop drinking.

Since society does not understand (and is afraid of) addictive drinking (it fears all abnormal behavior), it quite irrationally blames the individual, who has no choice, and punishes him unmercifully with social stigma, fines, imprisonment, and asylums, all in the name of justice, the protection of society, and, laughably, the protection of the individual himself. Actually, society is itself suffering from stress illness and reacts as naïvely and emotionally as the addictive drinker. It's just as dumb to worry about the stigma of society and let it drive you to drink as it is to apply it to yourself. Stop it.

Let's kill the bogey man of false assumptions and irrational fears. A bogey man doesn't last very long once the night light goes on, and you can see that he is only a dirty shirt hanging on the bedpost. Put stigma where it belongs, slipped into a book of fairly tales, and you have won your first battle to overcome denial.

False Pride

Another face of denial is false pride. Whether you're a banker or a baker, you become a bailer very quickly and without thought in a sinking boat. There's no false pride in that situation. If your lifeboat is sinking because alcohol has knocked a hole in the bottom, you will bail with whatever comes to hand, while stuffing rags or anything else in the hole to cut down the flood. Or will you? As should be obvious, it is not intelligent to stand on the deck singing "Nearer My God to Thee" at such a time, because you aren't the "sort of person who bails, old boy."

This book offers several kinds of "crutches" in the part entitled "How to Get Dry and Stay That Way," the short-term goal of each addictive drinker desiring to get well. These crutches include such actions as the taking of Antabuse, going to a recovery home, the attending of meetings of Alcoholics Anonymous. And you're a damn silly fool if you don't use some of them when your alcoholic leg is broken. As they say in A.A., "It takes what it takes." If you are making the best intelligent choices for *you* at every stage of the game, and following through on them, you cannot fail to win in the end, and you'll gain a lot more self-confidence and happiness along the way. It's part of what self-mastery is all about, and stress is reduced any time you feel you're running the store for a change, even on crutches. That feeling brings true pride.

I will never forget one day. (It turned out to be a turning point in my recovery.) I was talking to a friend, an ex-addictive drinker. I was running on about some of my successes of the past. Suddenly he broke in on my monologue, saying, "Look, I don't give a damn how great you were. How great are you today?" His words were like a stomach punch, but they brought me back to reality with a thump.

Addictive drinkers love to dwell on past glories, to build tottering egos and to wallow in self-pity for what might have been, if only stupid, selfish, uncaring people and vicious fate had not betrayed them. These people also love to build beautiful dreams of wonderful things they plan to do (or be) in the future. They don't spend much time living in the present, however, because that's pretty grim when you're only sober temporarily, and you don't often get much of value done when drunk.

If you're not feeling very great today, it's really not such a big deal. It just seems bad right now. I know how real that feeling is. The whole idea in recovery is to realize that you can get well, and soon. A year may seem like a long time, and that first year of recovery does seem long, but in terms of the rest of your life it isn't long at all, and you keep seeing improvements on the way. The main problem is that addictive drinkers want everything yesterday, and that's what the problem is all about. In the real world you don't get everything you want yesterday, so you have to bring yourself to face that. You do that one day at a time, because that keeps everything bite-size, so you can handle it.

The idea of living a day at a time (operating in the present) is easy to understand intellectually, but it's hard for an addictive drinker to practice. It's a matter of changing some attitudes, and as has been stated, it's hard to change attitudes quickly. Learning to live a day at a time is fundamental for a recovering person, because if he doesn't, the problem of recovery looks so vast and so slow that it appears only reasonable to give up. That's why a lot of people quit after getting off to a good start.

To learn how to live a day at a time, start with an hour at a time. Decide that for one hour you will not let yourself think about the past or the future. If you start to, stop. Think, "What shall I do now instead?" When the hour is up, choose to do another hour, and do it. If one or two hours are all you can take, quit at the end, but not before. That way you didn't fail. You chose to stop. Next time shoot for three or four hours. If this sounds silly, it's not. And it's not just a dumb psychological game. What you are doing is conditioning yourself to live in the present. Now—today—is the time to act. What can you do today to help yourself get well? Decide and do it. You'll feel better, proud. That is, really proud, not falsely proud. (See "Planning One Day at a Time," page 140.)

BODY CHEMISTRY OF THE ADDICTIVE DRINKER

The addictive drinker's body chemistry, too, is different, so different that all by itself it can and does cause abnormal levels of mental and emotional stress, at least equal in severity to that caused by his poor handling of stress in general, his poor accommodation to the world as it really is, and his denial of his drinking situation—each of which contributes to an abnormally high total stress level. The addictive drinker's particular body chemistry will be discussed in the early-treatment part of this book, "How to Get Dry and Stay That Way," where I describe a variety of specific actions by which the craving for alcohol, as well as stress from all causes, can be reduced.

Many people have observed that addictive drinking often runs in families, suggesting that the illness can somehow be inherited. I believe that it is not addictive drinking that is inherited but one or more of the physical abnormalities that so often lead to this addiction.

ON BEING DIFFERENT

I have said that I see the addictive drinker as different in four fundamental ways (described in the four sections above), but I believe he is also different in other ways.

If you have wondered for years why you felt different from so-called normal people, even before you had a drinking problem, I suggest that the reason you felt that way is because you were and are.

You were and are different from the non-addictive person for all the negative reasons we discussed, and for some others that come later in our discussion (little things, important things). Many of these negatives need to be worked on and straightened out. That's the bad news. However, there is also "the good news," as the jokes go.

You are different from others for some very positive reasons, which place you squarely above the average run of people. I have no statistics to go on, because there are none to my knowledge, but I am sure of my conclusions after close observation of hundreds of recovering and recovered addictive drinkers. These positive differences are just as real as the negative ones.

I am convinced that addictive drinkers are generally different in all or most of the following ways:

1. Taking into account each person's education and background, I find us to be more perceptive in our observations of the world and what goes on in it. We see through the cracks in society's systems and people's façades.

2. We are much more idealistic, and care more about people and standards than average people do, however much we may *appear* to disregard all standards and care only for ourselves when we get into real addictive drinking.

3. We are invariably individualistic to a marked degree, and one of our major problems in life is to make ourselves conform to rules and systems that are imposed on everyone by society and that frequently make very little sense, in whole or in part, when applied to us as individuals.

4. Then, as the idealists we are, seeing through the cracks in society and people as we do, we are constantly infuriated and frustrated by the blatant stupidities and unfairnesses we see surrounding us on every side.

5. Because of the above, we tend to be, or try to be, improvers and changers, in order to make bad things better. Of course, without improvers and changers, humans would still be living in caves, throwing rocks at the animals, but here we come into direct conflict with the great majority of people, who are generally against change because it disturbs the even tenor of their lives. Their reactions to our efforts for change and improvement are, therefore, usually negative and discouraging, making us feel more different, more alone, and more misunderstood.

6. Addictive drinkers, before their illness begins to destroy them, are more highly motivated to excel and usually do so. This leads invariably to a certain amount of envy, backbiting, and other forms of attack by others, with a similar result in our feelings of being different, alone, and misunderstood.

7. We are often very imaginative, tending to be far more creative than the average person, as shown by the tremen-

dous frequency of addiction in the histories of writers and creative artists of all kinds.

8. We are more adventurous and daring, and more easily bored by dull people and routine. I know that one of the reasons why I liked to get drunk, when I was young especially, was that I never knew what would happen, but could usually expect something different and exciting.

9. Perhaps we are born that way; perhaps it's because of all the above positive factors, and the negative ones too, but, one way or the other, we tend to be more sensitive—to hurt and beauty, to unfairness and love, to fear and fun, to hate and humor.

With all this, is it any wonder that we are so often in conflict with ourselves and with society? It's harder to be different, to run up the down staircase. That's one reason why we drink too much. It takes great self-confidence to be different and enjoy it—and considerable emotional control. Building self-confidence and learning to handle emotions are vital in recovery.

Key to the Test on Page 6

If you answered yes to at least four questions, you have at least a potential addictive drinking problem. If you answered yes to more than six, you are an addictive drinker.

Part Two

How To Get Dry And Stay That Way, The Short-Term Goal

WITHDRAWAL FROM ALCOHOL

There is a country-Western song, "Do You Want to Make Love or Do You Just Want to Fool Around?" I can tell you how you can stop drinking and stay dry, but it won't do you any good to have that information unless you have decided very honestly, to the depths of your being, that you are going to stop drinking so that you can start living again. It is essential that you decide that you are willing to go to *any lengths whatsoever*. Later on, it gets easier and easier, until the compulsion goes away entirely; but in the beginning, only a *total commitment* will do the job. If you're anything like me, you've tried to quit many times before *and failed*. Maybe you've finally come to the point, as I did, where you quit even trying. If so, maybe you've said to yourself a thousand times, "If only I could, but I can't, so the hell with it!" The actual failures, plus each time you have said, "I can't," have added up to what psychologists call a *failure syndrome*, a negative attitude—another dumb habit, but it's a beaut. However, the whole point of this book, of the group known as Alcoholics Anonymous, and of all the other valid therapy and treatment groups is essentially the same. With help, every person in the grip of addiction can break the habit if he's willing to learn to grow as a person and to make one hell of an effort. Over a million people have done it, and more are doing it every day. However, only very recently have we learned to do it with any degree of efficiency and certainty of success.

The whole denial system is really a way of playing games with your own mind and with the minds of other people, so that neither you nor they can see the reality of your serious drinking problem. However, as the addiction progresses, the point is reached at which you can't fool other people any longer. It becomes too obvious. But your situation is different. You can and do succeed in fooling yourself successfully for a much longer period of time, because of denial. Thus, a vital part of the first step toward recovery involves learning to be completely honest with yourself.

Total self-honesty comes very hard at first because you have been fooling yourself for so long that it is a deeply established habit. In addition, this particular habit is even more difficult to deal with, because, like having a KICK ME sign stuck on your back without your knowledge, you are suffering the results without being able to see the reason why it's all happening. I can tell you about denial, but you can't just reach back and pull it off like a KICK ME sign. So what can you do? To beat denial you need the help of other people who understand the problem. (Denial is only one of the reasons why you can't get well all by yourself, as I will be stressing from time to time.) Other people who understand the problem can see your KICK ME sign and tell you when it is showing. This is one of the most important things a counselor specializing in stress-drinking problems will do for you in the early stages of recovery. This is what people in A.A. can do for you, too. Whenever you make a statement minimizing your drinking problem or suggesting that you feel that you're in pretty good shape now that you're dry—and maybe never did really have a serious drinking problem—you need someone around to remind you that you are falling into denial again.

I know this sounds unpleasant. Nobody wants to feel like a little kid who has to be told the same thing over and over again; but how else are you going to deal with something you can't hear, see, or smell? In fact, it doesn't have to be unpleasant. If you inform people at A.A., your counselor, or anyone else that you want them to tell you when your denial is showing, they will respect you for having the intelligence to face the problem and deal with it sensibly. Since you chose to ask them to do this for you, they will do it more easily and more often. As a result, you can overcome your denial faster. You've taken one more step forward to overcome your problem. You have every reason to respect yourself for doing that. You can speed up the process of recovery in many ways when you know what you are doing and why; the above is a good example. Also, every time you take a positive step, you're making another move toward taking control of your own life, and every time you do that, the compulsion to drink is pushed back a little farther.

For many years people in the stress-drinking treatment field believed that each individual had to hit bottom before he could be helped. "Hitting bottom" meant reaching a point of total personal desperation and hopelessness so deep that pride (and denial) collapsed, at least temporarily, and the individual was finally able to see his real situation. Only then would he be sufficiently motivated to ask for help. Only then would he be willing to listen, learn, and follow directions, in order to begin the recovery process. However, even in the dark days when so little was understood about the nuts and bolts of recovery, it was well known that "bottom" came for different people at dramatically different levels of addiction and deterioration. For the largest number "bottom" was literal bottom (which explains the use of the term), marked by loss of family, home, job, and everything, including self-respect.

More recently, treatment people have found, most dramatically in Industrial Alcohol programs, that bottom can be "brought about" (on purpose) far earlier than it would normally occur if left entirely to chance. This is a delicate matter, but it is being done by professionals with a high degree of success on a fairly large scale. Some combination of employer, family, and significant friends is gathered together in one place, the stress drinker is called in, and each in turn tells him "how it is" from his point of view—with no holds barred. The personal crisis—bottom—almost invariably occurs during the meeting. (This is described fully in "To Those Who Love Them.")

Further, it is now entirely possible to bring the drinker's compulsion down to *willpower-controllable levels in the first two hours* of his recovery effort (see pages 82–84). Only personal crisis can smash denial in the most serious cases, but this information alone is often enough for many to find the motivation necessary to decide to try recovery. However the crisis comes about, good information on the availability of dependable help and its effectiveness must be on hand, so that the person in crisis can find hope and be motivated to get into a program of recovery before the crisis passes, allowing him to return to drinking for lack of belief in a practical alternative. Solid information is vital for both purposes.

Today, with our vastly improved understanding of the recovery process and with all kinds of therapy, professional counseling, and specialized facilities available, free or at reasonable cost, the picture is much improved. The old belief that recovery was practically impossible (so why even try) is no longer justified. Now such belief is nothing but an excuse for not being willing to make the effort, since anyone can do it if he really wants to. It's never going to be easy, but it is much easier today than it used to be, and after all, *you do it only one step at a time.*

There are three ways to stop drinking "cold turkey" (suddenly stopping all consumption of alcohol in any form) and two ways to "taper off." However, before we discuss how the quitting is done, it is strongly recommended that you consult *a doctor who is a specialist in stress-drinking problems** for

---

*The nearest office of the National Council on Alcoholism can usually furnish the names of such specialists or refer you to someone who can. There is more about the National Council on page 68.

a complete physical and his professional opinion as to whether *you* can safely quit cold turkey or must taper off. If you happen to be on tranquilizers, you will need his recommendations on how to get off them as well, since *you cannot recover from stress drinking while on tranquilizers.* (See "Tranquilizers," page 115.)

Sudden and complete withdrawal from alcohol, tranquilizers, or both can cause a seizure (almost identical to an epileptic seizure and potentially very dangerous) or, in the case of alcohol alone, delirium tremens (an extreme form of delirium caused by withdrawal from alcohol).

Assuming that you have had a physical and that the specialist in stress drinking (not just any doctor) has told you that you can safely withdraw from alcohol cold turkey (the vast majority of people can), that is the choice I recommend most strongly. Doing it this way can be extremely uncomfortable, especially if you have been drinking heavily and eating very little, but it is far from unbearable. On the other hand, it is often remarkably painless, especially if you have been eating regularly; working in three detoxification centers, I have seen hundreds of such cases.

My reasons for recommending this choice are simple. First, stress drinkers do not like pain or to be uncomfortable, and they are accustomed to drinking to relieve hurt or discomfort. I drank when I was sad, depressed, angry, lonely, or in any way uncomfortable, and it always helped. When I had the flu, I stayed quietly sloshed until it was over and suffered very little indeed. The point is that people who do not drink the way we do or did have learned to put up with reasonable amounts of pain and discomfort as a normal part of living, and we have to learn to do the same if we are to begin to live normal lives again. If you have decided to recover, you might as well deal with reality from the start, and you will feel better about yourself for having the guts to *choose* to do it this way. Remember that feeling better about yourself in regard to what you did "today," not what you did years ago or are going to do someday, is one of the basic keys to getting well—it creates *true* pride and self-confidence.

Another reason for recommending a choice of cold turkey is this: you are in denial, as we have discussed. If you arrange to go through withdrawal using drugs, so that you feel nothing in the process, you will never have the vivid memory of just how sick you were. It is that memory which serves as a reminder when you wonder if you ever really were a true stress drinker and you begin playing with the idea of trying it again to prove that you were not! Also, once you have gone through cold turkey, you are likely to think twice before taking that first drink and setting yourself up to go through it all over again. It's your choice. Recovery means a lot of hard choices, especially for the first few months, and it isn't very encouraging for your future success if you start off by choosing the easy way (tapering off).

How to Do It Cold Turkey

The three ways of doing it cold turkey are: at home without professional help, in a detoxification center that uses or allows this method, in a recovery home that uses or allows this method. By whichever method, the worst will be over in two or three days.

Cold turkey is done at home by a large percentage of highly motivated addictive drinkers. If you decide to stay home, and your doctor concurs, you should make sure that you will not be alone and that the person who is nearby is aware of the following:

While addiction to most drugs, including alcohol, involves both emotional and physical dependence upon the drug, withdrawal is almost entirely a physical problem which occurs whenever the addicted person stops using the drug suddenly or cuts down his regular intake dramatically. The symptoms of withdrawal are different from those of a hangover. They may include: involuntary shaking of the body, especially the hands, inability to sleep, sweating, depression, headache, a feeling of weakness, inability to keep food down, alcoholic seizure, and delirium tremens ("a state of mental confusion and clouded consciousness, resulting from intoxication or shock and characterized by anxiety, tremors, hallucinations, delusions and incoherence"). D.t.s (delirium tremens) and seizure occur in only a small percentage of cases and do not usually result in any permanent harm. Cold-turkey withdrawal from certain other drugs, barbiturates especially, is far more dangerous and should *never* be done. It can easily kill you.

An alcoholic seizure is almost identical in appearance to an epileptic seizure. If standing or sitting, the victim falls to the ground suddenly, with no exterior warning signs beyond a slight glazing of the eyes, often hard to detect, or frequently a sudden moan or cry. In a seizure the person becomes instantaneously and completely unconscious, the effect being similar to a complete short circuit in a piece of electrical equipment. The whole body is convulsed by muscle spasms, which may be violent or slight. The first concern should be to prevent physical hurt, which may result from the person involuntarily hitting or kicking solid objects near him. He should be rolled immediately on his side—with his face to the side. A constant check should be kept on his respiration, so that appropriate action can be taken to clear the breathing passages in the event of any blockage caused by swallowing the tongue or regurgitating material from the stomach. A pillow or other soft object should be placed under the head, and the body should be covered with something to keep it warm, to avoid shock.

Consciousness normally begins to return without other action in about three to five minutes, usually accompanied by considerable disorientation. Often the patient does not know his name, where he is, etc., but this is nothing to be concerned about, as he usually returns to complete consciousness and to his normal state within a few hours. When he is reasonably aware of his surroundings and can understand simple instructions, he can be assisted to a car, where he can sit or lie down while being taken to the nearest hospital for treatment and observation.

The best way to prevent seizures is to understand that they are primarily fear-induced, and it is important to allay fears in every possible way during the whole period of withdrawal, for this and other reasons. The atmosphere surrounding the patient must be calm and peaceful. This is most definitely not the time for arguments or disruptions, and the people around him must be calm, relaxed, friendly, and totally supportive in every way. This is the time for pampering, especially if a hard line has been used on the drinker when he was drinking.

If he starts seeing or hearing things that aren't there (d.t.s), don't play along, and don't worry. (This is common in those having serious withdrawal problems and is best treated matter-of-factly, even humorously.) Tell him that the things aren't really there, that he is just having an hallucination, which is normal and will soon pass. Keep talking to distract his mind, joke about his having his own private home movies. People can usually be talked out of d.t.s if the person doing the talking is relaxed, clearly certain that nothing bad is going to happen, and able to keep the conversation light and distracting. Suspecting that a low blood sugar condition is a factor in seizures and d.t.s, I suggest the following: He can smoke all he wants to and should be encouraged to eat whenever possible anything reasonably easy to digest. The more solid food he can keep down, the better he will feel. Use fructose in coffee or in any drink (lemonade, etc.) or food in which table sugar is normally used. Also, push sweets—but only those made with fructose. Fructose helps cut down the craving for a drink at any time: it simulates the quick "shot," the boost that comes from booze to which the drinker is accustomed, but does not trigger depression, anxiety, and the other unpleasant effects that follow the ingestion of table sugar (sucrose) in most addictive drinkers. (See page 125 for the relationship between alcohol and sugar in the addictive drinker who has a low-blood-sugar problem, as most do.)

The cold-turkey approach is used exclusively in detoxification centers on the Social Model Detoxification plan. At present these are found only in California and the Toronto area.

If you are in such poor physical shape that quitting cold turkey at home is inadvisable, you will need to enter a "detox," a recovery home with detoxification services (some do not have these), where quitting cold turkey is allowed (ask about this and request it), or a hospital which offers cold-turkey detoxification services (again, some do not). For information to help you choose which of these places is most appropriate for *you*—how they operate, what they cost, etc.—see the sections on each below.

If you are going to go cold turkey at home, I recommend most strongly that you join Alcoholics Anonymous prior to starting. This single move can easily make the difference between success and failure, since the A.A. program and people can offer you tremendous help and support during this difficult time. (See the five sections below about Alcoholics Anonymous for any questions you may have about this worldwide organization.)

As I have said, you cannot do it alone if you are to have any real hope of success. It is not like dieting. Alcohol addiction is a very serious and complex illness, and you will need all the help you can get to ensure success. Use it, starting now. You buy insurance for your house and car. This is your life and happiness we are talking about.

How to Taper Off

Tapering off usually involves the taking of various drugs, under medical supervision, in a detox, recovery home, or hospital. In the facilities that charge fees, especially the expensive places, making the process of withdrawal as painless and pleasant as possible is good for business. The patient is put "under" (drugged) and sleeps through the major discomfort of withdrawal, while the drug dosages used as substitutes for alcohol are gradually reduced. Then, when the worst is over, the patient is allowed to regain consciousness and often is placed on tranquilizers. He is given food in a pleasant, relaxing atmosphere for several days, until even the residual signs of withdrawal have ceased.

A common alternative, often used in recovery homes and a few hospitals, is alcohol itself. Patients are served a carefully measured drink, prepared by the staff, every three or four hours, the alcohol dose being progressively reduced over a period of days. The number of days and rate of dose reduction are roughly determined by the staff's estimate of the seriousness of the patient's condition on entry. Medical supervision may or may not be involved in recovery homes where this type of tapering off is used, but if not, you can be sure that the staff people have had plenty of experience and know how to look after you, if the facility has been recommended by a reliable source. Like the drug method, this approach is almost entirely painless.

Tapering off with alcohol is occasionally done at home, but to be successful there, it must be supervised by someone who really understands the problem, who can be absolutely hardhearted in carrying it out, and who is sufficiently respected by the drinker to be able to enforce the regimen. Even so, this approach is not recommended, because it so often fails and because it requires a great deal of someone's time. Wives, husbands, or other members of the family are completely inappropriate for this role, because of their emotional involvement with the drinker.

NATIONAL COUNCIL ON ALCOHOLISM

This organization offers a unique service to anyone faced with an addictive drinking problem, whether it be the drinker himself or someone deeply concerned about him. The organization is unique because many offices do not offer treatment of any kind and therefore have no ax to grind. Even in those that do, pre-treatment counseling is free and there is no pressure or requirement that you take any other kind of counseling that may be available. It is unique also in that it is an independent organization supported entirely by voluntary donations and is, thus, free from pressure or control by powerful groups, such as medical-psychiatric associations or the government. Its sole functions are to disseminate facts about addictive drinking and to counsel individuals who have no idea where to turn for help by answering their questions about addictive drinking and telling them what kinds of help are available in the community and where to find them. Its name for this advice, "pre-treatment counseling," explains it nicely. There is no charge for these services. Also, the council offers all kinds of excellent literature. There is some variation in structure from office to office. Some offer various forms of therapeutic counseling as well as pre-treatment counseling. (There is also some variation in funding methods for therapeutic counseling; in some cases, there may be a charge for this type of counseling.)

Throughout this book I shall be recommending various kinds of facilities, treatment therapies, and groups, but I can't tell you where to find them in your area, not can I answer your specific questions in a book. The nearest office of the National Council can. It has offices in every big city and in many smaller ones. See "National Council on Alcoholism" (may also be listed under "Alcoholism") in your telephone book, or call the New York office and ask them where your nearest office is: (212) 935-7070.

When you go to the council office, you do not have to give your name or address if you don't want to, and everything you say will be held in strict confidence.

Having worked for the council for some time as a pre-treatment counselor, I would like to make two specific comments. First, the council could easily get plenty of money from powerful interest groups to support its operational costs if it were willing to accept the strings which are invariably attached. It does not accept such money—in order to be free to give you honest and unbiased information, the kind you need most right now. However, I have noticed that very few people who come for its excellent information and advice leave a donation, probably because they are so upset at the time and are unaware of how important such donations are to the continued success of the organization. Please, don't forget to make a contribution; you will find the understanding and counsel more than worth it.

Second, the council trains its pre-treatment counselors, most of whom, except the office manager and secretary, are unpaid volunteers. Unfortunately, the problem of addiction to alcohol is so complex that a pre-treatment counselor, however excellent his training course, cannot hope to have all the answers or to become really good until he has had considerable experience in actual counseling, with the added learning and understanding that come with it. Therefore, don't just walk in the door and ask for counseling. You may well get the newest volunteer there. Say that you are an addictive drinker or someone personally involved with one and ask for an appointment with their best pre-treatment counselor. If you are an addictive drinker, you would be well advised to ask for a recovered addictive drinker counselor. He will almost certainly be able to do a better job than one who has not experienced the illness himself.

ALCOHOLICS ANONYMOUS

A.A. is a remarkable human institution. The organization has grown until it now covers every part of the United States. In fact, wherever you go in the world—on vacation or business—you will usually find A.A. It is a warm place in a cold world for people who want to recover. There is more caring and concern among the members for one another than you are likely to find in any other human institution. The reason is simple: A.A. is saving the lives of its members, giving them back their self-respect, a sense of worth, and hope for the future. You can't beat that kind of direct personal motivation, and that is why, as stated earlier, to date more people have overcome their drinking problems in A.A. than by all other methods and therapies combined.

There are no dues or fees. All gifts of money or property from any source are refused, and the organization is supported entirely by voluntary donations from the members at meetings. Each group is autonomous, free of any outside control by the A.A. headquarters in New York or by any other body. There is no hierarchy in any group, the only office being that of group secretary, the man or woman who makes the arrangements for meetings, chooses a chairperson for each meeting, sees that the building is opened, the chairs set up, and the coffee and tea put on. Even the secretary holds office for only a limited period of time, handing the responsibilities on to another member after a few months at most. There is only one requirement for membership: a desire to stop drinking. Nothing else counts. Race, religion (or the lack of it), economic or social status, none of these is important. In fact, you can even attend drunk, as long as you don't disturb the meeting. Yet, all this being true, it is very rare indeed that a meeting does not start on time.

Since A.A. offers by far the best *single* approach to getting well, you would think that persons with a drinking problem would be insane to pass A.A. by or to drop out after only a few meetings; yet this is exactly what happens in a large number of cases. Why? Are the dropouts, in fact, insane? I don't believe so. I am convinced that they don't go or that they drop out because either they don't understand the process of recovery from a drinking problem, do not understand how A.A. works to help a person to achieve that recovery, or have completely wrong ideas as to what A.A. is in the first place. (See the sections following for more about this: "Common Misconceptions about A.A.," "Why and How A.A. Works from a Stress Point of View," and "Misguided Reasons for Dropping Out of A.A.") And, of course, false pride and the constantly waxing and waning compulsion to drink encourage any form of rationalization that will appear to justify giving up the struggle.

All authorities agree on one thing: *Recovery from a drinking problem requires a change of living habits and changes of thinking habits. There is no question about this. It is a fundamental fact.* But changing oneself and one's way of life is always hard, especially in the beginning. Many people don't even realize that it's possible. It is far easier to continue with the same life pattern, however miserable that may be, than to change it. That, and not knowing how to change the pattern effectively, are two of the major reasons why it is a widely accepted statistic that (at present) roughly thirty-four out of thirty-five people with drinking problems keep on drinking to insanity or death.

Choosing to go to A.A. or any other form of treatment, and choosing to keep on going after you get there, are decisions to change yourself, and you *will* change if you keep going; but it will not be easy, and you will have second thoughts about it many times. There is another factor, too. When most stress drinkers finally decide to do something about the problem, they very much want to reduce the amount of misery in their lives, but they do not want to stop drinking *entirely.* The latter is next to impossible to do at the start, and drinking at this stage is the most important necessity of life. Is it any wonder that so many never go to A.A. or soon drop out? We are dealing with addiction, and addiction is a kind of temporary but repetitive insanity, in the sense that when the compulsion is on you, you do not act in a rational manner. So, at the time when you are sane and sensible, you must act to protect yourself from drinking when the compulsion comes on strong, and you must reduce the severity of the compulsion in every possible way. This is another reason for the earlier statement that you cannot get well by yourself, and thus another reason for finding people in A.A. to help you get through each time, until the compulsion goes away.

A.A. is listed in the telephone book under "Alcoholics Anonymous" or "A.A." If it isn't listed, local police can give you the number.

What a Meeting Is Like

Meetings are usually held in churches or temples (of *any* denomination, since A.A. is not church-oriented) or at A.A. oriented "clubs."* I have attended meetings in banquet rooms of restaurants, private homes, business offices, schools, libraries, and on boats. The physical location is unimportant—it's the people and what happens.

When you arrive, you will usually find people setting up chairs, putting out ashtrays, placing free literature on a table, and making coffee. Other members will be standing or sitting in small groups, socializing. If you are new, someone will probably introduce himself and other members, but don't count on it. There are no official greeters, and you may not be noticed at first. If you're not, pick up a piece of A.A. literature to read, or introduce yourself to someone, telling him you are new.

If you're shy about attending your first meeting alone, call A.A. and someone will pick you up, take you there, and help to make it all easy and comfortable. Don't hesitate to call. You can be absolutely sure that whoever comes knows just how you feel and sincerely wants to help in every way. Normally, it will be a woman if you are, and vice versa.

When the meeting starts, everyone sits down at one or more tables or in rows of chairs. There is no special seating

*Such clubs are set up and run by groups of A.A. people but are neither supported by nor under the direct auspices of A.A.

order except for the secretary and/or chairperson and one or more speakers, who sit at the head of the main table or on a platform if the meeting is in a hall.

The chairperson opens with a moment of silence, followed by a group recitation of the Serenity Prayer (nondenominational). The definition of Alcoholics Anonymous is usually then read, followed by a portion of "Chapter 5" or some other section of the book *Alcoholics Anonymous*, also called the "Big Book."

Then the chairperson usually asks if anyone is there for the first, second, or third time. Introduce yourself: "Hello, my name is Mary, this is my first meeting." If you do not wish to say anything, tell the A.A. friend who brought you or the chairperson before the meeting. One or the other will do it for you. Of course, you can go alone and say nothing. However, the new member is the lifeblood of A.A. and the most important person at the meeting in the members' eyes. (Everyone there remembers his first meeting and how frightened and shy he almost certainly felt.) Your first meeting *should* be given over to you (common A.A. practice); that's what the people want, if you'll only let them know. If you do, what will happen? (If you don't, by the way, they may choose to talk about a subject you may not get much out of because you're new and don't have the necessary background.)

If the group is small enough, the chairperson will normally call on each person going around the table or at random. If the meeting is very large, he usually calls on volunteers until the time is up. Each person usually begins by saying, "My name is [Betty, George, Vivian, etc.]; I am an alcoholic," and then offers his thoughts. (You do not have to say that you are an alcoholic now or at any time. Each person normally chooses to say this sooner or later, to remind himself once again that he is an addictive drinker, which he must never allow himself to forget. I believe that doing this at every meeting also helps each person to achieve the emotional acceptance of his addiction that we talked about before, thus helping him conquer denial.)

After identifying himself, the individual will say whatever he feels may be helpful to a first-timer. He may talk about his first meeting or his first week dry or something with which you can identify and, therefore, feel more comfortable about. Some will offer advice which is especially important for new members to hear. One item will almost certainly be, "Get some phone numbers after the meeting and use them, especially if you think you may be going to take another drink." This is absolutely vital. Do it if you do nothing else. You need the help of people who care about you and understand what it's like—now more than at any other time in your life. These people are offering it, and they mean it. They mean it if you should call at 3:00 a.m., just as much as at high noon. If it will help you to overcome your false pride or shyness, you should also know that all members believe that by trying to help you they are helping themselves to stay sober and grow. They believe this absolutely, and so do I. So don't think they're only doing you a favor. They really do want you to call, and that call is your ace in the hole against that first drink, if everything else fails. Call, too, if you're lonely, or just to chat. That's okay also.

Here's what happened to me. When I finally hit bottom and called A.A. for help, a U.S. Air Force officer came to tell me about A.A. For the first time in my life, I was talking to someone who obviously really understood my problem, as four psychiatrists had not, and he took me to my first meeting, sober but none too steady. It was amazing. I went home afterward and didn't have to drink. I went again the next night, still dry, and the miracle happened a second time. The third morning my wife went off to work, my boys to school, and I was alone. Suddenly I wanted a drink more than I had ever wanted one in my life. I tried walking for a while. No good. The feeling was getting worse. I tried reading. Couldn't concentrate. Then I became really desperate, and although I wasn't used to calling strangers for help, I called Fred, an A.A.-er who had said that he was retired and would welcome a call at any time. We talked a bit; he could see that talking on the phone wasn't going to be enough. He said, "Look, I've got an idea. Let me make a phone call, and I'll call you back in ten minutes. Can you hold on that long?" I said I could. He called back in eight, asking me to come over to his house. We talked endlessly, went out for a sandwich together, and finally my craving for a drink went away. We went to a meeting. Next morning I was fine again, and now I had gone four days without a drink.

That night I spoke up, told the group how Fred had helped me. When the meeting was finished, a man came over to me and said, "I think you might like to know something I heard about Fred." It seemed Fred had had an appointment with his doctor to find out the result of some tests he had taken to determine how serious his kidney condition was. When he had asked me to wait ten minutes, he was calling the doctor's office to put off the appointment to another day, so he could tend to me. Examples are not usually as dramatic as this one, but it may give you some idea of the real depth of concern A.A. people have for one another, even when they are strangers who have only just met. It's a most unusual kind of human bond.

At the end of an A.A. meeting a chairperson may ask if you wish to say anything. Don't hesitate to express what you feel, but if you don't want to say anything more than "Thank you, all," that's okay, too. In fact, if you are terribly shy, you don't have to speak much at meetings for as long as you like. All you have to say at any time is, "My name is So-and-so, and I'll just listen, thank you."

The basic idea behind every meeting is "Come here believing and feeling any way at all. Take what you can use from what you hear, and pigeonhole the rest. It's your life. We'll help if we can." You will never be asked to say you believe in anything such as a creed, only that you "have a desire to stop drinking." That's it.

The chairperson usually closes a meeting with announcements (while the collection basket goes around); then the group stands, usually holding hands, to repeat in unison the Lord's Prayer. If you don't want to, don't. That's okay, too.

New members are not expected or even allowed in most cases to put any money in the basket until after the third meeting. The donation given is what you can afford—a dollar, a quarter, a penny, or nothing. And don't be embarrassed if it's nothing. I know of no other place where people will so readily believe that you really can't afford to put anything in if you don't. That's because everyone knows that the worst miser in the world would give money to an organization which was directly helping to save his life, and that you will too, whenever you can.

After a meeting people stand around talking for a while. This is the time to meet new friends—and get those phone numbers!

Common Misconceptions about A.A.

1. "A.A. is for skid-row bums, and no respectable person would be seen there."

In reality, the membership is a cross-section of people from all walks of life, including representatives of all the professions and a large number of business executives—male and female.

2. "I might meet someone I know there, and then it would be all over town that I'm an alcoholic."

This is why A.A. is named Alcoholics Anonymous; it is the sacred duty of every member to respect the anonymity of every person who attends, and it is rare indeed when a member breaks this trust.* Furthermore, if you meet someone

*It is one of the Twelve Traditions (quite different from the Twelve Steps) of A.A. that members do not break their *own* anonymity at the level of press, radio, and films. This tradition exists for an excellent reason. It is felt, rightly in my opinion, that if a person does this and then returns to drinking, his public example may damage the A.A. name and discourage others from believing that A.A. works. Nevertheless, I break my anonymity here, because I see no alternative. I believe that people are dying because some of the things I am saying about A.A. are not generally known or have not been said at all. They must be said. If I should drink again, and I cannot predict the future, however strongly I believe that I will not, it will not be you know, he is almost certainly there for the same reason you are and just as concerned about his anonymity as you are. Thus, he is unlikely to break yours. Concern for anonymity is also a major reason for there being two kinds of meetings in A.A., open and closed. Anyone is welcome at open meetings, but only people with drinking problems are allowed at closed meetings. So go only to closed meetings at first, if that makes you feel more comfortable. In the large cities there are even special unlisted meetings for people in highly sensitive positions: doctors, lawyers, clergy members, movie stars, and important public officials. (The local office of A.A. can refer you.)

3. "A.A. is an organization of religious fanatics and psalm singers."

There is no psalm singing and no organized religion of any kind.

4. "I can't go into a meeting, shaking like this, and I look too awful to be seen anywhere."

If you're in that kind of shape, you will be especially welcome, and if you call A.A. as I did, a member will come to see you *wherever you are* to tell you about A.A. and take you to a meeting, if that will make it easier for you. No matter what kind of shape you're in, many of the people at the meeting have been where you are, or worse, and all will understand. They are all ex-stress drinkers. They know. A.A. is the ultimate come-as-you-are party. The whole idea is to come as you are now, so that you can learn how to go other places as you want to be later.

---

the fault of A.A. I go to A.A. now about once a month—to share the fellowship, to give something back, to take others, and to remind myself regularly of the necessity to follow my personal program for sobriety. Going to so few meetings is heresy to many A.A. people, but I must live my life as I see it. (For years A.A. was essential to my sobriety, but I have now developed a private program, which seems to meet my needs well, and I no longer feel dependent on any outside institution to stay sober. This, to me, is the true goal of recovery.) So, if I am proved wrong, don't blame A.A. Blame me. I accept full responsibility for my own life. No institution or other person can be responsible for my sobriety.

5. "If I go to A.A., I have to admit in public that I am an alcoholic."

Not so. The only requirement for membership is a desire to stop drinking.

6. "Maybe I'm not eligible."

Anyone who wants to stop drinking is automatically eligible for membership and welcome at any regular meeting, open or closed—with one exception: a few meetings are stag, all men or all women. There are also meetings especially for gay people. (The local A.A. office can tell you about these, too.)

7. "You are not welcome at an A.A. meeting if you have been drinking."

Not so. A fair number of people feel that they have to have a couple of drinks to find the courage to go to their first meeting, and some come back after a slip, still under the weather. (Needless to say, you don't do this very often.) In either case, you are particularly welcome, as long as you do not disturb the meeting. After all, A.A. is *for* people who drink too much when they shouldn't.

8. "If you don't believe in God, A.A. can't help you."

Again not so. A great many people who come to A.A. lost faith in God years ago, or never really had it in the first place. Some are able to find faith again after a while in A.A., some find a new faith, and some recover in A.A. without faith in any God at all. There is no question that faith in God—or some Higher Power—is a tremendous help in recovery, since it offers a source of limitless support and power to call on whenever one feels that he has come to the end of his own resources. Such belief is a source of strength and hope at any time, thus, a tremendous stress reducer. However, there is a very real danger in "faith," which in no way lessens its importance or value if it is understood and guarded against: Do not ask God or your Higher Power—or A.A., for that matter—to do for you what only you can do for yourself. Too many people make this mistake.

9. "All you need to get well is A.A.; it's all there."

The individual does find that by getting to meetings every day and hanging in there, he has managed to stay dry for a considerable period of time, has gotten better physically and mentally, and sees his life improving in all kinds of ways to such an extent that it is common to experience a sense of euphoria as a result, the "pink-cloud period," as A.A.-ers put it. So it is understandable when all this has happened already to assume that if he just keeps on with more of the same he will continue to get better and better until he is finally well. "Faith in a Higher Power and plenty of meetings, that's all it takes." Not so. Full recovery means working up through stages. Getting dry and learning ways and means of reducing stress in your life is only the first stage. You can't stay in this stage and wait for the magic to continue. It won't. This is the time to begin active work to speed your own recovery. I have seen far too many people in A.A. who never really moved beyond stage one and are dry but very unhappy, because they didn't know there was so much more that they could do for themselves, both inside and outside A.A.

I strongly recommend that you plan your recovery program to include other growth therapies and exercises in addition to A.A. A.A. doesn't claim to have all the answers, but some people in A.A. will recommend as strongly as they can against your doing anything else besides A.A., and you should not be surprised when this happens. Their reason for taking this position is basically sound. Because the field of alcohol addiction treatment is still very young, there are many charlatans and others offering relatively ineffective treatments, or making claims for treatments they offer that are untrue and dangerously deceiving. As a result, many A.A. people have come to distrust anything that is not A.A., and you should be extremely careful in choosing other programs for the same reason. Some of the best of these will be described and discussed, along with the potential dangers, in later sections of this book.

Why and How A.A. Works from a Stress Point of View

By the time they call for help, most stress drinkers have become seriously isolated emotionally, and often physically, from family, friends, and nearly everyone else, except for those who drink as they do. They have been repeatedly embarrassed and have felt misunderstood and rejected for years, to the point at which they often feel terribly alone even in a room—or a bar—full of people. The emotional isolation and the feelings of which I speak are not easily seen on the surface, especially by the stress drinker himself. Doing everything he can to rationalize his real position and feelings, he probably has himself convinced most of the time that he is getting along quite well with people. Deep down, however, in moments of depression, and often when drinking, the nagging sense of isolation, lack of understanding by others, and naked fear are very real and have been for a long time.

The individual begins to withdraw more and more into himself, frequently turning for human warmth to the only people with whom he can feel at all comfortable, those who are similarly addicted. And still it gets worse, until in many cases the individual begins to withdraw into the bottle from all people, closing himself away completely—in his home or some other private place—to drink and suffer for days or weeks at a time.

I am not suggesting that everyone who reads this has reached anything close to the final stage of almost total withdrawal from the human race. If that were the case, you would probably not be reading this at all. But if you are a stress drinker and capable of honest self-examination, you will identify with some of the above. The moment of truth, the moment of realization that you can't do it alone and must find help, comes for each person at dramatically different stages of addiction.

The reactions of various people to their first contact with A.A. are as different in degree as are the stages and degrees of the addiction. However, the most fundamental reaction felt by nearly all people to some degree is one of amazement. Suddenly, after years of progressive feelings of loneliness, misunderstanding, rejection, and difference from other people, the drinker feels that here he is not alone, is understood, is not rejected but welcomed, and is among people who may feel "different," too, but who seem very much like him in basic ways. And these people, amazingly, are all stress drinkers addicted to alcohol by their own admission; yet they are sober, apparently happy that way, and obviously in the process of getting well.

The second reaction is disbelief. It can't be true. But the disbelief is short-lived, because the feeling that it is all really true is too strong to be denied, and intensifies with each meeting and each contact with A.A. people. These people really do care about him, want to help him, and have the knowledge to do so. Can you imagine what such a realization can mean to a person, in terms of *relieving and reducing his level of stress?* And he knows that this stress fix can *hold* his compulsion to willpower-controllable levels—at no charge. If the psychological part of compulsion is nothing more than an abnormally high level of stress demanding relief, is it in any way surprising that people who have had to drink every day for years to keep from going insane can suddenly stop drinking entirely by simply attending A.A. meetings regularly? It happens all the time.

One of the first things that strike a new member attending his first few meetings is the incredible openness and honesty which all but the newest members display in talking about their problems. Here are people easily admitting to robbery, crimes of violence, every kind of drunken excess, fears of every kind; things that, in the new person's experience, were so embarrassing that he considered them unmentionable, except possibly to a priest in confession. He hears every sort of personal problem brought up and discussed openly, each person at the table offering suggestions for solutions from his own experience. And, most amazing of all, he sees that the people bringing up these unspeakable problems do so without apparent embarrassment, and are listened to and answered with respect and consideration. Fantastic! And he also sees that the answers and suggested solutions are often very good indeed.

To an outsider raised in our culture, the idea of people discussing their personal problems with each other, especially with relative strangers, undoubtedly sounds terribly embarrassing, thoroughly inappropriate socially—for a man, "unmanly"; for a woman, "unladylike." In our society people are taught from childhood to keep their feelings and problems to themselves. Ask anyone in our society, "Well, how are things with you?" and the almost inevitable answer is, "Fine, great, couldn't be better," regardless of the real state of affairs. Thoreau said long ago that most people "lead lives of quiet desperation." He meant "most people," not only stress drinkers, and one of the major reasons why this is so is that we have all been taught to pretend to the world that everything is fine, when it is not only not fine but so bad that we are utterly terrified and at our wits' end to think of any solution at all. Almost never does one hear a reply to how-are-you, such as, "If I don't have a drink in the next five minutes, I'll go out of my mind," or "I'm so scared of losing my job that I can't think of anything else all day and can't sleep at night," or "I don't know what's the matter with me, I'm impotent all of a sudden, since I quit drinking, and it's really messing up my efforts to put my marriage back together." Almost never does one get that sort of reply—except in A.A.

In my case, I saw myself on the straight toboggan slide to skid row, with no way to get off. I hated myself for being the way I was, and I felt, over and over, day after week after month after year, that I was in a steel box, running round and round on a treadmill that went faster and faster, with no way out. The most terrible part of this experience was that I was going through it entirely alone. I couldn't bring myself to talk about it, even with my wife, and so she thought I didn't care and drank because I enjoyed it, regardless of what it did to her and the children. I cared more than I could say, but I was powerless to do anything about it. Can you imagine the fantastic sense of relief A.A. brings to a person who feels as I did—to find that he can talk to someone who understands and cares and, what's more, may be able to offer suggestions as to how to go about dealing with his problems? *The stress level falls another ten notches.*

Once a person is free to open up about his secret fears and humiliations and to share them with others, those fears and humiliations begin to shrink, and they finally disappear. Then he is free to look more deeply into himself, to dredge up more and more of these feelings, until all of them have been brought out and dealt with. The relief of stress resulting from this whole process is tremendous, and the way has now been cleared for the individual to look easily into his inmost self *on a regular basis*—to see and to recognize what is happening, so that he can take appropriate actions to deal with stress-creating emotions and feelings before they reach dangerous levels. *This is the beginning of self-awareness, without which there can be no recovery and no personal growth.* The psychiatrists can do it, but A.A. does it too, very well, and the price is right.

I include this section on why and how A.A. works *from a stress point of view*, because "How It Works," Chapter 5, of the book *Alcoholics Anonymous*, in my opinion, does not begin to answer the question, and because there are people (like me) who need to understand what they are doing, before they become terribly frustrated, lose faith in the program, and drop out of the organization best equipped to save them.

A.A. came into existence many years ago, in 1935, long before anyone had any clear idea why people became addictive drinkers and when psychology was in its infancy. The fundamental ideas and principles on which A.A. was founded (which are still in use today) came primarily through inspiration and trial and error, a fantastic achievement, but not one easily explained in practical terms (such as stress relief) by A.A.-ers themselves. Knowledge about stress drinking problems and recovery is still young, and A.A. people are amateurs, not professionals. They don't talk in terms of stress at all, nor of accommodating to reality, nor even of what is being learned of the connection between hypoglycemia and addictive drinking; they really don't know how A.A. works (beyond quoting Chapter 5 in the 1935 "Big Book"), except for a general feeling that after they turned their wills and lives over to a Higher Power, marvelous things began to work for them. That, and "utilizing the program." "The program" includes a number of slogans, which they do discuss and which work wonders, especially when applied directly to one's life (not just bandied about) and used with common sense as to degree. One of these is "One day at a time." Another is "Don't get too lonely, too hungry, or too tired." Both of these are great stress reducers, as anyone can see.

One expression often heard in A.A. is: "Do you walk like you talk?" You will find those who are really sober and enjoying life, not just talking, as some people do in A.A., and you will find those who are not only walking like they are talking but who were much worse off than you. When you see them, you will begin to have some solid confidence that you can do it, too. Put simply, as a friend of mine did, "If that son-of-a-bitch can do it, I know sure as hell I can." This feeling of confidence reduces stress tremendously and makes you feel awfully good.

"The geographical cure never works" is one A.A. answer to addictive drinkers wanting to move from one place to another in the belief that, if they can get away from their old drinking friends and associations, they will be able to stop or control their drinking. Since these people never realize that it is not the alcohol that is the problem but their basic attitudes and approach to life, the A.A. statement is right. However, the geographical-cure idea *is* essentially sound. It is just a question of how you look at it, your attitude.

If you move your body every night one block from your old bar to an A.A. meeting, you have made a change in your mental and social environment equivalent to crossing oceans and climbing high mountains. If you move physically from a job you hate and a climate that has been bugging you for years to a job you enjoy, even at less pay, in a climate that you really like, and move at the same time from the bar to A.A., then you have increased your odds on getting well significantly by making a total geographical change. Any move you make, physical or otherwise, that helps you to function more efficiently, be more comfortable, and feel better about yourself is a step toward recovery. As I shall be repeating from time to time, action is the key to getting well.

"Don't take the first drink." This is central to the A.A. program. And they will tell you that when you feel that you want a drink, or even feel uncomfortable, the best answer is to take appropriate action. It does no good to sit around and feel sorry for yourself. In fact, doing that invariably makes it worse. One man I know was in bad shape one night. He called his four A.A. friends and found them all away. But he knew what he needed, to talk with some other people like himself with the same problem. So he went down to the local jail and asked to be put in the drunk tank overnight. (There's always someone there!) By this action, he was ensured that he wouldn't drink that night, and he felt good about it, because he had chosen to put himself in that position. (Positive practical action.) He had the most vivid possible examples of why he did not want to drink to talk to and look at all night, and he managed to convince one man to come to a meeting the next day.

Sometimes being with A.A. people is the only means of staying away from that first drink, and you may well find that you feel more comfortable and relaxed when you are with them than you do at any other time, even in your own home, which may well have become a place of bitterness, guilt feelings, and general misery. It's beautiful when you find out that the safe port is always there when the storm starts raging, and that feeling and knowledge reduce stress still further. No other form of therapy offers this safe port twenty-four hours a day. Can you afford not to have a safe port when you know that at present you can't handle emotional storms at sea?

Now that we have talked about the most direct elements of A.A., which relieve stress so efficiently that it is possible for a majority of new people to get and stay dry instantly if they really want to, we come to what I consider to be the heart of A.A., the most subtle element and the most important for recovery: attitude change. There are many, many ways to reduce stress in your life, but changing negative attitudes to positive ones is more fundamental and important than anything else.

Going on all the time in A.A., and one of the major reasons for its success, I believe, is what I finally came to realize is active behavior modification (without the science of behavior modification itself ever even being discussed or considered).*

When you choose to go to A.A., you are *choosing* to be programmed from negative thinking to positive thinking, and as you begin to get better, there are various techniques (outside the A.A. program) you can use to speed up this reprogramming process and make it far more efficient than it would be if you simply sat around waiting for it to happen. Discussion of these techniques is one of the purposes of this book, so that you can use them if you choose to: see Part Four, "Choosing Your Own Self."

When you attend your first meetings, you may be negative about a great many things. You may be full of resentments toward people and an unkind fate, disgusted with yourself as a person, lacking in self-confidence, uninterested in doing much of anything constructive for money or pleasure, and terribly self-centered, because your problems have become so huge that you can think of little else but them and yourself. "There are people who have an appetite for grief, plea-

---

*Formal behavior modification is a new science that works with both animals and man. Very simply, behavior change is brought about by rewarding the desired behavior and ignoring all others. It is interesting that within a very short time it no longer is necessary to produce an instant reward every time the desired behavior is repeated. Eventually, this new behavior becomes automatic, a new habit, whether it be a new physical habit or a new mental habit (attitude).

sure is not strong enough and they crave pain, mithridatic stomachs which must be fed on poisoned bread, natures so doomed that no prosperity can soothe their ragged and disheveled desolation. They mis-hear and mis-behold, they suspect and dread. They handle every nettle and ivy in the hedge, and tread on every snake in the meadow"—Emerson, "On Man and God." Such is the person with negative attitudes toward life. He frequently cries out, "Poor me!" and escapes into the bottle. People are used to this in A.A., and they will listen to your sorry tales of woe and your self-pity up to a point, because they know that it will help to get it out, and too, all of them have had "poor me" periods themselves. But the people who have been in A.A. for a while are much more positive than you are, and they have learned that complaining and self-pity do not solve problems. So they will keep looking on the positive side of your problems and mention these positive aspects so that you can begin to think positively, too. In the meetings almost everything that is said is positive in nature, because the people are learning to live positively; and every time you show a positive reaction of any kind, they will be pleased, and you will know it. Every time you show a positive reaction, you will feel better inside, and more a part of the group. These are your instant rewards for positive thoughts and attitudes. On the other hand, you will find no reward for complaining and expressions of "poor me," at least not from those who are getting well. They don't need or want that anymore in their lives, and you will sense this even when they don't tell you so outright.

The more positive your thinking becomes, the more stress is relieved, the better you begin to feel about yourself, the more compulsion decreases, and the more often and more effectively you begin to take positive action to solve your problems, instead of uselessly moaning about how tough and unfair people and life are. Once you begin to do this, it gets easier and easier, and better and better, all along the line. The ever-present danger is that things will get so good that you will let the growth process (the recovery process) slip into neutral and coast. When you coast, remember: you have to be going downhill. But many, not realizing this, drop out of A.A. at this point.

Misguided Reasons for Dropping Out of A.A.

1. "I tried some meetings, but they just weren't my kind of people, and I couldn't identify with them." In time you will find that you can identify quite well with any A.A. group, however different the social or economic conditions of the people may be compared with your own. It is vital to understand this, especially if you live in a small town or relatively isolated area, where there may be only one group available to you. The truth is that "your kind of people" right now are, first and foremost, people who drank too much and now are getting well.

In the first months of recovery you are like a passenger who has to jump into the water to escape a sinking ship. At such a moment, with your life in the balance, you would accept help from anyone willing to offer it. There are all kinds of people in A.A., and I received valuable help from all kinds, not just from people with backgrounds like mine. One of them, a former ex-con and stick-up man, now one of the kindest, most gentle men I have ever known, spent hours patiently getting across to me things I had not been able to hear from anyone else, things I desperately needed to learn. All people who have been addicted to alcohol and fought their way back to sanity, decency, and self-respect have truly suffered and learned some basic lessons about successful living, the lessons that count far more than money or social position, or trade skills, or the number of college degrees you may have. I found that all real A.A. people, not the ones who are just fooling around with it, are my kind of people, but I didn't think so at first. If you think you're better than they are, they'll know and understand that you need more time. They won't push you, though they may get a little exasperated with your stupidity sometimes and say some pretty rough things to you to shock you into listening. If they do, it's only because they care. You can be willing to do whatever is necessary to get well, or you can pass by on the other side of the street, where there's no reconstruction work going on. Also, there's a great little bar just down a way on that side, where you can find some instant "friends" and the oblivion that passeth all understanding.

In most urban areas there is a whole spectrum of groups to choose from, and I strongly recommend that you shop around, trying all of the meetings near enough to attend. Not only will you find one or more meetings where you feel especially at ease, but also you will find that the variety of experience prevents the boredom that can occur if you are always listening to the same people. It also makes the whole A.A. adventure more valuable by giving you many points of view. After shopping around, most people find one meeting that becomes their favorite or "home group," to which they go more or less regularly, attending others when they want a change and some new ideas. If no A.A. people are your kind of people, you can be sure that the fault is not theirs. Give them and yourself a chance.

2. "I've been to quite a few meetings, and as far as I can see, everybody who's making it believes in God or some 'Higher Power,' and they talk about it to the point where it drives me up the wall. That's the main thing that keeps them sober, they feel. Well, I still can't manage to believe in anything at all, no matter how I try, so I guess I couldn't make it anyway."

Not so. Fortunately, I felt this way and said so. An old-timer collared me after the meeting and told me privately that he never had believed in a Higher Power and still couldn't after twelve years of sobriety in A.A. It is easy to draw the conclusion that everybody in A.A. believes in a Higher Power, because those who don't never seem to say so; but, in fact, over the years I've found quite a few people like me who were also managing to get well in A.A. without a Higher Power. One of the "Twelve Steps" in A.A. *is* that you are willing to turn your will and your life over to a Higher Power. I found that when I turned my will and my life over to "absolutely nothing," simply doing what I could each day and then relaxing about it, the same miraculous things occurred.

3. "A.A. becomes too boring after a while. There just isn't enough depth to the program. At first it sounds interesting, but after a while you realize that they just keep on repeating the same old slogans and discussing the same old subjects at meetings. I dropped out from pure boredom."

This objection is common, especially during the first months in A.A. There is very often an initial high, the "pink-cloud period," followed by an often rather sudden sense of disillusionment and the old despair.

One of the most difficult things a person trying to overcome a serious drinking problem needs to understand and accept is the fact that the process of recovery is slow and largely imperceptible to the individual in some of its *deepest and most vital aspects.* You cannot see your attitudes changing. You can only become aware of the fact that they *have changed* after they have, and it takes six months to a year for such change to become really noticeable to the individual himself.

It is also a fact that growth does not occur in a straight upward line. Sometimes we're forging ahead nicely; at others we're standing still or going backward, the last two largely because our emotions frequently get the upper hand during the first year or so of recovery.

For a long period in recovery, as much as two years, you must expect fairly frequent and often sudden, powerful mood changes, periods of boredom, depression, and a sense that the whole effort just isn't worthwhile. This is what A.A. people call "stinking thinking." These periods are a painful part of recovery and a major factor accounting for much of the boredom feeling in A.A.

When you arrive at a meeting and hear that "Resentment" is to be discussed (again!) or you hear "Easy does it," in somebody's reply, don't just shake your head and say to yourself, "I've heard that twenty times already!" Immediately start thinking about it in *today's* situation, *your* situation: what happened at the shop, what your daughter (or mother or husband) said and did at breakfast, this morning's appointment at the office, this evening's before-meeting conversation—in every way that you can apply it. As someone said to me when I thought of quitting because of boredom, "Look, your head is in a different place every time you come in here, isn't it?" I agreed that it was. "All right, then; if you listen to what is being said and apply it to where your head is at the moment, to the way you are *feeling* at the moment, won't the thoughts you have be different every time you do it?" As with many A.A.-ers in that first year or second, I had thought that *intellectual understanding was all that was required,* the way someone hears something so that he can explain it to someone else or pass a test on understanding it. Not so. When "one day at a time," comes out in the meeting, no matter *how many* times, ask yourself how you are doing with that, not thinking about past or future, not *needing* the past or the future. Repetition of your personal thoughts about slogans which make sense is the best way to change attitudes there is. It's an exercise in reprogramming yourself.

4. "I couldn't stand that humility stuff."

I couldn't either, and every so often, over the years in A.A. meetings, the subject of humility would come up and I would feel very uncomfortable. I enjoyed most subjects, and the discussions were always useful to me in some way, but not "humility." There was something wrong there every time. I listened to all sorts of "humble" statements in which people put themselves down, refusing to take any personal credit for their own recovery—statements like, "I didn't do anything myself; I owe it all to my Higher Power and you beautiful people."

I don't care what anyone says: I remember the first two years of my recovery vividly, and if there is one thing I am absolutely sure of, it is that I had one hell of a lot to do with it, with all due credit to indispensable outside help. I was the one who got myself to meetings when I didn't want to go. I was the one who stayed dry between meetings when I was alone and screaming for a drink. I was the one who said over and over to myself, "How long, O Lord, how long?" and hung in there.

And I tell you another thing: I take great pride in that achievement. I think it was heroic, and I think that every other sober addictive drinker who has done the same thing is a hero. I further believe that feeling this way about it had a lot to do with my recovery and with my present sobriety and happiness. I think that feeling that way about it will help you, too.

Now I think I've figured out why humility was a bummer for me for so long. In the discussions we were talking about pride all the time, but we didn't distinguish between the two kinds—false pride and real pride, as discussed earlier. And that failure meant that we were saying all sorts of silly things and thinking them, too, a good part of the time. Don't let this common confusion bug you in A.A.

It was false pride that kept me believing that I could stop drinking alone, without any outside help; but it is real pride that keeps me believing today that I'm worth enough to other people and to myself sober to justify my staying that way, and so, on that basis, I am willing to do whatever is necessary to accomplish this.

5. "All my life I have been taught never to accept something as true unless I have examined it thoroughly and found it to be true. In A.A. all I hear is, 'Don't analyze it [the program], utilize it!' and 'Just keep coming back and things will get better.' Why, for chrissake? I have to understand why and how it works, so I can believe in it and trust it."

This was my biggest single problem in A.A., and I have met many others for whom this was also their biggest problem. I agree that it is dangerous for a person newly dry to try to analyze anything so complex as the recovery process in A.A. At this early point, he may easily become confused and misled in his thinking, and end up out of A.A. and into drinking again. I tried and kept trying, because I had no alternative if I was to find a way to make the program work for me, because I didn't have a Higher Power and had to find something else to hang on to. It was a long time before I began to make headway, and I do not recommend this kind of analysis to new people. (I *was* badly confused and misled in my thinking for a long time because of it.) I hope that my own interpretation of "Why and How A.A. Works from a Stress Point of View," will go a long way to helping you, so that you won't have to go through all that misery.

6. (After a period of some months in A.A.) "Looking back on the days when I was drinking too much, I realize now that it was only fairly bad for the last two or three years. In fact, I never did those crazy things I hear some A.A. people talking about. Maybe I was never really addicted at all. My life was in a terrible mess at that time, and a lot of people drink a little too much when they have problems. I certainly don't feel that I have to have a drink now, and I have no desire to get drunk at all. Just one or two drinks at a party like everyone else. I ought to be able to do that, and if I feel any compulsion to drink more, then I'll really give it up for good." ("A.A. was great, but I don't need it anymore.")

This is the old denial, of course, still going strong.

When you find yourself beginning to think this way, you must recognize a serious threat to your sobriety and well-being. Probably most stress drinkers come to this stage and have to experiment with drinking again, only social drinking, of course— To my knowledge, and from talking about it with many professional people in this field, I have found that *not one true stress drinker has ever succeeded in returning to social drinking without, sooner or later, returning to true addictive drinking and all the hell that that involves.* (The fact that a heavy drinker, unlike an addictive drinker, can do this only confuses the question.)

But, you ask, if learning to deal with life and its stresses more effectively is the answer to overcoming a stress drinking problem and finding freedom from compulsion, why, then, should a person who *has done all that* not be able to return to social drinking? *Why should he start stress drinking again after he has learned to control stress?* A reasonable question. The answer, I believe, is simple. A very real part of it may be connected with the effect of alcohol on our particular body chemistry. In addition, we are creatures of habit. That is, we all become conditioned over a period of years to think and act in certain ways quite automatically, without conscious thought, as has been noted. The process of recovery is a process of reprogramming our automatic computer with new, positive habits of thought and new attitudes toward life; but never assume that the old programming, old habits of thought have disappeared, just because you have superimposed a whole new program on top of the old negative one to such an extent that it never even shows through anymore.

The old programming is very much alive and well, and it is lying there like an old deeply grooved record in your unconscious memory bank, ready for instant replay. Consider the years of your life which led up to your stress drinking, and then add to that long conditioning process the long conditioning of the drinking years! By the time you quit drinking, you may well have spent more than half your life practicing and refining the habits of thought and outlook which led you to full addiction and that final day of desperation when you called for help. Is it reasonable to assume that you should be able to return to social drinking, when to do so means again putting into your brain the same mood-altering substance with which all those years of old conditioning became so intimately associated? The conditioning of the recovery process can never be more than a hard veneer over the old conditioning. Break that veneer thoughtlessly with a few drinks and you will see how quickly the old demons reappear. It's like Pandora's box. Try it if you must, if you think you really will be the very first of thousands. No truly rational person would do so when faced with such odds, but stress drinking is not a rational illness, and there are sound reasons for speaking about "the insanity of alcohol."

If you do decide to try social drinking again, and a large percentage of people seem to have to try it to convince themselves by getting drunk again, I can tell you an apparently amazing thing you may find. Some people have one drink, and that's all it takes: they get drunk immediately. But with me and many others the first drink, or even the first two or three, seemed to have absolutely no effect at all. After six months in the A.A. program without a drink, I took my wife out to dinner on our anniversary and decided to have one glass of wine before dinner as a symbol of our celebration. I did and had no desire for more. A week or so later we went out again, and I had one martini. Same thing: no desire for more at all. Five days later I was alone in the house, and for no reason that I could remember afterward, I went to the liquor cabinet, got out the gin, and got smashed. Why? After only six months I was just "dry," not even halfway on the road to real recovery. My defenses against stress and the terrible compulsion to drink were very weak indeed, although I thought them strong. When I took that first drink, a glass of wine in a social situation, I automatically dropped most of my defenses. I released the catch of my Pandora's box of powerful, negative addiction conditioning. After that, the final flipping wide open of the lid was absolutely predictable. It was then only a question of time. When you put that old, deeply grooved record on a new record player, it plays the old song, not a new one.

If you do start drinking and get drunk again, it is vital to know one thing about A.A.: you are always welcome back, even before you get sober. Don't be stupid and decide that you can't go back, because you will be too embarrassed to face the people. That's false pride again. They are used to this sort of slip (drinking after a dry period) and are doubly glad to see you when you return, because they hope that maybe now you have learned the fundamental truth about yourself and will be able to recover this time. I knew one man who had setbacks with fair regularity for five years before he finally made it, and he was still welcomed back after so many slips that we lost count.

I believe that there are four basic reasons for a slip: (1) The person stops going to meetings regularly, thereby giving up his periodic opportunity to have his total stress level reduced to manageable proportions, as usually happens in meetings, and thus allowing that level to rise to a point at or too close to his stress threshold. (2) He has failed to identify or deal effectively with one or more important stress-creating areas of his life, and these, over a period of time, cause his total stress level to rise too close to his threshold. (3) Some unusual and highly stress-causing event occurs in his life, for which his adaptive growth to date is insufficient. (4) His deep desire not to appear different from other people by not drinking and his egotistical need to prove to himself that he isn't different in this respect leads him to rationalize his way to the belief that, in fact, he is not different and can drink again.

Stress drinkers find a thousand reasons to justify their drinking before they stop, and they are equally able to find an endless list of apparently sound reasons for dropping out of A.A. before they have truly begun to achieve real sobriety and happiness. So it would be impossible and fruitless for me to try to list and discuss them all. However, it is probably fairly safe to say that if you find yourself considering reasons for dropping out of A.A., it is a sign that you need more meetings rather than none at all.

DETOXIFICATION CENTERS, RECOVERY HOMES, HOSPITALS, AND HALFWAY HOUSES

All of the above facilities offer services for addictive drinkers, and it is important to understand how each fits into the overall picture of addictive drinking treatment so that you can decide which one of them might be appropriate for you and at what stage of recovery.

All offer a protected environment specially designed to

help stress drinkers get off alcohol completely, either immediately or within a matter of days, or, as in the case of the halfway house, to stay off after the detoxification process has been completed. Of those that offer detoxification service, some do it cold turkey, others use the tapering-off approach.

The Detoxification Center

The purpose of a detoxification center—whether it is located in a hospital, a recovery home, or is an independent facility—is to sober up and to help an addict safely through withdrawal (detoxification) under controlled conditions. A person normally stays in a detox for three or four days. In some, the individual is free to walk out at any time. In others, he either commits himself or is committed by a suitable authority. During his stay he is usually given information on addictive drinking and referred to other appropriate facilities and services, in preparation for the day when he "graduates" from the detox and continues his treatment.

Experience has shown that if the normal symptoms of withdrawal are not blocked out with drugs, this is one of the best times at which to reach the addicted person, whose denial is at its weakest point during cold-turkey withdrawal. In fact, the experience is often so vivid, so thoroughly miserable, and so directly indicative of its own cause that the drinker in involuntary withdrawal due to commitment frequently decides to seek help even without pressure from other people. As I have said (it cannot be emphasized enough), drug-free withdrawal will never be forgotten, and this memory can serve as an important stimulus to hang in there during the early stages of treatment. On the other hand, when enough drugs are used, withdrawal can be made completely painless, so that a few days later it is as though it had never happened. Then the opportunity to break through the denial system and get the addicted person into treatment is completely lost, with the almost certain result that he will return to drinking, until he becomes sick enough to return to the detox for a second (or fiftieth!) time around—unless, of course, he dies first, which often happens.

The severity of withdrawal symptoms is roughly proportional to the severity of the drinking problem and the physical condition of the individual. However, there is a large variable from one person to another. A few people never have hangovers; many go through withdrawal easily even after years of daily heavy drinking. All of the reasons for this variability in individual reactions to long-term abuse of alcohol may never be known, but one factor seems certain. While it is true that alcohol abuse causes more direct physical damage to the body than abuse of any other drug, including heroin, it has been widely observed that those addictive drinkers who regularly eat good meals during their drinking careers suffer far less damage and generally find withdrawal easier and less likely to result in a serious threat of d.t.s or seizure. (If you who love the drinker can't do anything else, try to see that he or she eats at least one good meal a day, without making a big issue of it.)

The majority of people go through withdrawal without going to any facility at all. For example, if the individual is usually sober during the day, even if he gets drunk every night, he probably does not have to go to a detox to withdraw. However, if he can't stay in a home environment with understanding family or friends to give him support through the ordeal, a detox is a safer bet.

Detox facilities vary tremendously in quality, but cost is not, by any means, the indicative factor. Some county-supported detoxes are excellent in all respects, if not luxurious, and are free or very inexpensive. Some are terrible, with poor supervision; sometimes residents go out regularly to get bottles for parties in the facility itself. Some private facilities are very expensive indeed, and no better than the good county detoxes. The most expensive private institutions are also the most likely to be the ones which block out all withdrawal symptoms to keep the customer happy and simplify their work at the same time. To find the best facility of the kind you want, contact the local office of the National Council on Alcoholism and/or A.A. (They are the ones who know.) Most detox facilities insist on the use of drugs, to some extent at least, but there are some, especially the Social Model detoxes, which are offshoots of a program developed in Toronto, Canada, where no drugs of any kind are used.

The Recovery Home

The recovery home often offers detoxification services, but its primary purpose is to furnish a quiet, pleasant, protected environment in which the resident has no responsibility except to stay dry and begin to recover physically and emotionally. When he feels up to it, he may be encouraged, even required, to do simple household or grounds chores for therapeutic reasons. If you feel that you're above that sort of thing (false pride), you may be able to avoid it, but the other people won't think very highly of you for it. Besides, if you're that "great," you can probably do it better than anyone else and take real pride in showing them you can.

Recovery homes usually offer a combination of individual and group counseling, lectures, tapes, and movies on addictive drinking, regular A.A. meetings, and various other kinds of therapy, such as occupational and diet.

Recovery homes have never been held in high esteem in this country, because of the social stigma associated with any aspect of alcohol addiction, and because people have often expected the impossible from them and then been disappointed when it was not produced. In part, the completely unrealistic expectation that the recovery home can "cure" the drinker is the fault of some of the owners, who have claimed cures or encouraged the idea that they could offer cure, in order to keep clients coming. In part, the idea came about as a result of the average layman's total lack of understanding of addiction. The hard truth is that it takes a lot more than thirty days or three months to get well, and you are never "cured." No recovery home can do either one, but it can offer a valuable service, the help you need at a vital stage in your recovery.

If you understand the real purpose and limitations of the recovery home, you can then decide whether—and/or at what stage—it would be appropriate for you, and you will not be disappointed when it does not produce results which you might otherwise have been led to expect.

Think of a recovery home as serving a purpose like that of a recovery room in a hospital, a quiet, safe place, offering special services for people in a very early stage of recovery. (It is completely inappropriate for the later stages.) If getting completely well means learning to adapt yourself to living in the real world, so that you can function far better than ever before and thoroughly enjoy the process, in spite of the hard knocks, problems, and unfairness of it, *that part of the learning process has to take place in the real world*. If you are living away from the real world in a specially designed, protected environment, from which the hard knocks, problems, and unfairness have been carefully removed, how are you going to learn to live in the real "here-and-now"? Recovery homes are like tranquilizers in this respect.

When a person has been drinking too much for years, always more and more, or has just finished a two-week binge almost entirely without food, he can be in very bad shape physically, mentally, and emotionally. Detoxification is only a short first step toward recovery, and a great many people are by no means well enough to go from there directly into outpatient treatment. Also, it is not unusual for a person who was "absolutely serious about recovery" in the detoxification center to be discharged and head straight for the nearest bar or liquor store. It is not unusual for such a person to go home with his family "to continue resting and recuperating" and then sneak off within hours or a couple of days to begin another drunk. All the old pressures hit him as soon as he leaves the detox.

If you are concerned about yourself or someone else, the safest place to go from detox is to a recovery home, if you have decided that you will do whatever is necessary to get well. Thirty days there will result in marked improvement, physically, mentally, and emotionally. (Less than thirty days is generally felt to be insufficient, judging by the experience of many people. You may decide that you need a little more time there. If you do, take it, but be sure that you don't make the mistake of staying in the nice safe womb too long. You can get hooked on that, too, and damage your chances of recovery.)

The value of a recovery home is, of course, dependent in part on the quality of staff, the program, and the services. However, there is a slogan that no addictive drinker in recovery should forget: "You alone can do it, but you can't do it alone."

"You alone can do it . . ." means just that. All the recovery home, A.A., addictive drinking counselors, or anyone else in the field can do is to tell you how and furnish the tools. You are the only one who can get *you* well. This being the case, your attitude on the day you finish detox and begin the recovery home process is crucial. You are there to relax, eat well, and recover physically, mentally, and emotionally, but that is not all. You are also there to learn all you can about addiction and yourself, and to get all you can out of the program and counseling offered. *Most important of all, you are there to get yourself together, and to work out in your own mind what you are going to do and how you are going to do it when you leave the home.* You have made—finally—a safe port for repairs after a terrible storm and serious damage to your ship. The repairmen can help you put your vessel in reasonable shape to continue the voyage, but you are the skipper who has to sail through whatever comes once you go back to sea, and you're not going to be ready for the open ocean for a long time yet. You can get the ship in shape if you work on it, but chart your course with a plan. Run along the coast and know where the safe harbors are, so that you can always run for cover when the storms come up. Working at sea and in the ports, you can keep improving your vessel, and then, when you are truly ready, you can head for any port you wish. Work on your cruise plan every day, practice it, so that you can sail out of the recovery home with confidence. Specific suggestions as to how to go about that plan are in Parts Three and Four of this book, "Choosing Your Own Situation" and "Choosing Your Own Self."

Many people get through withdrawal at home, get off to a good start in outpatient treatment, and find that something is still wrong. This happened to me. I was constantly trying to force myself to do things I wasn't emotionally ready for, but I didn't realize that. And, too, every failure worried me to death. The atmosphere at home, my relationship with my wife and sons, was killing me—for reasons I now understand but did not at the time. My work situation was bad, too. Unaware of how to deal with these problems, and suffering considerable stress as a result, I kept having slips, three of them in a year, and realized that I could not continue that way. I decided that what I needed was a large piece of uninterrupted time, free of all the pressures of my daily life at home and at work, to think out my situation and come up with a better and more complete plan for recovery. I went to a recovery home for thirty days, did what I described above, and haven't had a drink since. I didn't find a cure there, but I didn't expect to. Of the eighteen people I came to know there, seventeen returned to drinking within days or weeks of leaving, I heard later. They were just sitting around at the home having a vacation, in spite of what they said. None of them left with a solid game plan, with one exception—he was the one who didn't return to drinking.

Thus, it is necessary to give this one loud warning: If you don't leave the recovery home with a solid, detailed game plan, including a strong support-and-stress-relief system like A.A. and a contingency plan for any special situation that can flip you out, you're dead—dead drunk.

Hospitals

Many hospitals still do not offer alcohol addiction treatment services, but more and more are beginning to do so. Some have elaborate programs, and many of these are highly regarded by alcohol addiction treatment people. However, I feel that a person should take a careful look at the other alternatives in this part of the book before committing himself to one of them. The basic question is: "What kind of facility will best meet my needs at the moment?" In my opinion, a hospital program is not the answer for at least 90 percent of addictive drinkers. Let us see why.

1. People in the Social Model Detoxification Centers in California, which use no drugs of any kind during detoxification, have found that even during detoxification, less than 5 percent of addictive drinkers actually require medical observation and intervention with drugs to prevent serious medical emergencies. After detoxification, the number of addictive drinkers needing hospitalization for physical treatment, for serious liver damage, for example, is even smaller.

2. Hospital programs are under the direction of either a doctor or a psychiatrist, and staffed by registered nurses, usually with special psychiatric or psychological training, and other doctors and specialists of various kinds. From their special training, all of these people are conditioned to believe in the use of drugs—tranquilizers especially—and in the psychiatric approach to the solution of people's problems with living. Except for real medical emergency, tranquilizers and other drugs are unnecessary in the treatment of addictive drinkers, and tranquilizers actively prevent the individual from getting well.

3. Because of the high degree of specialization and training of the above staff people and the tremendous costs of all the equipment and services offered by any large hospital, the cost to the patient per day is exorbitant, often four times as much as a similar program in an average recovery home with a good program.

In sum, if you are physically sick enough to require a regular hospital, or insane enough to require a mental hospital, then a hospital program is probably right for you. If you do not fit in either category, I submit that you can find excellent treatment—maybe even better care—at far less money elsewhere. Why pay hospital rates, when all the physical testing and psychology stuff is far cheaper on an outpatient basis or in a recovery home? (Many insurance plans are beginning to provide at least partial compensation for certain types of rehabilitation programs.) A hospital program is really a recovery home program with medical frills. It makes no sense to me, except under special circumstances.

Having made the above statement, I feel that several points need to be added:

We have learned a great deal of inestimable value from the research and writings of medical professionals—to such an extent that I believe we would not have our present knowledge and understanding of addictive drinking without their contributions. The problem is that the highly specialized education and orientation of the vast majority of medical and psychiatric people has been insufficient and inappropriate for the proper diagnosis and treatment of this much misunderstood illness, with the outstanding exception of those few who have specialized in this field. Since effective treatment is so new, and developing so fast, full-time work and study are the only ways any of us can learn about addictive drinking at the present state of the art.

I feel it is my responsibility to warn you against putting your usual confidence in the medical profession with regard to treatment for addictive drinking until it has had time to develop proper training and procedures for its personnel. We are still a long way from that day, however, as is clear from two present facts: (1) The profession with the highest incidence of alcohol addiction and drug abuse is still the medical-psychiatric profession. (2) A laymen's organization of amateurs, A.A., is still credited by all authorities with far more success in helping addictive drinkers to get well than all other groups combined, including the medical-psychiatric profession.

My warning here is general but not against all such institutions and individuals without exception. If a particular doctor, psychiatrist, or other medical professional is recommended to you as a specialist in the field, by someone who is knowledgeable on the subject (preferably not a medical person, someone in the National Council on Alcoholism or A.A., for example), then use him by all means. The same would apply to hospital programs, especially if your company or a rich aunt is paying the bill. All I am really saying is that, if a treatment program or treatment person is primarily medical, psychological, or psychiatric in orientation, watch out. That is not where the best treatment for addictive drinking is usually found, and prices tend to be excessively high, especially when compared with the results being achieved by others at far lower cost.

Halfway Houses

The halfway house is the next institutional step after a recovery home. The name implies that it is a house for addictive drinkers who are halfway on the road to recovery; but, in fact, there is a great deal of variety from one house to another in the actual stage of recovery of the residents and no one in any kind of halfway house is even close to being halfway to recovery. In some urban areas where the halfway house has been fully developed, there are quarter-way, halfway, and three-quarter-way houses. They may be generally described as follows:

The quarter-way house is really a small recovery home, generally state-supported, for the addictive drinker who cannot afford a private recovery home. The house is usually staffed by former addictive drinkers—one, two, or three people—who offer a simple recovery program and oversee the running of the house, doing formal or informal counseling on the side. All the residents help with cooking and other chores. The focus of the whole operation is on recuperation and the first stages of recovery. After an initial orientation period, during which residents may not leave the house, they are allowed to attend outside A.A. meetings. Usually they go as a group at first and then are given day and weekend passes, as the staff feels they are ready to handle them without drinking. Residents may not hold outside jobs.

The halfway house is similar to the quarter-way house, except that the recovery program is less time-consuming. There is more freedom for residents to come and go outside the house, with or without formal permission of the staff, and the residents are encouraged and usually expected to work inside or outside for pay. The staff and members of the local community often help in finding jobs for the residents.

The three-quarter-way house is like the halfway house, but has a minimal or no organized recovery program. All residents have outside jobs, with complete freedom to come and go.

In some areas the so-called halfway house fulfills all these functions, each individual advancing from stage to stage while living in the same house.

The basic idea behind all these houses is to create a protected environment for the recovering addictive drinker, where he can find community, friendship, understanding, education about alcohol addiction, and support along the whole road to recovery. The goal for each person is to reach a point of personal growth at which he is finally ready to leave the shelter of the house and return to normal life in the larger community. However, when each person leaves, he is strongly encouraged to continue some form of outpatient support system to help him through the transition period and, afterward, to ensure his continued growth to a mature sobriety. This is essential if he is to have any reasonable expectation of success.

The quarter-way houses are usually free or charge according to the individual's ability to pay, and they operate with state or county financial support. In houses where they have outside jobs, the residents usually pay board and room. In all cases, the cost is held to a minimum, so that residents can begin to have their own money in their pockets, can pay off old debts, and can build a stake for their eventual return to independent living in the community.

You now see that there is a complete institutional track to follow—from drunk in detox, through a recovery home and/or quarter-way house or the halfway-house system, to final return to the community as an independent person. All along the way there is support, education, personal growth opportunities, and community, in a safe, controlled environment, with freedom and responsibility increasing as the individual grows to handle it.

The quality and availability of these facilities from one place to another varies tremendously—from nonexistent or awful to complete and excellent. The National Council on Alcoholism, the County Health Department, and A.A. are the best sources of referral.

Synanon, a Special Case

Synanon offers a highly unusual, unquestionably radical solution to the problem of how to get dry and stay that way. However, it works very well for those who choose it, in spite of some recent bad press. It might be the answer for you.

Synanon is not just another therapy method to help you for a while to learn a different way of life. It *is* a different way of living, which lasts for life if you want it to. In fact, it is a world apart from the rest of the world, but you can leave it whenever you desire. Started for drug addicts and expanded to serve people addicted to alcohol, this unique organization now also accepts anyone who has serious problems in coping with life, if he sincerely wants what is offered and appears able to fit in and benefit from it.

Most addictive drinkers' problems can be solved by far less drastic means, but there are those who are so thoroughly confused, so emotionally unstable and lacking in self-confidence, that total reorganization, retraining, and restructuring of their lives by authoritarian rule is the only answer. As I see it, Synanon is an oasis for people in this category, their best hope to find the massive discipline and restructuring that are essential for them in an atmosphere of total security, love, and understanding. Synanon offers all this at a cost which ranges from nothing to many thousands, depending on the individual's ability to pay.

If I had a child who was in serious trouble repeatedly with the law (especially if he was involved with drugs and/or alcohol), I would rather have him go to Synanon's "Basic Training" for young people than to see him at any of our present-day correctional facilities. I believe that Synanon's youth program is doing essentially what our correctional facilities should be doing but aren't.

Synanon, based in California,* has three huge live-in facilities: a ranch north of San Francisco, a converted factory in San Francisco, and a center for elderly people and beach recreation in Southern California.

In A.A. it is suggested that you turn your will and your life over to your Higher Power. Synanon says turn your will and life over to us. A.A. and other outpatient treatment facilities offer guidelines, direction, and help in solving problems and living according to a new and better way of life. They offer no guarantees. Synanon says, come to us, full-time, for the rest of your life if you wish, and we will take care of you until you die. And they apparently do.

The organization is totalitarian. The rules are absolute. However, it is all done with love and for your own welfare. Your life is completely disciplined and planned, from morning to night, year in and year out, for as long as you need it. You have no financial worries, nothing to fear; you work, play, and live in a totally protected environment—and so do your children, until you are ready to begin to cope a bit with "the jungle out there." You will find just about everything that A.A. offers to help you find yourself, gain self-

*Their address is 6055 Marshall-Petaluma Road, P.O. Box 786, Marshall, CA 94940; telephone: (415) 663-8111.

confidence, and put yourself together—in perfect safety.

Synanon wants you to come for life, and many do, finding a peace, fulfillment, and joy such as they have never known. Others stay for whatever time they need to get the necessary discipline, organization, and skills, and then they return to the real world to live normal lives.

Without a doubt, Synanon is the supercrutch to end all crutches, taking over total responsibility for your life and welfare, for whatever time is necessary. In return, you give Synanon all your worldly possessions, your freedom, and your labor. (Everybody works according to his ability, interests, and the needs of the organization, at first inside the walls, and later—perhaps—outside in a regular job, but still living in.)

This may sound like a high price to pay, and it is, but it's well worth it if that's what you need. You are free to take your freedom and your life back whenever you feel ready and able to do so.

I visited the facility in San Francisco, and I can honestly say that I have never seen so many ex-addicts anywhere so relaxed, comfortable, and apparently enjoying the whole experience. But I would regard Synanon as a last resort, and I would suggest that you visit their facilities yourself, talking with people like you, and with those who are the management now, before committing yourself or a minor to them. However, if they are still offering what I observed in 1974, it is a viable program for people who can be helped by nothing less.

ANTABUSE

Antabuse is another possible weapon in the fight to stay dry, another option. Recovery is in large part a matter of discovering and expanding good options, until you are free to choose whatever is possible in this world, but it all starts with the choice to stay dry.

Antabuse (also called disulfiram) is a substance, generally prescribed in pill form, which has no mood-altering or other side effects. Its purpose is to make the body violently allergic to alcohol in any form. A person feels and is perfectly normal while on Antabuse, as long as he keeps himself completely clear of alcohol. However, if he takes any form of alcohol, the body's reaction is dramatic. The skin turns red, or even a purplish color. Violent stomach cramps, vomiting, and a pounding headache are accompanied by marked body temperature changes. The total effect, according to people who have tried drinking while on Antabuse, is worse than any kind of pain or illness they have ever experienced. They say that it is so bad you want to die. The reaction lasts for several hours and also includes impressive changes in blood pressure, both up and down. Obviously it should be taken only under a doctor's care, after a suitable physical examination (during which the physician determines whether you are allergic to it),* and *should never be slipped into the addictive drinker's food or drink without his knowledge*, as has been done on many occasions by spouses who did not understand the dangers involved.

Antabuse has long been given to addictive drinkers as a *cure* by doctors who did not understand the addiction, on the assumption that since you can't drink while on Antabuse, all you have to do to avoid drinking is continue to use it daily. This idea is absurd, because it does not begin to take into account the problem of stress and resultant compulsion. A person on Antabuse does find some real relief of stress with Antabuse, because he feels safer, but this relief by itself is not enough to keep the total stress level within manageable limits. That has to be done by other means.

---

*In the event your doctor finds you allergic to Antabuse, as a few people are, he will prescribe another substance which functions in essentially the same way.

Thus, a person on Antabuse alone suffers stress buildup like any other stress drinker, and sooner or later reaches a point at which the compulsion becomes too great. He no longer has a choice and must stop taking his daily pill, so that he will be able to drink again—to relieve the stress. Antabuse by itself is virtually useless.

The only valid reasons to take Antabuse are *to gain some peace of mind (stress reduction) and to buy time* for other treatment or therapy to take effect. It must be the drinker's own decision to take it, and he *must be able to stop taking it at will.* Free choice is essential.

The advantages of Antabuse were very well expressed in a letter from a friend of mine who chose to take it every day for eighteen months.

> When I got up in the morning I felt great. I didn't want a drink and had no compulsion. But before I took Antabuse, each day was a battle, from about ten o'clock on. I could feel the pressure building steadily and the need for a drink with it. It got worse and worse, and I had to decide perhaps fifty times a day whether I was going to give up and drink or keep hanging in there. This constant battle was nerve-racking and kept interrupting everything else I was trying to do. Then I started Antabuse, and all that was over. Sure, I still wanted a drink just as often, but with that stuff in me, I knew I wouldn't do it, and that took a lot of the pressure off. I didn't have to decide fifty times a day anymore. I made the big decision just once a day—in the morning when I took the pill. All the rest of the day, I was then free to concentrate on other things. Also, the fact that I had chosen to take it myself gave me the feeling that I was at last in charge of my day again, the drinking anyway, that I was no longer a puppet on a string. That was a marvelous feeling for me after years of believing that there was absolutely nothing I could do.

Antabuse also helps in another special way. As has been mentioned, stress can rise to a level of high compulsion before a person knows what's happening. When this occurs, the person on Antabuse has a time safety factor of several days off the pill before he can start drinking again (five days on the average between cessation of the pills and the safe resumption of alcohol). Since he has to wait before he can drink and will be very uncomfortable because of his high stress level, he has strong motivation to seek stress (compulsion) relief by every other method he has learned in his program to date. If he does this, he will probably find enough relief to bring his total stress level down to manageable proportions again; and if that happens, he again has the choice and can go back on the pills without ever taking a drink at all. Antabuse is a good insurance policy.

Antabuse is often looked upon as a crutch and rejected on that basis out of false pride. Maybe you don't "need to use a *crutch.*" Maybe you can do it with A.A. and other therapy. Lots of people do. It's your decision. Antabuse *is* a crutch. No doubt about it. Of course, if you had a broken leg— But here it's different somehow, and many with the terminal illness of addictive drinking, a far, far more serious problem than a broken leg, reject the Antabuse crutch, which could well be the crucial factor in helping them to stay away from that first drink long enough to get well into recovery. We will never know how many people would have made it if they had added Antabuse to their programs; but we do know that those who use it succeed more often than those who do not. I am convinced that those who turn down Antabuse do so out of false pride, stemming from a low self-image, and the resulting desperate need to convince themselves that they are in control of the situation by not submitting to the use of a crutch. In fact, they know deep down that they haven't been in control for years, but that is frightening to face. Better to pretend that everything is really not so bad, and maybe it won't be. It's the denial we talked about.

A.A., with or without Antabuse, is the only means presently known, outside of a hospital, recovery home, or halfway house, by which an addictive drinker *can stop drinking sudden-*

ly and have any real expectation that he will be able to stay stopped. "Suddenly" is the only way. The idea of tapering off by oneself is a pure delusion, a mental game which we always lose. It is true that addictive drinkers can stop by using willpower for varying periods of time. Periodic addictive drinkers can count on a month, or three months, or whatever their "dry cycle" may be; and even daily drinkers can go dry for astonishing periods on occasion, but in either case the drinking day always returns. Since you need at least a year dry in order to get a good start on your recovery program, it is only good common sense to take *every* precaution. "Or do you just want to fool around?"

Note: Antabuse is so effective that even such things as aftershave lotion, cough medicine, mouthwash, Geritol, and the like will cause a very unpleasant reaction, since most of them contain alcohol. So care must be taken. It is not a big problem, but it is important to be aware of it. Just get in the habit of reading labels. Cooking with wine, by the way, is normally no threat, because the alcohol cooks off. The taste, however, may be enough to trigger desire for a drink in the early stages of recovery, and you may choose to forgo wine cooking for a while for that reason. Later you will enjoy it more than ever, because you will find that the flavor of foods is enhanced when you haven't knocked your taste buds into the ropes with three martinis before dinner.

BIG NOTE: One hospital, with a large section for addictive drinkers, long ago recognized that even the best and most experienced members of the staff had great difficulty in trying to determine which patients were really serious about recovery and which were just talking a good game. (Addictive drinkers are all great con artists.) They finally found one thing that proved to be a good indicator. Those who elected to take Antabuse turned out to be the serious ones, the ones who tended to make it most often after leaving the facility. The ones who didn't, didn't. Your own decision in this matter may tell you something about how serious you really are.

TRANQUILIZERS

My sole purpose in devoting a whole section to tranquilizers here is to emphasize that YOU ABSOLUTELY CANNOT RECOVER FROM ADDICTIVE DRINKING IF YOU ARE ON TRANQUILIZERS.

As I have stated before, the subject of addictive drinking and its treatment was not taught in American medical schools until very recently, and the vast majority of doctors and psychiatrists in the country know very little indeed about it. In recent years there has been a tremendous amount of literature and publicity about the wonders that can be achieved with tranquilizers. I am sure you have seen at least one article describing how tranquilizers are making it possible to empty whole wards of patients from mental institutions and hospitals.

It is true that an addictive drinker is usually a nervous person, especially when not under the direct influence of alcohol, and tranquilizers are great relievers of nervous symptoms. Therefore, it is not at all surprising that doctors and psychiatrists by the thousands are prescribing tranquilizers for their addictive-drinker patients in the firm belief that they are helping them avoid the nervousness underlying their compulsive use of alcohol. In many cases the doctor does not even know that his patient is an addictive drinker, because the drinker usually does everything he can to conceal the fact. The result is the same.

There is great danger in prescribing tranquilizers for addictive drinkers, a danger most people are unaware of. They do not know and frequently are not told, or don't "hear" it if they are told, that when you combine alcohol and a tranquilizer (both depressant drugs), you get what is called in medicine "the synergistic effect," which can relax you until you're dead. When you add one unit of alcohol and one unit of any other depressant drug, the result is not two. It is more like the equivalent of four or six in total depressant effect, and when you depress the involuntary system, which controls heart and breathing, to a certain point, the patient dies. While it is rare for a person to drink enough alcohol to depress the central nervous system sufficiently to cause death (he passes out before this stage is reached), it is not uncommon for people to reach coma and death when two depressants are combined. This frequently occurs when the individual takes only the prescribed dose of tranquilizer, especially if he does so during a long period of heavy drinking.

As many people do not know, it is common to "trip" on tranquilizers alone by taking more than the prescribed dose. The effect is similar to being high or drunk on alcohol. Many addictive drinkers know this, and a large number combine heavy doses of each—alcohol and tranquilizer—because you can go higher faster that way. Once a person starts taking tranquilizers while drinking, a second vital factor comes into play. He starts overdosing by mistake. When a certain degree of drunkenness is reached, whether induced by alcohol alone or alcohol in combination with other depressant drugs, the memory ceases to function well, and cases have been documented in which a heavy drinker took a tranquilizer or his normal sleeping pill (another depressant) dosage *four or five times,* each time thinking that he had not taken his pill yet!

YOU ABSOLUTELY CANNOT RECOVER FROM ADDICTIVE DRINKING IF YOU ARE ON TRANQUILIZERS. While it is certainly true that you cannot recover if you are dead of an overdose of combined depressants, that is not what I mean by the above statement. As I have said, recovery is a process in which a person learns to face reality squarely, and to function in that reality as effectively as possible. If recovery requires that you learn to recognize and deal effectively with reality, how can you expect to recover when you are living in a chemical haze that effectively blunts your perception of reality, that makes everything that is wrong with your life seem okay?

The day I moved out of my home, leaving behind my family of twenty-seven years, I had been dry only six months. In spite of the fact that I had seen my divorce coming for many months and had learned how to reduce my total stress level enough to stay dry, I was totally unprepared for the massive emotional stress of the final act. As I packed, tears were streaming down my face, and I felt compulsion rising like a rocket. It was all too much. I couldn't stand it, and I *knew* instinctively that nothing I had learned to date would be enough to pull me through. I was going to drink, no matter how I fought against it. At that moment I thought of a possible alternative, not a good alternative, but a better one, I thought, than drinking. (The A.A. people had told me that I had to be willing to do anything whatsoever to keep from drinking.) So my last act before leaving home and family was to go to the medicine chest and take a prescription dose of Thorazine, which was still there, a leftover from my last psychiatrist. I drove to a friend's home, and we sat and talked. As time passed the Thorazine did its work, and I will never forget the experience. I was not at all drunk on the prescription dose; I felt mentally alert and normal except for a dry mouth. What was amazing to me was that, having been off all mood-altering substances for six months and thus fully aware of how frightened, incredibly uptight, and desperate for a drink I had been only hours ago, everything was now, suddenly, okay. I wasn't afraid or tense, and I had no compulsion to drink. I was actually chatting about my situation and discussing my plans for the future, as though we were talking about plans for a two-week vacation! It was fantastic to me. Oh, yes, tranquilizers work all right! They remove virtually all stress with unbelievable efficiency.

There is a positive function of stress, whether normal or abnormal. It is not all bad. It functions exactly like physical pain, another form of stress, to warn the individual that something is wrong and action is called for to set it right. Since stress of any kind is painful at high levels, it is one of the most basic and effective motivating factors in life. Stresses are flashing red warning lights on your safety board and the motivators for corrective action. Tranquilizers short out your *whole* safety board and cut off the power to your corrective-action machinery, allowing you to go paddling along in happy ignorance of the fact that your life is in a terrible mess, which only full awareness of that reality and hard work can put right. Ignorance may be bliss, just as drunken oblivion is a form of bliss after great pain, but it doesn't help you to get well. It makes getting well impossible.

You have to learn to hurt to get well, because the hurting is the only thing you can count on to motivate you to find out what you have been doing wrong, and to get you off your miserable duff to take action and start doing things right for a change.

I am happy to say that I never took another dose of Thorazine or anything else after that one, which got me through the initial trauma of leaving, and I can honestly say that tripping in sober reality turns out to be far more fun and far more beautiful.

An example of the danger of "tranquilizer cover-up" as it affected one man's life may be helpful. His name is Willy, an addictive drinker, unmarried, a middle-aged man who was still living with his parents. Over a number of counseling sessions, we put together a program by which he could stay dry, and then he could begin the process of growth toward true sobriety and happiness. It went well; in fact, too well, it seemed to me. There were no slips and none of the nervousness and tension usually associated with the early months of recovery. As a result I became suspicious. I had asked him earlier about tranquilizers, of course, and he had answered in the negative. However, now he finally admitted that he was on a strong tranquilizer by his doctor's prescription and was quick to add that he had never taken more than a prescription dose and had not considered that as really being "on tranquilizers." This was the answer, of course, to why he was appearing to recover painlessly. The tranquilizer, even in prescription dosage, was sufficient to replace the alcohol addiction by relieving his stress, especially in conjunction with the stress-relieving program on which he had embarked.

I did my best to convince him to get his doctor to take him

off the drug, and he did talk about it with his doctor, but the doctor was adamant. According to his view, Willy was far too nervous to function safely without it and must continue. I talked with the doctor on the phone to no avail.

So Willy continued with his tranquilizer. He did not drink, but neither did he choose to make any of the meaningful changes in his life-style that I considered necessary and strongly recommended. He said he would like to make some: such as moving out of his parents' home, away from his father's lifetime domination (difficult to believe, I know, but Dad was still there and still dominating) and his mother's constant mothering, and starting a small cattle ranch, his life ambition, for which he had plenty of money. But he couldn't make the break. Finally, it became obvious that I could help him no further until he was willing to drop the tranquilizer and get on with his life in some sort of sensible way, so I terminated our sessions with an explanation to that effect.

Nearly nine months later he called me up, drunk, asking for help again. After three weeks of steady drinking plus his regular prescription drug, Willy was a very sick man, and I took him immediately to a detoxification center. When he came home, still shaky but feeling vastly better, he went to his doctor and told him that he was going to go off the tranquilizer no matter what he said. With dire predictions about the result, but with no alternative, the doctor told him how to "come off," and he followed directions to the letter. Five days later he was off the tranquilizer for the first time in years and absolutely shocked to find that he felt perfectly all right. He had dropped his how-to-stay-dry program shortly before getting drunk, predictably, but started back again with a vengeance; three months later he moved out of his family's home and bought a small ranch and stock near Sacramento. Although the ranch has not been a great financial success (he says he expects to do better as he learns to avoid his early mistakes), he is still dry two years later, with no need for mood-altering drugs of any kind; and I would say that he has grown into a healthy level of sobriety. He found the sources for personal growth he needed and is today several times the man he was, before he ever started drinking.

NEVER STOP TAKING ANY KIND OF DEPRESSANT DRUG COLD TURKEY (alcohol excepted, if approved by an addiction-specialist doctor). *Such sudden and complete withdrawal from some of these drugs can lead to convulsions and death.*

The *transfer* of addiction is very easy and very common—from hard drugs (heroin, for example) to alcohol, or from alcohol to tranquilizers. In these cases of transfer, there may be improvement in overall behavior: the heroin addict does not have to steal anymore, because alcohol is relatively cheap; or the violence associated with alcohol abuse disappears with the switch to tranquilizers, because their effect on the body is somewhat different. But the addict is still an addict and cannot get well until he frees himself from all mood-altering substances.

BODY CHEMISTRY, THE PHYSICAL SIDE OF ADDICTIVE DRINKING

Ninety-five percent of addictive drinkers are hypoglycemic;* that is, they suffer from an abnormal sugar metabolism problem, which frequently causes their blood sugar level to fall below normal. The result is depression, headaches, feelings of anxiety, insomnia, nervousness, a general negative view of people and/or circumstances, loss of energy, and loss of emotional control (Jekyll-and-Hyde behavior).

*Ninety-five percent is the statistic most often mentioned, and Dr. Abram Hoffer, eminent psychiatrist and biochemist, has said in his books, the latest one *Orthomolecular Nutrition: New Lifestyle for Super Good Health* (1978), that "all or almost all alcoholics have hypoglycemia."

A candy bar, a piece of cake, or a drink (a "shot") will quickly furnish a "pick me up" to the hypoglycemic person (whether addicted to alcohol or not), reducing or ending the symptoms of depression, anxiety, etc. However, this is only the short-term effect of the *sudden* raising of his blood sugar level. Very soon after the blood sugar is raised by sugar or alcohol, the pancreas is triggered to shoot out insulin in a decided *over*reaction. This burns up the sugar and sends the blood sugar level to below normal again! The ups are higher, and the downs are lower as this cycle continues—for months or years.*

This seems to explain the drunk who is-happy-then-becomes-depressed (and maudlin). And it seems to explain our manic-depressive personalities when sober. This repeated action/reaction process, the long-term effect of heavy sugar (or alcohol) intake, causes the body's metabolism to go further out of balance. The out-of-balance nature of this illness has caused it to be termed "hyperinsulinism," referring to the overreaction type of insulin shoot-out. Left unremedied, this imbalance may lead to degenerative disease, most often diabetes or cardiovascular disease, chronic obesity, and/or addictive drinking. May this also not account, at least in part, for the progressive nature of alcohol addiction *even when the drinker has been dry for years?*

In your youth you may have been one of those elementary school kids who was a sweets freak. Or it may be that your alcohol addiction brought on the hypoglycemia. It happens both ways. In alcohol addiction, the hypoglycemic individual is usually off the sugar because he's on the sauce, or he may swing back and forth during periods of drinking and being

*According to a recent paper, "Functional Hypoglycemia: Ubiquitous Malady," by Drs. D. Cooper and C. Pfeiffer (Brain Bio Center, Princeton, N.J.), one of the factors creating this overproduction of insulin is continual abnormal stress. During stress (including anxiety, fear, etc.) the adrenal gland must constantly supply adrenaline. Eventually the gland is exhausted. Since adrenaline antagonizes or puts down insulin activity, hypoglycemia is the result of the exhausted gland.

"on the wagon." (One woman in recovery explained to me that she had been off desserts for five years; when she pinned it down, that's when she started drinking wine with meals, gradually increasing to wine between meals as well.)

Since nearly all addictive drinkers are hypoglycemic, they "need a drink" frequently for no other reason than to raise their blood sugar level so they can feel more normal. They don't know it's low blood sugar, of course; they only know that two or three shots will make them feel an awful lot better. We don't drink addictively just because we have living problems or just because we want to get high. It's a complex equation. But, clearly, alcohol is doing a lot more to and for a hypoglycemic person than it does for other people. And it is fair to say that an addictive drinker has a hyperinsulinism illness, as well as a stress illness.

The doctors have been busy on this question of addictive drinking as an illness for a long time, and the medical literature is extensive. Most of it is made up of highly theoretical discussions of various possibilities—missing enzymes, DNA abnormalities, etc., but little is of much practical use at the present time. However, a new class of medical researchers into a new area of study appears to have struck pay dirt at last, and they are achieving some truly spectacular results. This new area of study is called orthomolecular medicine. It may be described as the science of determining that combination of nutrients, including vitamins, trace minerals, and essential amino acids, which will produce optimum health for *each* individual.

A major discovery in this field is the fact that far greater extremes of biochemical individuality exist in people than was previously believed. For many years a large number of medical tests have been interpreted on the basis of so-called norms. If a test showed a patient to be within the limits of those norms, he was assumed not to have a problem in that area. The discovery that many people do not fit these norms and need far more or less of certain substances (biochemical individuality) for normal health means that thousands who have been tested have been inaccurately diagnosed as not having a problem in a certain area, when, in fact, that was the area of the problem precisely.

One dramatic example concerns a girl who had been diagnosed professionally at different times as a behavioral and learning problem, having minimal brain dysfunction and learning disabilities involving visual perception and auditory memory. The behavior problems were especially difficult for the family, including as they did unprovoked temper tantrums, with ranting, raving, and swear words at any time of the day or night. Her parents, noting that she was better after eating fried oysters, ate an awful lot of fried oysters, in addition to trying to keep her on a sugar-free diet to manage her hypoglycemia, which had previously been found to be a part of her problem. Finally, with the parents' clue of the fried oysters, orthomolecular doctors, who were aware that oysters contain a relatively large amount of zinc (more than twenty times that in roast beef, which is the next highest food source), found out by testing the girl that her metabolism required vastly more zinc than that of normal people. When she was given a suitable zinc supplement, all the previously mentioned symptoms disappeared.

Roger J. Williams, the nutritional biochemist who pioneered in this field in the 1950s at the University of Texas, has written:*

> In the literature pertaining to alcoholism there are a number of references to the "X" factor involved. What is the "peculiar element" present in the life of alcoholic addicts and absent from the lives of those who can drink moderately?
>
> From the beginning of my study of the problem of alcoholism, I have been convinced that distinctive body chemistries must be involved in the answer to this question and that an important "X" factor [or factors] must lie in this realm. Many of those who have looked at the

**Alcoholism: The Nutritional Approach* (University of Texas Press, 1959).

> alcoholism problem, in what has become a traditional manner, completely ignore the biochemical individuality which seems clearly to be of import. This attitude of unawareness, this head-in-the-sand stance, cannot persist indefinitely in the face of the facts which are now apparent. It cannot always be taken as an axiomatic fact that alcoholism is fundamentally a psychological and a psychiatric problem. The psychological factors enter but physiological and biochemical factors are involved too, and to be ignorant of these is to be ignorant of the disease itself.

Reference to Dr. Williams's work in the field of biochemical individuality is still being made today in new writings in orthomolecular medicine, and no one yet has said it better.

The second discovery concerns malnutrition. With respect to general malnutrition, one report mentioned by Dr. Carl Pfeiffer* describes a study at Jersey City Medical Center in which it was found that 83 percent of patients admitted to the hospital had at least one vitamin deficiency, and 68 percent had two or more such deficiencies. With respect to the malnutrition of addictive drinkers as a group (as well as drug addicts and schizophrenics), he states that *all* are on the upper end of the spectrum of biochemical need and that they have shown *particular* deficiencies in some nutrients.

If biochemical individuality and alcohol addiction's malnutrition can create by themselves such apparently wild emotional imbalances, and if hypoglycemia, "our special problem," can produce by itself emotional symptoms which are associated with addictive drinking—and the dry-drunk syndrome I talk about on page 142, the problem of our body chemistry must be taken into account in any serious effort to recover from a drinking problem.

**Mental and Elemental Nutrients:* "A Physician's Guide to Nutrition and Health Care," by Carl C. Pfeiffer, Ph.D., M.D., and the Publications Committee (Brain-Bio Center, Princeton, N.J., 1975).

What to Do about Hypoglycemia

Many addictive drinkers have suspected for some time that they are *carboholics*. Some call themselves *sugarholics* (when off the sauce), but they have no idea what to do about it except to stop eating "everything I like." Obviously, this source of heavy stress (hypoglycemia) must be either ruled out (you don't have it yet) or dealt with if your total stress level (compulsion level) is to be reduced to manageable proportions. Equally obvious, any such reduction in your total stress level makes getting dry and staying that way far easier and more comfortable.

To rule out or to confirm hypoglycemia a Glucose Tolerance Test (GTT) is necessary, and here, as in the field of addictive drinking treatment as a whole, there is controversy and disagreement. Those doctors who use the GTT routinely in their work and really know how to interpret it are the ones who find hypoglycemia in nine out of ten addictive drinkers and 50 percent of headache sufferers. Those who do not, claim that it is rare. The proof of the pudding, as far as I am concerned, is that, of those addictive drinkers who take the steps indicated to deal with hypoglycemia, a high proportion find marked relief of some or all of the related symptoms.

Just as doctors do not agree about the relative frequency of hypoglycemia, they also differ dramatically in their knowledge of how to administer and interpret a GTT, to such an extent that it is common for doctors to give a GTT and cut off the testing of the patient's reactions too early to get a conclusive hypoglycemic reaction or to look only at certain normative figures in the test results rather than *the rates of blood sugar rise and fall* (fall especially!), which are far more significant.

Therefore, if you choose to have a GTT, specify to your doctor that you want at least a five-hour test and that you want the specific results of your test. Then *you* do the interpreting yourself. It is easy, and the best explanation of how to do it is given in a Bantam paperback, *Dr. Atkins' Superenergy Diet* by Robert C. Atkins, M.D., and Shirley Linde (1978). (Don't be turned off by the title; that's a gimmick to sell books. You will find the book itself excellent, and it may make a significant difference in your life.)

If you don't want to bother with the GTT at this point (unless you know you need it), Atkins's book offers a do-it-yourself hour test to see if the GTT is indicated. Or you can just assume the nine-to-one odds that you have some degree of hypoglycemia, take the steps indicated below for at least a month, and see if they make a noticeable difference in the way you feel.

Limit your use of substances that trigger the release of insulin, which lowers your blood sugar level: table sugar, including brown sugar (substitute fructose as described below), coffee (substitute decaffeinated coffee), tea (make tea weak, limit four cups a day), colas, which contain sugar and caffeine, and, of course, alcohol, which acts like table sugar in the body.

It is the addition of fructose in the diet that enables the change from table sugar or alcohol or both to be made with relative ease, from the first days of "just dry," including the withdrawal period itself. Fructose does everything for you that regular sugar (sucrose—a combination of glucose and fructose) does, is about two-thirds again sweeter than sucrose (three teaspoons of fructose equal five teaspoons of sucrose), and significantly reduces the compulsion to drink alcohol. Unlike regular sugar, fructose does not trigger the insulin overproduction characteristic of hypoglycemia.

Switching from sucrose to fructose is easy on the taste (nobody can tell the difference). At home one simply uses fructose as table sugar is normally used; in cooking, remember the three-to-five-teaspoon ratio. (It's better for your family, too, since many doctors say that Americans eat damaging amounts of table sugar.) Fructose is also available in pill form, which solves the problem of away-from-home coffees, etc. Dr. Atkins suggests:

> You can take two fructose tablets (2 grams each) every two hours, making about sixteen tablets distributed throughout the day. Or you can make lemonade with it, using about six teaspoons to a quart, and drink it throughout the day. Or you can use fructose as you would ordinary sugar. To get the full antihypoglycemic effect, you may need a teaspoon or two of fructose each hour, which effectively curtails insulin release. Or you may need to use it only at certain times of the day. Test it for yourself, watching for the point at which you experience an energy letdown. If you feel fatigue, tension, or uneasiness, then you know it's time to take fructose again. Sometimes you will feel relief in minutes.

Dr. Atkins explains the addiction to ordinary sugar and sweets of the hypoglycemic person (when not drinking) as follows: "Sugar causes an unbearable degree of hypoglycemia and the symptoms are relieved by the ingestion of more sugar." The ingested sugar triggers an insulin overresponse, which then pushes the blood sugar below normal again, a vicious cycle. Used correctly, fructose will break this cycle and give you a steady, assured source of energy without any of the letdown of ordinary sugar. Atkins also includes the fact that fructose should be taken with a magnesium supplement for the best effects, indicating the proper amounts, and mentions the need to have your triglycerides checked periodically by your doctor while on fructose.

The switch to fructose can be of inestimable help to an addictive drinker by (1) raising the blood sugar level quickly any time a pick-me-up is needed, without the resultant "down" and other unpleasant effects experienced after eating regular sweets, and (2) keeping the blood sugar level up on a regular basis without triggering an insulin overresponse and the resultant increase of that same malfunctioning over a period of months and years, which leads so often to diabetes and other problems.

A large proportion of American processed foods contain forms of sugar (also labeled as corn syrup, dextrin, sorbitol, and mannitol), so it will be up to you to decide how far you want to go to avoid it. It's almost impossible today in the United States to eat processed foods (including ketchup, relish, soup, peanut butter, tartar sauce, cheese dips, frankfurters, luncheon meats, and frozen items) if you want to avoid sugar without switching entirely to the foods on the dietetic shelf of the market and/or patronizing your nearest health-food store. As you feel you can make more choices in your recovery program, you may want to eliminate your sugar intake entirely, but the stopgap measure of switching to fructose now whenever possible should go a long way toward making you feel better.

Note: Smoking also causes a fall in blood sugar, loss of energy, and other nasty things. However, most emphatically I do not recommend that you stop smoking now. However bad smoking is for you, getting drunk is worse right now, and if you try to quit both simultaneously, you will surely drink. Wait at least a year or more before you tackle smoking.

What to Do about Other Biochemical Deficiencies

Not only does stress cause addictive drinkers to seek the only relief they know, alcohol, but stress, as well as alcohol itself, can also cause nutritional deficiencies which, in turn, cause more stress and so more physiological urge to drink alcohol. Experiments with rats by Williams at the University of Texas proved that stresses and annoyances, such as flashing lights and jangling cowbells going day and night near their cages, were actually driving the animals to drink, even when the food was good enough to prevent their drinking alcohol under ordinary circumstances. In other laboratories it has been found that rats subjected to stress had an increased requirement for certain food elements, such as pantothenic acid (a member of the vitamin B-complex family).

Dr. Pfeiffer of the Brain Bio Center supports this idea of nutritional deficiencies creating compulsion to drink because of biochemically created stress. Two nutrients stand out in any picture of such deficiencies in addictive drinking. One has been widely used therapeutically in the United States, even within some A.A. and Alanon groups: niacin, also known as vitamin B_3. It is an aid, not only in getting dry, but in "maintaining alcohol abstinence by helping to prevent the craving for alcohol," according to Pfeiffer and others. It is effective in reducing the craving for alcohol most likely because it raises the blood sugar levels in the hypoglycemic person, and combats fatigue as well. The other nutrient is pangamic acid, also known as vitamin B_{15}, which is used extensively in the Soviet Union, not only to reduce the compulsion to drink, but also in treating cirrhosis of the liver and alcoholic hepatitis, as well as increasing the sense of well-being and comfort in recovering addictive drinkers. Its value has recently become recognized in the United States (it was discovered by an American!), and it is now readily available, especially in health-food stores.

Pangamic acid is considered by the Russians to be effective also in cases of insomnia. If you cannot find this vitamin, you can substitute another nutrient, inositol, which will help you sleep. Atkins says, "I have found 2000 mg. of inositol taken at bedtime to be a remarkable sleeping medication in many patients; and 650 mg. makes an effective daytime sedative. And how much safer it is than sleeping pills!"

What problems, other than craving for alcohol and insomnia, might you have in drying out? Perhaps it is more correct to ask, "What nutritional deficiencies are normally associated with long-term alcohol drinking?"

To quote Dr. Atkins again: "Alcoholics, in fact, are almost all severely deficient in folic acid [part of the B complex]. They cannot absorb it or vitamin B_1 or B_6 from food even a week after they stop drinking." What does folic acid deficiency produce? "According to folic acid expert Dr. Victor Hebert," Atkins writes, "the symptoms may include irritability, forgetfulness, weakness, tiredness, diarrhea, headache, palpitations, and shortness of breath." To this list Dr. Pfeiffer adds: agitation, moodiness, depression, delusions, hallucinations, and paranoia. I will personally confirm its great value in correcting these symptoms, and add one more—the decreased sex drive seen in heavy drinkers. One alcoholic relabeled it 'frolic acid.' " Dr. Pfeiffer thinks that 90 percent of addictive drinkers suffer folic acid deficiency and says that they are also "particularly susceptible to vitamin B_1 deficiency." He lists both physical and mental symptoms, the latter being "apathy, confusion, emotional instability, irritability, depression and fear of impending disaster." (Vitamin B_1, also known as thiamine, is now used routinely in the treatment of addictive drinkers in hospitals and, according to Dr. Abram Hoffer, "has been clearly shown to have saved lives among alcoholics.")

Much of what was said about folic acid can be said of vitamin B_{12}. It is lost in those who consume alcohol in large quantities. Pfeiffer and other doctors of the school of orthomolecular medicine stress the close relationship between B_{12} and folic acid. They advise women who are taking estrogen (for replacement during menopause or for other reasons) that with the addition of vitamin E and the combined B_{12} and folic acid supplements, the estrogen dose can be substantially reduced or discontinued, to avoid possible undesirable side effects, including the exacerbation of low blood sugar and diabetes. At any rate, if you are taking the birth control pill (which contains a small amount of estrogen), you have an increased need for these vitamins. Since deficiencies of these and other vitamins are associated also with addictive drinking, you have a double problem.

To sum up the case for vitamins, Dr. Pfeiffer writes: "Nutrient programs involving a high-protein diet, large (mega) doses of niacin, vitamin C, vitamin B_6 and occasionally vitamin E have been successful in treating more than five thousand alcoholics, in all stages of the disease."

And the case for trace minerals? First of all, zinc is necessary for the absorption of vitamins B_{12} and A. And, too, Dr. Pfeiffer, reporting on research at the Brain Bio Center into physical impotence in males, found that zinc supplements alone could solve the problem in many cases. Since psychological impotence is such a common problem during recovery from addictive drinking (see "Sober Isn't Sexy—at First, page 193), the addition of a regular zinc supplement to one's diet would, at least, minimize the likelihood of physical impotence. Also consider the fact that studies show most Americans to be deficient in zinc, which serves other nutritional needs as well. (It would appear that the old folk medicine idea that "eating oysters puts lead in your pencil" was almost correct.)

According to Dr. Hoffer, another possible deficiency common to addictive drinkers is a lack of magnesium, which tends, with the associated deficiencies in thiamine (B_1) and niacin (B_3), to cause delirium tremens. He also says that hypoglycemic people need bone meal or dolomitic calcium tablets (combination of magnesium and calcium) twice a day.

If you want to find an orthomolecular specialist for testing and prescription in the areas of diet, vitamin, and trace-element therapy, write the Academy of Orthomolecular Psychiatry, 1691 Northern Boulevard, Manhasset, New York 11030. The academy keeps an active referral list of its fellows throughout the country for this purpose. (Their telephone number is [516] 627–7260.) A current referral list is also maintained by two other agencies: the Canadian Schizophrenia Foundation, 2135 Albert Street, Regina, Saskatchewan, Canada S4P 2VI and the Huxley Institute for Biosocial Research, 1114 First Avenue, New York, New York 10021 (telephone: [212] 759–9554).

There is one more very important aspect of the whole picture with respect to the physical side of alcohol addiction. It can best be described by an observation made by Dr. Pfeiffer:

> Tests have repeatedly shown that diet can affect alcoholism regardless of genetics or environment. A rat placed on a typical American diet of coffee, refined

> foods and soda, will eventually avoid the bowl of water in his cage and selectively drink from the bowl of whiskey. A diet high in carbohydrates, especially of the refined variety, can produce a drunken rat whether or not he has a mean mother or an alcoholic father! This pattern has been discovered in humans as well. . . .

If you are a "carboholic," as we mentioned, you may want to go the whole route, including a hypoglycemic diet. Your orthomolecular specialist can tailor it to aid your recovery. I would *not* suggest switching to a special diet for hypoglycemics at the just-dry stage—wait until you are well into recovery—because, like quitting smoking, there is too much stress involved in such a change at the same time that you are coming off alcohol. Getting off alcohol and sugar (substituting fructose instead) and taking supplementary vitamins and minerals, especially those which are known generally to be needed by addictive drinkers, is enough "switching" at first.

In the meantime, you could not have a better list of vitamins and trace minerals to give you what you need right now than the one Dr. Atkins recommends (below) in his Diet Revolution Centers. (How to increase and decrease vitamin and mineral dosages according to how you feel is described in his book.) There are no harmful side effects since what the body doesn't need of the water-soluble vitamin B group and C will be sloughed off in urine, and the doses listed for the minerals and vitamins A and D are not toxic. However, the minerals and the fat-soluble vitamins A and D should not be taken in dosages larger than those listed. (Some people experience flushing and tingling of the skin after taking niacin, but this effect subsides quickly. To avoid gastric distress from the acidity of such vitamins as niacin and C, don't take them on an empty stomach.) The fat-soluble vitamin E has a special note, as increased dosage beyond the listed 200 I.U. is recommended for women, as stated in the text.

The following is a list of the *total* dosages of each nutrient to be taken each day. The daily amount of vitamin C and the vitamin B group (including PABA, niacin, niacinamide, and calcium pantothenate) should be divided into three doses to be taken after meals:

Vitamin A	10,000 I.U.
Vitamin D	400 I.U.
Vitamin B_1 (thiamine)	100 mg.
Vitamin B_2 (riboflavin)	75 mg.
Vitamin C	1,500 mg.
Niacin	50 mg.
Niacinamide	100 mg.
Calcium	600 mg.
Vitamin B_6 (pyridoxine)	200 mg.
PABA	1,200 mg.
Calcium pantothenate	150 mg.
Folic acid	3.6 mg.
Vitamin B_{12}	750 mcg.
Vitamin E (d-alpha tocopherol form)*	200 I.U.
Magnesium	300 mg.
Manganese	6 mg.
Zinc	45 mg.
Choline	750 mg.
Inositol	450 mg.
Biotin	300 mcg.
Rutin	45 mg.
Bioflavonoids	300 mg.
Iron (as ferrous fumarate)	18 mg.
Iodine (as kelp)	225 mcg.

*If you start with 200 units and gradually build (increasing by 200 units every few days) to 600 or 1200 units, or whatever you need, most toxicity problems will be avoided. Take with any meal, but not simultaneously with iron-containing preparations.

WHAT DO I SAY WHEN SOMEONE OFFERS ME A DRINK?

This is a question I have heard discussed hundreds of times by groups of addictive drinkers in early recovery. It is a vital question for several reasons: (1) When you first stop drinking, it is wise to decide how you are going to handle the problem before it comes up. Otherwise, you are apt to panic and accept a drink, just because you don't know how to say no to it. (2) Your answer to the question may need to be carefully thought out, because you may not want to admit to having any sort of addictive drinking problem, because of the potential damage to your position caused by other people's prejudice and lack of understanding. Only you can assess your own position and decide what is best. (3) Your answer can reveal a lot about your stage of recovery to counselors or other addictive drinkers in recovery. (4) Your answer can serve as bait to bring other addictive drinkers or people who care about one out of the woodwork to ask questions about the illness and about possible treatment. Your answers to these questions may then serve to save someone's life, by encouraging him to seek help. Your answer can also lead to a group discussion of addictive drinking, thus giving you the opportunity to make your specialized knowledge available to everyone, while shooting down a variety of old wives' tales about alcohol, addictive drinking, and its treatment, and thus you can reduce the stigma with which we all have to deal.

If you are in a highly sensitive public position—doctor, public office holder, religious leader, actor, etc., there may be no way to get around the necessity to cover up your addictive drinking problem. Much more commonly, you may be so ashamed of having such a problem, because you have accepted the stigma of society and because you are still worried about what other people will think about you, that you feel you must cover it up. (If you do, you will get rid of those fears as you recover.) In either of the above cases, the following answers have worked well for many people:

1. "No, thank you. My doctor has put me on a medication which, he says, will not work properly if I drink any alcohol." (If you're on Antabuse, this will be quite true, and there are other medications to which this statement applies as well.)

2. "I've started a program to get myself in shape again and decided to stop drinking as part of it."

3. "I don't feel like drinking right now. Could I just have a Coke or a cup of coffee?"

4. "Booze makes my ulcer kick up, so I've decided to be good to myself for a while."

5. "I decided it wasn't doing me any good and gave it up for a while."

6. "No, thanks. I guess I've become allergic to it. It makes me feel sick to my stomach when I drink now."

The function of a good host is to make his guests as comfortable as he can. That means he gives them what they want without asking potentially embarrassing questions. However, there are two kinds of bad hosts: the one who is an addictive drinker himself and so can't imagine that anyone would refuse a drink, and who wants everyone there to drink so that his own drinking will appear more normal, and the one who thinks it's the duty of a good host to press alcohol and food on his guests. Both can be difficult to deal with, but the answer is the same for both. Stick to your guns, and continue to refuse, whether they like it or not. If the person is too difficult, you can leave or decide not to go to his home again. Recovery is a matter of making intelligent choices. This often means removing yourself from uncomfortable places when you feel it necessary.

After I stopped drinking, I learned an interesting thing. Aside from the two bad hosts mentioned above, normal people couldn't care less whether you drink or not, as long as they're getting theirs if they want it. Why should they? It's not the big deal in their minds that it is in yours. They really don't think that much about it. It also came as a surprise to learn that some 30 percent of the American people don't drink a drop at any time—for a variety of reasons. People who don't drink are not as rare as dodo birds by a long shot, although in San Francisco and New York, where the percentage of addictive drinking is believed by some professionals to be as high as one in five in the adult population, they might appear so.

A simpler and more honest answer is "I don't drink. Have you a Coke, a cup of coffee, or tea?" There is no reason for you to have to explain why you don't drink alcohol. If you don't like spinach, you don't eat it, that's all. You don't feel any need to go into a long explanation about it. Why do so about a drink? You don't drink, that's all. If they press you, you can say a variety of things: "Don't like it." "Don't like what it does to me." "It makes me stupid, and I'm dumb enough as it is." "Do you really care?" "Look, I don't drink. Let's not make a federal case out of it." Nobody has any right to press you for your reasons. It's bad manners. You can even say, "Look, it's my life. Let me run it the way I want to, please." They'll get the message.

It's really quite funny the way addictive drinkers in early recovery manage to convince themselves that nobody knew about their problem at all and that they must continue to try to hide it. All the neighbors heard the family fights, saw the drunken parties, the unusually large number of bottles in the trash cans, heard what your children told them or their children about Daddy's or Mommy's drinking, saw you weaving up to the door late at night over and over, and all the rest of the signs. I never drank in the morning when I had to teach, because I knew I couldn't fool the kids. So I'd take a big B_{12} shot for the hangover, force food to settle my stomach, put Revlon Touch-and-Glow makeup on my blue nose and Visine in my red eyes, and go to class, feeling pure and confident. After I stopped drinking, I went back to one school for a visit and learned that I had had a reputation for drinking in the morning among all the kids, because the odor of alcohol on my breath and from my body—even after a shower—was so strong from the night before that they thought I must have been drinking that morning! If you have been drinking addictively for any extended period of time, you can count on most of the people around you knowing it. That being the case, there is another and often better way to answer the question.

"No, thank you. I don't drink, because I'm a recovering [recovered*] alcoholic [addictive drinker]." I've been saying "recovered alcoholic" and, more recently, "recovered addictive drinker" for years, and the response is interesting. It was a real surprise to me at first. What I usually get, if anything is said at all, is, in one form or another, "Say, that's great. I really admire you," or, "You mean you really were an alcoholic and you were able to quit entirely?" Recovered addictive drinkers say this in public so rarely that it usually comes as a surprise to people, and they are almost invariably favorably impressed. I wondered about this at first, because I was very much aware of the general stigma, and then I figured it out. When someone believes that an addictive drinker is a bum, a person with no character, no willpower, and then hears me say that I was addicted and recovered, he has to think that I am one helluva guy, with lots of character and willpower, because he has surely read or heard stories about how the addict almost never makes it. It's funny that stigma can actually make people think well of you, rather than the other way around.

The real advantage in using this answer, however, is the good it gives you a chance to do. When you say, "I'm a recovered alcoholic [addictive drinker], it is usually true that the person or persons who hear you have never met "one of those people," and they are almost always fascinated, curious, and full of questions. That's why your answer often leads to a group discussion of the whole drinking, treatment, and recovery question. Or it leads to someone sidling up to you in the course of the evening to say, "Excuse me, but I heard you say you were a recovered addictive drinker— Now, I have a friend—" Of course, the friend is usually standing right there in front of you, but in either case, the

*See "Recovering vs. Recovered," page 268.

opportunity to help someone, and even save his life and the happiness of his family, is there for you to use as best you can.

What you say when someone offers you a drink is nobody's business but your own, and nobody has any right to question you about it. If they do, it is your privilege to respond in any way that seems appropriate. The one thing you cannot do is allow yourself to feel so insecure, so desirous of appearing to be something you are not in order to please others, that you let them control you and make you do things that make you feel worse about yourself. If you do that, you'll drink again. Your only alternative is to stand up on your own legs and look out for yourself, however wobbly those legs may feel at first. Nobody else will do it for you, and you will be surprised to find how much stronger those legs become after a few weeks of regular calisthenics. They don't push me around anymore when they offer me a drink, I can tell you. I have even said, when really pushed, "Look, when I drink either I get violent and smash up the furniture, or I puke on the carpet— Do you want that?" That usually stops 'em.

PLANNING YOUR OWN RECOVERY

It should be understood that a great many addictive drinkers never enter a detox, halfway house, or recovery home. They manage to get well using outpatient services—from initial withdrawal right on through the whole growth process. Others do this only in part, choosing to use one or more of the live-in facilities in the early stages of their growth process. Every possible combination has been right for someone. *There is no one way to get dry and stay that way. Each individual must choose his own*, that combination of inpatient and outpatient facilities and services which makes sense to him in dealing with his problem. And each must incorporate into his planning his decision as to how he will deal with the problem of what to do when someone offers him a drink and how he will deal with the variety of other problems that arise. The essential point is that getting well begins with the single choice either to take action and recover or to give up and die a drunk. From then on, recovery is a matter of making intelligent choices and expanding one's options until the sky is the limit.

Action is the name of the game in getting well. And this is why: During the just-dry period the addictive drinker is a rational person taking rational steps to get well one minute, and in the next moment an emotional animal in excruciating pain, with body and mind crying for the only relief he knows—a drink. He is on a seesaw all day long: "I will not drink. I understand what I have to do. It makes sense, and I know it works." Then: "But, my God, I've got to have a drink. It's driving me crazy." When the stress level is down, he can be a rational person; when it is up, his reason is hanging by a thread. If you don't have a plan of action all worked out in advance for the times when you get really depressed, completely discouraged, too weak and too tired to fight anymore, or just can't go another five minutes without a drink, *you will drink.* Also, certain people and situations can drive your stress level to the point of explosion in minutes. At such times don't expect to be able to think and make decisions. With a game plan for when high stress moments occur, you can be prepared for these situations and stay away from that first deadly drink. Otherwise, forget it. A recovery home or some other protected environment is a good place to work out and contemplate (practice in your own mind) situational game plans. Parts Three and Four of this book contain specific suggestions to help you do that. If you choose to go to a live-in facility for thirty days or more, I suggest that you take this book with you to help you work out some of these plans.

There are forms on pages 146 and 208 of this book which will help you in roughing out your basic plan of attack for getting dry and staying that way, and will help you with the more sophisticated planning discussed in Parts Three and Four. I found these forms helpful for people I was counseling, because, once on paper, the plans became more concrete in their minds and also could be used at a later date as a point of reference for deciding what changes in their programs would be appropriate. When I was first getting sober, I worked out the various elements of my plan at different times, but never put them down on paper, and consequently never had a sharp, clear picture. I now believe that writing down the plan is helpful in giving one a sense that he *has* a concrete plan and a direction in his life, and it is then easier to put into practice.

In my opinion, A.A. should be choice number one in any addictive drinker's recovery plan. It offers much in one free package that can be found nowhere else, except in bits and pieces.

Planning One Day at a Time

It is helpful if you start living one day at a time as soon as you feel you can take this action. Not only will your just-dry days be made easier with one-day-at-a-time living, but the hours which were formerly used up in drinking will need to be filled in pleasure-giving ways—or you will drink again. As I said in Part One, starting with one or two hours a day is the best way to begin.

Take a Sunday (or any free day) right after you've quit drinking. Have a good big breakfast. If you aren't used to that, do it anyway, even if you have to wait a couple of hours before you can face it. Your whole body is trying to make a big adjustment, and it needs food. Your nerves especially are in terrible shape, and they need food to recover. Don't read the paper or listen to the news. It's all bad, and you don't need bad news. (You will hear anything really important from other people anyway.)

Choose to practice "one day at a time" for an hour or two while keeping busy, taking a walk, or raking leaves, cleaning your guns or oiling your sewing machine, spray-painting the garden chairs or sorting tools in the cellar—whatever, but *do* something. (This before or after breakfast; it's your day.) After that, maybe golf or tennis, maybe a good book, or doing something with your children (at the playground, at their favorite ice cream shop) for an hour or two (whatever time you planned on). (If you are to be free this day—and on subsequent days in the just-dry period—find someone to take your small children for part of each day.) In the afternoon, visit or call an A.A. friend, especially if you're uptight. If there's an A.A. club around (open twenty-four hours a day in some urban centers), spend some time there. Join the Y and get a list of all their programs and classes, or join an athletic club, or start a new hobby. (Today? Yes!) Do anything, but do something new and different, even if you don't feel like it.

Keep in mind that you are learning how to live in the present and to have fun all over again, without booze; and you have to start doing things before you can enjoy them. It does no good merely to sit and think how pure you are in the just-dry period; you have to have some fun, to enjoy life sober, or you'll get drunk again. If you get tired, take a nap or rest for a while, but don't start feeling sorry for yourself. If that starts, get on the phone to an A.A. friend or join other people who are not drinking so you can come out of yourself and start thinking about something else. Remember, no thoughts about past or future (not even planning your "day at a time" for tomorrow!) if you can possibly do it—all day long. Keeping busy is the best way to do that.

By evening you should be tired enough to sleep, though this may be hard to do if you're just off the sauce. (Even so, it will pass in a week or so. See page 129 for sleep help.) If you're still awake, just lying there, think about the day, what you did, how you made out with the hours which you structured and called "one day at a time" hours. If you had to push yourself to do some of the things, take pride in that, talk to yourself about it, consciously, to build up your self-image and self-confidence. Say to yourself, "Well, I put away the magazines scattered all over the den, started a new book, talked to Joan about Billy's problem, watched a game with Dan, washed one load of clothes, prepared breakfast and supper, set out everything for a help-yourself lunch, went to an A.A. meeting and to a coffee bar afterward with two new friends from the group. Not bad. Oh, yes, I didn't take a drink today. Pretty good, really, and maybe I'll decide not to drink tomorrow, too." That's right; you do that only a day at a time, too. *Never* decide to quit forever. That's a terrible thing to think about, and it is meaningless, anyway. Maybe you will choose to drink tomorrow. Who knows? After all, you are running the store now. You make the choices, even the choice to drink again.

The Dry Drunk

The "dry drunk" is a curious but serious phenomenon that occurs from time to time during recovery. This is what happens: A person has stopped drinking and begun to make progress toward recovery. He has achieved some real hope of ultimate success in his battle with the bottle, feels better physically and mentally, is beginning to feel much more positive about life and people, and is taking steps toward getting himself and his life straightened out. He may even be almost euphorically happy much of the time, the "pink cloud" feeling previously referred to. Then, often quite suddenly, or by degrees over a period of days, all that changes. He becomes tense, negative, highly critical of other people, extremely self-centered, and impatient with any person, thing, or event which thwarts him even in the smallest way. His statements in general become grandiose, highly judgmental, and quite unrealistic. The total effect is behavior that is irrational and childish in the extreme. Associated with all this is a general mood of depression and loss of interest in positive activities and projects, including his recovery program. Nothing seems worthwhile, and everything is wrong. The dry drunk is a very unpleasant and dangerous condition—unpleasant for the dry drinker, who is miserable, and for everyone around him, and dangerous, because it frequently results in a return to drinking.

Here is another reason for the statement that the addictive drinker cannot do it alone. Even when the dry drunk comes on suddenly, the individual is sometimes not aware of it. He knows that he suddenly feels lousy, that everything is somehow different, but he doesn't realize that the people around him and the world are the same, that it is his mental state which has changed. If he thinks about it at all, he usually concludes that he has been looking at the world through rose-colored glasses and now suddenly sees it as it really is—dirty, hopeless, frustrating, and worthless. However, if he has learned what a dry drunk is, a sudden mental flip-flop back to the negative, supercritical, defeatist, self-hating thinking of his worst drinking days, and that it need be only a temporary time of discomfort, which must be lived through and dealt with by taking positive action, he can take those actions and come out of it. That is, he can if he recognizes it for what it is, or if there is someone there to recognize what is happening and make him aware of it. However, telling an addictive drinker that he's on a dry drunk is not an easy thing to do, and the person who does must be someone whose judgment and knowledge of alcohol addiction he respects. Otherwise, he will reject the statement as absurd, because, having made some notable progress in recovery, he cannot now accept the idea that his life is still unmanageable, that he still has a long, long way to go before he can be truly well and in full command of himself at all times. It's denial again, coupled with a depressed state—a time for action.

What action? First, take a look at your diet, especially with respect to the eating of sugar and the resultant hypoglycemia "attacks" I described earlier. Did you switch to fructose as a sugar substitute? (Many addictive drinkers leave booze for sweets and lots of table sugar and, as time goes on, increase their intake of sugar, making their insulin response even whackier. One man I know drives around with bags full of sweets in his van at all times; he's also fighting slips throughout the year, and is in and out of A.A. like a jack-in-the-box.) Are you taking the vitamin and mineral supplements? If you did not choose to do this, I suggest you do now. They can be vital.

What other action can you take to ensure that you won't go on to that first drink? You can put yourself with positive people who understand dry drunks. Go to an A.A. club, meeting, or friend; tell someone how you feel, that you suspect you may be on a dry drunk, and get their reaction and support. What usually happens is this: Eventually during such a get-together of A.A.-ers someone will bring up a problem which *you* have dealt with successfully, and you will find yourself working hard to get him to see the solution. By the time you are done, you are out of yourself, out of your depression, and out of your dry drunk. Suddenly you will feel fine again.

Addiction is a self-centered illness, and the best answer to most of the unpleasant emotional states that occur in recovery is to get out of yourself by becoming involved in the lives of other people or in some form of creative activity—painting, carving, building—activities which make you give of yourself, instead of feeling "poor me." It's a fundamental rule: Any time you find yourself criticizing others, complaining about the world, and feeling "poor me," you're in trouble. That's the signal to take action. When you do, it works, if you give it time, and then you have won the battle and can feel proud of having done so. That is, you have taken one more successful step toward self-conquest and can feel that much better about yourself as a person competent to deal with himself and his world. Essentially, recovery is a process of learning to put up with unpleasant emotional states or living problems, while taking action to change those states or overcome the problem. Dry drunks are almost standard procedure, and only temporary, if you can recognize them for the imposters they are. "Knowledge is power."

When can you expect a dry drunk to occur? Any time. I had a recovering addictive drinker friend who had been in

A.A. for four years. He was easygoing, always inconveniencing himself to help others (a real "people pleaser"), a carpenter, happily married and apparently now well-adjusted. One day he picked me up to go shopping for supplies in the city, and I met a new Frank as I got into the car.

"You know that BMW with the busted muffler I left to be repaired? He promised to have it by six last night, so I could pick it up this morning. You know what? The dumb bastard wasn't even there. I saw his wife, and he hadn't even started on it. Just took off to do something with his brother!" We stopped at a red light, and when it changed, the car ahead delayed perhaps three seconds before starting to move. "Jesus Christ, move it, you son-of-a-bitch! These damned drivers out here are the worst in the world. No goddamn consideration for anybody!" He then shifted down, floored it, and screamed past the slow starter, giving him the finger and cutting sharply in front of him. All the way to town it was the same, a constant series of foul-mouthed imprecations at and disdainful comments about every driver on the road. In the stores the same thing—cheap, shoddy merchandise, all the prices were robbery, the clerks stupid, and the restaurant food not fit for a dog.

All this may sound like exaggeration, but it is not. The whole afternoon was like that, a real Dr. Jekyll–Mr. Hyde kind of personality change—in short, a dry drunk. They're not all that sudden and dramatic, of course, but the change is always remarkable to anyone who knows the person well. It's no fun to experience or to deal with, but it's no big thing if you can recognize it for what it is and know what to do about it.

What really happens, of course, is that stress has built up in the person over a period of time to a dangerously high level, in spite of the stress relief in his recovery program, and the dry drunk is the response. The fury at the slow-starting car, the supercritical ranting and constant complaining about everyone and everything, are all unconscious reactions to vent the stored-up emotional pressure. That is why the behavior appears so irrational and childish. The cause is the emotional pressure, not the person or event, and the violent reaction is proportional to the pressure, not the action or event.

When do dry drunks stop? At some point of personal growth after enough of the physical and emotional problems creating abnormal stress have been isolated and taken care of. Frank had successfully completed getting dry and choosing for himself a better situation than he had had in his drinking days. He had achieved a reasonable measure of personal growth in A.A., but by no means had he achieved the upper levels of personal growth that I will be discussing in Part Four, "Choosing Your Own Self." Also, he had done nothing about the physical aspects of his illness. As a result, while apparently in no danger of a return to drinking, his life was and is today punctuated at irregular intervals with dry drunks, explosions of temper, and thoroughly uncomfortable periods of depression. This is so, and will continue to be so, because he is unaware of the fact that there is much more to do and much further to go—not to recover, but to live richly.

EARLY RECOVERY PLAN

Consider each of the following, and note or check beside each what you plan to do about it. Because of denial, be sure to choose to do more than what you think of as your minimum need.

Make appointment with a counselor at the National Council of Alcoholism (to answer my questions, refer me to groups and facilities, and help me to make some of the necessary decisions below) ______

GETTING DRY

1. Cold turkey? (If yes, medical exam by doctor—addictive drinking specialist preferred—is strongly advised.) ______

Do it at home? ______

At detox, recovery home, or hospital? ______

2. Taper off?

At detox, recovery home, or hospital? ______

ALCOHOLICS ANONYMOUS

1. Call A.A. and ask that someone come to talk to me about it? ______
2. Go to a meeting by myself? ______
3. Length of time I should prescribe for myself in A.A.? (Most strongly recommended: 90 meetings in 90 days and regular attendance for at least two years.) ______

ANTABUSE

(Medical exam for possible allergy recommended.)

1. Make appointment with doctor for allergy test? ______
2. Length of time I should prescribe for myself? (At least one year is strongly recommended.) ______

DRUG WITHDRAWAL. Tranquilizers and Other Mood-Altering Substances, Including Marijuana Yes!

(Essential for recovery as noted. Can be done simultaneously with withdrawal from alcohol, but only as recommended by a medical specialist. THIS IS A MUST, EXCEPT IN THE CASE OF MARIJUANA. See A.A. or National Council on Alcoholism for name of a doctor to advise you.)

BODY CHEMISTRY. Fructose, Vitamins and Minerals, Coffee, Tea

1. Take Glucose Tolerance Test (GTT)?* ______
2. Take home test to determine need for GTT?* ______
3. Assume 9-to-1 odds I have hypoglycemia and switch to fructose sugar—

---

*See *Dr. Atkins' Superenergy Diet.*

Wherever I use table sugar? ______
In all cooking at home? ______
Eat only sweets made with fructose? ______

4. Take the entire list of recommended vitamins and minerals? ______
5. Quit coffee or limit to 4 cups a day? ______
6. Switch to decaffeinated coffee? ______
7. Quit tea or limit to 4 cups weak tea a day? ______

FACILITIES

1. Synanon? ______
2. Quarter-way or halfway house or recovery home after detox or if already dry? ______

What will I say when someone offers me a drink? ______

____

PRACTICE A DAY AT A TIME? ______
When? ______
For how long? ______

Have someone close to me read "Dry Drunk" section and agree to tell me when I show signs of being on one? ______

Ask one or more people in my therapy group to do the same? ______

Have someone close to me read "Denial" section and agree to tell me when it is showing? ______

Ask one or more people in my therapy group to do the same? ______

When I have a strong compulsion to drink, I will

____

When I become seriously depressed, to bring myself out of it I will

____

What have I decided to do about my drinking buddies?

____

How do I plan to make new friends who will not threaten my sobriety?

____

Many things in life are unfair. That's reality. What kinds of unfairness bother me most?

______________ ______________ ______________

______________ ______________ ______________

______________ ______________ ______________

How will I deal with each of these in the future?

______________ ______________ ______________

PART THREE

CHOOSING YOUR OWN SITUATION, THE LONG-TERM GOAL

GOING BEYOND JUST DRY

The physical and emotional effects of long-term alcohol abuse occur so gradually that they are not even noticed by the person doing the drinking and not for a long time even by those closest to him. However, they are very real. To take just one example of the physical effects: brain-wave comparisons have shown that the patterns of stress drinkers are distinctly different from those of people who do not drink heavily, and that it takes about eighteen months completely free of alcohol for them to return to normal. During all this time, the quality of thinking processes and judgment is improving.

While your body and mind are recovering, you are not only learning more about stress drinking—which, we hope, is now in the past—but you are beginning to learn stress reduction—how to pinpoint your problem areas and apply the appropriate techniques to straighten them out. This is the most crucial phase of recovery, the period when all stress-reducing mechanisms are least effective, when you have hardly started on changing attitudes, and therefore, your abnormal stress level, which causes the compulsion, is still fluctuating dangerously near your threshold, the level at which you will drink in spite of all the willpower in the world.

Also during this just-dry time, your relationships with other people are likely to be in terrible shape, at a time when you need the full support of friends and family desperately. Furthermore, you may have decided that you must give up your old drinking buddies, in order to stay off the stuff, and there hasn't been time to make new friends among nondrinking people or people who, at least, don't drink enough to make friendship with them a threat to your sobriety. (By the way, A.A. offers you the best and fastest way to make new friends.) In sum, this is the most difficult time of adjustment, when you are in the poorest position to handle it. This is the time when your return on your investment of great effort and real suffering is far from satisfying. It's like starting a new business. You have to work like hell and just hang in there for a long time before the real profits start to roll in. Of course, it is only on the basis of the real hope and confidence that the profits will eventually roll in that you make the effort at all, and fortunately, there are some immediate profits to help you keep going. Therefore, it should be of some help to you to know that all the time and effort you are spending, and all the discomfort you are going through, lead to much more, as you will see, than just getting dry. After all, that is just the short-term goal.

Removing Stress from Your Situation

If you have a serious drinking problem, we can assume that your life is not working out at all satisfactorily for some reason or reasons and you are in a bad situation. How do intelligent people get into such situations?

The major reason is that they innocently make long-term commitments at an age when they are not properly prepared to make such commitments and they have very little choice but to do so—bad marriages, jobs that turn out to be inappropriate for their skills and interests, buying-on-credit traps, life-styles they can't afford, and so on. Compounding these mistakes of judgment is their lack of knowledge that such errors can and must be rectified as soon as it becomes clear that they are serious errors, *regardless of the cost*, because failure to do so can ruin one's life. Instead, seeing themselves as irrevocably committed—because of children, because of raises and retirement benefits, because they "need" all the things bought on credit, because pride makes the lifestyle a "necessity"—they plug on for years, trying to make an impossible situation work. It won't. Now they are in a trap, and as the years roll by, the intolerable stresses of the situation build and build. Addictive drinking results and further compounds the problem by adding new stresses.

Living is an art that requires special skills and wisdom, which we usually do not have in early life. That is a fundamental problem of being human. Therefore, it is not surprising that so many people are destroyed by this lack, and *they are most certainly not to blame for it.*

Once you have recognized that your situation is bad, perhaps even a mess, and that you are in kindergarten when it comes to knowing how to direct your life intelligently, the solution, of course, is to acquire the knowledge you need as quickly as possible, so that you can straighten your situation out and begin to function as a person in control of his life, probably for the first time.

Stress, however caused, must be dealt with, but emotional stress is by far the most subtle and difficult to attack. It is just too nonspecific to get hold of! So now is the time to look below the tip of the iceberg to see what lies beneath the surface, beneath the stress. When we look under the water, we find fear. Fear is the major cause of emotional stress, but it is possible to defeat it. Tranquilizers can and do reduce stress (just as alcohol does); they make you "less nervous," in fact, quite *fear*less. But they can't remove the fear or its causes; they can only lessen your awareness of it. A belief in a Higher Power can help in the same way, but faith does not remove the fear or its causes either, although it does help with the short-term goal of getting dry and staying that way. So let's learn how to attack and deal with fear effectively.

You start to remove large chunks of fear by changing

those aspects of your situation that generate a great deal of anxiety. The just-dry period is the best time to begin this process, which I call mature life planning—specifically, to improve your immediate situation, and generally to start dreaming and planning for bigger things to come. Stress drinkers are great dreamers, but as the illness progresses, the productive, realistic kind of dreaming stops and becomes unrealistic fantasy. Now is the time to start dreaming again, the good kind, and there is an altogether pleasant way to go about it. Thinking ahead about all the good things you might like to be working for and achieving, even though they may seem far in the future just now, is the best way of making the difficult early days of recovery more hopeful and pleasant.

After you have resolved the major fear-producing problems in your immediate situation, there will still be residual fears and new ones coming up in the future. How the individual can pinpoint and attack specific fears, one by one, is part of a later discussion, "Choosing Your Own Self." But, first, let's begin to think about how to resolve some of those major fear-producing problems in your situation right now.

Life is a pretty complicated business, divided up as it is into many different compartments: family, work, friendships, outside interests, religious faith, etc. If you really want to get anywhere putting some *sense and order* into it, you have to follow a logical plan of attack, actually take an inventory of your situation, your circumstances, whereby you divide your life into segments and examine each with great care. Only in this way can you see clearly what is right and good in each *for you* and what needs to be changed to make a consistent plan for achieving your overall objectives. This is where you identify the areas that are creating massive stress (fears) and decide what changes are indicated to put those areas right.

The biggest problem addictive drinkers have with the kind of logical, sensible examination and planning of one's life that I am suggesting is that they are used to looking at themselves as the helpless victims of other people and circumstances. They resemble, to me, the British troops dug in at Cassino in World War II. There they were, sitting in slit trenches half filled with rainwater, with no protection from the weather at all, stiff-upper-lipping it and miserable. The Americans, on the other flank of the allied front, had taken the trouble to build elaborate underground shelters furnished with chairs and tables from bombed-out buildings. Each had a sign, some very carefully painted, giving the name of the establishment, MARY'S PARLOR, FRANK'S BAR & GRILL, etc. By comparison with the British, they were living in great comfort and splendor. Yet both groups were in the same circumstances with the same materials at their disposal. One group planned and made the effort. The other apparently assumed there was nothing to do but accept and put up with a miserable situation. They thought they had no control over their circumstances.

If your life has been mostly sitting in a muddy slit trench in the rain and you have decided you don't like that, do some planning. Get off your duff, and start building Mary's Parlor. It doesn't have to be much at first to be an awful lot better.

If life planning is to be of real use to anyone, stress drinker or otherwise, it absolutely must be *flexible*, that is, capable of adjustment, adaptation, and change. And it must be kept *simple* in the early days of recovery, because "long-term drinking is bad for thinking." Stress drinkers are famous for setting up elaborate, rigid plans, and then moving heaven and earth to make them happen. I did frequently. They also tend to get drunk a lot in the process. Or for two weeks straight when it's over!

To develop a well-thought-out plan, you have to start somewhere, so let's begin with housing . . .

HOUSING

For openers, we will look at how one man finally recognized that a very important positive factor in his life had become a negative factor and a source of massive stress. Once he was able to see this, he could turn it into a positive factor again in a matter of days. It did happen, and it did work out beautifully for him, becoming a key element of his recovery.

Paul had a small plumbing contracting business, an attractive wife, and two sons—one in college and one married and in sales. He also had a drinking problem, which had been causing increasing problems for some years, but the situation was not yet too serious in his own mind. (Denial.) If you had asked him, he would have said that he was quite happy. After all, "everyone has problems," and his business was doing very well.

Then, one day, he came home to find his wife gone and a letter in his easy chair. She could no longer live with his drinking, had taken her personal things, and asked only that he agree to a divorce. (Here was instant massive stress.)

In a daze he went to the kitchen for a drink, and "came to" some three weeks later in a detox, where the police had brought him. Aside from a few disjointed and hazy recollections of isolated events, he could remember nothing. His clothes were torn and filthy, and he had only seven dollars in his wallet. He was over five hundred miles from home. (A long blackout.)

As soon as he was over the shakes, he left the detox, used his credit cards for some clothes and a plane ticket, and flew home. From the airport he went directly to his best friend and business partner and told him the whole story. It was a long session, but his friend was understanding and they both agreed that he should try A.A., which he did. He was ready, and it "took" for him from the first meeting.

Six months later he was staying dry and feeling somewhat better, but he still loved his wife and was terribly lonely. He was getting along all right at work, at the restaurant where he ate lunch with friends, and in A.A., but whenever he came home, his house was a constant reminder of happy times with his family, depressing him to the point of almost drinking several times. He moved to a motel, which, while better than the house, was far from ideal; he was still very lonely. Then he sat down to consider his alternatives. There had to be a better answer.

(By the way, it took six months for the gravity of the situation to force upon him the fact that the house had suddenly shifted from a positive factor in his life, as it was before his wife had left him, to an almost entirely negative factor and a major threat to his well-being. Through a process of rational inventory taking, he could have seen this sooner, avoiding a lot of misery and painful emotion, which is very dangerous in the just-dry period.)

When he sat down to consider his alternatives, he came up with these: another smaller house, a condominium, an apartment, a residence hotel with housekeeping services, or a mobile home. But he discovered an interesting yet discouraging thing: none of the alternatives was very attractive to him, and he couldn't seem to choose any one above the others. The motel where he was seemed as good as the alternatives, so he decided not to decide just then.

Most people find it hard to make good decisions, and addictive drinkers in the early stages of recovery often find it particularly hard, because they have lost a large part of their old self-confidence and drive and are often in a highly emotional state, a normal result of the illness. This being the case, it is important to realize that the decision not to make a decision is the only sensible one to make at times. It may also be that none of the alternatives you have selected is attractive because none solves the problem, as it turned out in this case.

Paul had always loved boats and the sea and boating people. As a boy and a young man he had sailed small boats for years. So, one Sunday, with nothing to do and feeling lonely as usual, he wandered down to the marina. He got talking to a guy who lived on a houseboat year round. Suddenly there was a housing alternative he had not even considered. "You know, that could be a ball," and as he talked boats, he learned about a beautiful 40-foot Alden sloop for sale which he could afford as soon as his agent sold his house.

Not long after that day he was living a dream which he

had never even thought possible. There weren't enough free hours in the day to work on that boat! While on board, he always had people around with whom he had a lot in common, people who discussed his projects with him, and he helped with theirs. The loneliness was gone. Again, had he dreamed as part of his inventory taking, he might have found this solution sooner.

Without question, the single greatest problem of most recovering addictive drinkers is loneliness (more on this important subject in a later section), the feeling that no one really cares about them and the lack of having someone to care for, someone to share their lives with. Of all the causes of stress, the fear that one's spouse (one's family) doesn't really care, or if there is no longer a family, the fear that loneliness will go on and on may be the worst. If loneliness is an important part of your problem, it must be solved or ameliorated in every possible way. Or none of your housing alternatives will look bright, either.

A woman I know, Nancy, sobered up, realized that her marriage of twenty-plus years was a hopeless dead end, and got a divorce. She had been a mother most of her adult years, had not worked outside of her own home since she married, and had recently developed a new hobby, weekend and summer hiking, which had included a backpacking trip to France. After her divorce she had no idea of what sort of housing she wanted, because she didn't like houses and she didn't want suburbia. If she wanted a house at all, it would have to be a very easy-to-keep one, because she had had a lifetime of home maintenance and she wanted no more of that. In the New England house where she had lived, the climate was hopeless for much of the year, and she often daydreamed of a tent pitched somewhere on the sunny slopes of the Mediterranean!

One evening some friends mentioned that their small villa in southern France was a burden: the tenant was leaving, the gardener was a problem— She jumped at the opportunity and made a deal to be both tenant and gardener for reduced rent. The tiny house, with tiled floors, stuccoed walls, and lack of industrial dirt, made housekeeping easy. The eternal sunshine was wonderful after gray New England winters. But most of all, she liked the pace, the midday pause when everyone stops working, and she liked the garden. She already spoke some French.

She had limited funds, so she had taken the cheapest cabin offered on an ocean liner, where she had three roommates who spoke no English, and she began using her French on the voyage. The small French village where she now lived had a central plaza, where Nancy set up a card table and a sign in French advertising conversational English classes in her new home. (She couldn't live on principle forever!) Her hourly charge was pitifully small by American standards, but so were her living expenses. She registered enough students, adults and children in small groups, to more than cover her rent and food, and arranged her classes so as to be free to do her daily gardening job, with time to have some fun, too.

Her dream became a practical reality (without the tent), with the added bonus that she had a built-in introduction to the people of the village and had a chance to see real French life as no tourist can ever hope to.

Millicent, another recovering drinker, hated the maintenance of her house, too, especially now that all three of her children were off on their own (one still in college). She was convinced that her sobriety would be in jeopardy if she didn't cut down on "this endless cleaning, for what?" She and her husband talked it over, decided they really loved their house, at least the living-room–kitchen–patio part where they "lived," so they cleaned out the rest of the house, including all their bedroom furniture, had a garage sale, and bought a convertible sofa-bed for the living room! (A lot of clothes went, too, in that sale, Millicent told me.) They made less than $1,500 on it, but that really didn't matter. They closed up those rooms and got down to "living simply instead of sentimentally," as she says. It was a dream of hers—to "simplify"—one she kept talking about but never did. How did it work out? Two years later she told me they had cut a skylight into the roof, and both of them had taken up painting! It's now a large studio (two walls were taken out), and they both work up there, sometimes together, criticizing each other's progress. "I never clean the studio," she said. "I don't either," her husband quipped, "that would be cheating."

Maybe you don't have a house to sell and leave or to stay in and "simplify." Maybe you are coming up from near bottom. I still recommend dreaming. I know a young unmarried couple (it could be an old couple, too) who were both addicted to alcohol, both recovering and serious about living one day at a time. They asked for and got an unfinished attic to live in. The deal was that they would finish it by their own labor while they lived there; the landlord would furnish the materials. They contracted for two years of residence, paying a nominal rent after the building was finished. By that time they expected to be well on the way to recovery, employed in outside jobs and able to afford other housing.

Dreaming and making dreams come true is one of the most exciting things about living. Don't miss it. But remember, it's not always possible to make dreams come true in a matter of days. (Nancy worked on going to France for six months and did not have her classes in English established until she had been there close to four months.) But you still go at it "one step at a time," just as in overcoming addiction. That's only a dream in the beginning, too. At least, that's all it was for me; I often had times when I didn't really believe I could make it. You probably will too, and those times are when you should do some serious questioning of your own situation. The housing factor is often vital.

Your housing may be weighing you down in financial ways; for example, high mortgage payments and maintenance costs while you're out of work or receiving a reduced salary as a result of problems caused by your drinking. Could a smaller house, a condominium, or some other option remove that financial burden and change your whole situation? (It doesn't have to be forever. We are living in the present now, remember.) Or perhaps employment in your field of work is so tight where you now live that the odds against your finding another job are too high. Is your housing blocking you from a move to another area where you are not known as a drunk, where it would be easier to get started again? Have you always wanted to live someday in a place you once visited and liked a lot? Now is the time to consider these things and make appropriate decisions, before you get locked in again.

A trailer, camper, motor home, a converted truck or bus, are possibilities which you may own already or could buy outright, while getting completely clear of mortgage and high maintenance costs. I remember Bob, a Vietnam jungle hero, who had truly hit bottom after his glory days were over. In recovery he finally got the idea that one thing he had to have to stay sober was mobility. Now he lives in a motor home, and he is on the job first thing in the morning—a block away, in the parking lot across the street, or right in your driveway—depending upon where today's job is. His motor home is tool shed, nearby refrigerator, and "recovery space" for a coffee or think break, but the best thing it is is wheels. He often invites guests to stay overnight (in the guest "room"), and since he fancies himself a gourmet cook, he rides his guests around to get "all the proper fixin's."

Jill, another recovering drinker, lives in a trailer park, but not in a trailer. She lives in a low-rent cottage (one of about ten) in the corner of the park, where she paints all day. She converted the small garage into a studio and wired up fluorescent lighting to simulate northern light, as she was not allowed to cut through the roof to make a skylight. She uses the pay phone for outgoing calls and checks for in-coming messages at the park office; otherwise she keeps a NOT NOW sign on her front door during the day when she is painting. She is a respected artist, wins awards, and is shown in some galleries, but she can't make a living that way, so she stays in the trailer park where people come and go (and do buy), where there are lots of people around for the fun times, and where she is a "unique fish" in the big pond of Connecticut. It is interesting that Jill, like Bob the mechanic, has hit bottom more than once, despite the help of half a dozen psychiatrists, and has finally made it largely because her house is more a base of operations than just a place to cook, clean, and come back to.

Don't let false pride—what "they" may be saying about you—prevent you from making such a move. Anything that promises to improve your situation financially, emotionally, or otherwise is worth any reasonable sacrifice. Such moves do not have to be permanent. They are means to an end, a better life for you. If that decision frees you from heavy financial burdens, you can also now get away for a hunting or fishing trip, see some new part of the world, attend more musicals right in town, or go to a learn-to-ski week, where you can keep busy while staying sober. When you begin to have this sort of fun without booze, then you will have the real pride in yourself you need to stay sober.

If you think you are so far down financially that there is no housing for you anywhere short of sleeping under the bridge, then look into secondhand tent trailers; they can be picked up for a fraction of their retail cost, because people usually buy them new. Two or three hundred dollars can buy a nice one in most places, if you look around. (The car to pull it can come later.) Then there are the live-in jobs, with house or quarters furnished as fringe benefits, or because you have to be on the premises most of the time for some reason. Such jobs include: skippering or crewing on a yacht; managing a motel, hotel, or hunting lodge; many service, janitorial, and farm-labor jobs; institutional jobs in schools, hospitals, colleges, summer camps, recovery homes, and homes for juveniles. Labor-contract jobs abroad often include housing, or you might live in as a companion, tutor, governess, or nurse. Most of these jobs also guarantee that you will not be alone too much, a great danger in recovery, especially for those who have recently lost their family or moved to a new area where they know no one. A.A. is always a tremendous help in this area, because even if you elect to get a job as a governess or chambermaid with a well-to-do family in one of the famous watering holes or resorts where the boozing goes on as much as the watering, A.A. meetings and instant friends will be there or nearby.

We must look at each problem separately—housing, job, etc.—for obvious reasons, but the interrelationships, as you can see, are often far more important than any one item by itself. A woman I counseled went to a recovery home for a period of rest and recuperation, made friends with the director and staff, and ended up as the director's assistant there, thus ending her loneliness problem and turning the recovery home into a halfway house and full-time job for herself—in one fell swoop.

Caroline's story is different again. It shows how direction, rather than results, should be your byword when considering where and how you will live. She was "nearing forty and starting down the hill," as she expressed it. She had begun a program of recovery for her addictive drinking, but her husband had not for his. She stayed with him for a couple of years, developing self-confidence in her program to the point where she left him and moved to Florida. Where she lived did not matter very much, but "contributing in some way" did—something "all of a piece; not just a go-to-work-come-home sort of life," she had decided. She had two talents she was proud of: cooking and diving. She posted notices on the marina bulletin boards in and around Tampa Bay, asking for "a job with a yacht going south" as cook and diver in exchange for a bunk and board. She wrote me that she had landed a job and had learned to sail and navigate as well. The skipper told her that the reason he had hired her was that she didn't drink and that she seemed so certain of her "direction." As he explained it, "I wanted someone who was together." She told me that was the nicest thing anyone had said about her in years.

LONELINESS AND INVOLVEMENT

You can be terribly lonely while living in a house full of people, even when the people are your immediate family. If they are bitter, angry, and have no understanding of addictive drinking and the problems of recovery, it can easily become an unbearable situation. In a very real sense, you may be feeling more alone and desperate under such circumstances than you would if you were alone on a desert island. Loneliness is primarily the sense that nobody really cares, that nobody understands. Because of the withdrawal, rejection, and family breakup so frequently associated with addictive drinking, loneliness is a major problem for us, one that must be solved or alleviated in every possible way if we are to recover. "No man is an island—" Or, perhaps, every man is an island—in search of an archipelago.

Loneliness and involvement are so closely intertwined that they can only be discussed properly together. Stop feeling "poor me." Stop waiting for people to be nice to you. (You'll wait forever.) Start being nice to other people. Start trying to be positive about things. Smile as often as you can, even if you don't really feel like it. Start giving of yourself to others.

If this sounds like preaching platitudes, it is, but how else can you say it? Let's get specific. If you are shy, insecure, afraid of people, and have no self-confidence, make it easy on yourself. Go to A.A., where everyone there felt that way at one time and many still do. *They* understand. When you go there, smile at people. Introduce yourself. Shake hands. Ask questions and listen attentively to the answers. Look for people who sit by themselves and speak to them especially. They are almost certainly more shy and frightened than you are, and you may be able to help them. By expressing an interest in them, you are showing them that somebody does care how they feel and what they think. You may find a friend who needs you more than you need him. If you have been dry even a week, talk to the newcomer who hasn't been dry a day. You have something to give him that nobody else has. It isn't much help for him to talk to people who have been sober for months or years; he can't identify with them, but he can identify with you. In his mind, "a week dry" is something that might be possible, and he will be all ears, wondering how you managed that first week. Your talking to him may be the only reason why he leaves the meeting with enough hope to try and to come back again. You just might save his life by being there and making the effort of "Hi, there!"

Talk to the old-timers in A.A., too. They have learned how to stay dry for a long time and how to get some fun out of life. They have learned how to make friends, how not to feel lonely all the time. You can learn a great deal from them if you forget your pride and ask the real question, "I'm terribly lonely. What should I do?" If you ask the questions that really bother you, they will know it and be flattered that you asked them.

Once you have become comfortable in A.A., you are ready for the next step, becoming involved somewhere else. The possibilities are endless. No matter how uninteresting all activities which other people clearly enjoy may seem to you at the moment, remember, you're a "people," too. It's the messed-up thinking, the lack of confidence in yourself to be able to do anything reasonably well without embarrassment that makes you feel the way you do. You can change that and start enjoying the process quickly, if you'll make the effort to get started. Start thinking about the things you used to enjoy. If you liked doing them, you must have known something about how to do them reasonably well or you wouldn't have enjoyed them. That's human nature. Maybe you loved football and made a team; you can't play anymore, but you might like being an unpaid assistant coach. I did that and thoroughly enjoyed it, making up my own plays, leading the calisthenics, supervising practice, and building team spirit. Once I got started, I couldn't wait to get to the field every day. If you bowled, join a bowling club. You'll soon have friends and invitations to do other things. If you like kids, go to a local school or your church or temple and volunteer to lead some children's or young people's group, or start your own afternoon arts-and-crafts club or a boys' or girls' 4-H club for neighborhood children. If you had a hobby, try it again and join a hobby club. Any hobby store can tell you what's going on in your area.

For about ten dollars a year you can become a member of the International Youth Hostels association (forget the "youth" in the title, a state of mind only) and receive continuous announcements of weekend hikes (all degrees of severity), bicycling and canoeing trips, even bird-watching and conservation walks in your area. During the week they offer workshops on backpacking, bike maintenance, and other studies of an outdoor nature. And don't forget your local 'Y' 's multi-program. Groups like these are made up of a hodgepodge of people who come singly, for the most part, for a hike or whatever, because usually these interests are not shared by spouse or present friends, and a lot of new friendships are often the result. Also, they are not slippery places:* people don't bring liquor *because they are busy doing something else.* One of the best benefits of including this sort of direction in your life is that a lot of same-interest people are congregating for an extended time together, weekends of backpacking and camping in beautiful places one could never reach otherwise, bicycling around the flat country of Holland for a couple of weeks, or visiting the gourmet cooking schools of France in a rented van.

Whether your interest was or could become archeology or Japanese gardens, there is a group who enjoys that, too. Your local high school and nearby college probably offer any number of adult education classes for a nominal fee. Another sailing friend of mine went to a local school's evening class on navigation, because she had sailed only a small 13-footer and wanted to move to coastal cruising in something larger. She wound up taking three navigation courses, a ham operator's course, and a diesel engine maintenance course—all a half mile from her home. (U.S. Power Squad-

*An A.A. expression: "If you don't want to slip, don't go to slippery places."

ron courses in all phases of boating are offered in your community, too, and they are free.)

A few days after I went to my first A.A. meeting, I woke up to find that it was Saturday, and I had nothing to do. (I usually "drank" my Saturdays.) It wasn't necessary for me to read something like this book to tell me that I had to find something interesting to fill my old drinking hours if I wanted to have the chance of a snowball in hell of staying sober. Years before, I had started to make a model of a sailboat I had owned and loved. In those seven years I had gotten the hull carved and some of the rigging made; it was about half done. It was always a difficult project, because you can't do the highly precise work of model building while you're half in the bag. I started again on the model and was able to finish it by working all day Saturday, all day Sunday, and after supper during the week. Nine days, after seven years for the first half! At last I had the model I had wanted for so long sitting on the mantel in the living room. This experience showed me graphically one of the great advantages of being sober: things get done again in a reasonable period of time, and pleasure, real pleasure, not some liquor-hazy illusion of it, is felt once more. For me that real happiness had been a long time coming, and I felt better about continuing the battle to stay dry and get really sober.

It doesn't make a damned bit of difference what you get involved in, especially if you are doing it with other people around. Anything can become a lot more fun than drinking. If you have come to the conclusion that you don't like the cellar because it's dark and cold and lonely, stop pushing the down button, the drink button, every time you get in the elevator. You know it goes only to the cellar.

Loneliness is terrible when it goes on and on, and it is especially staggering when it is brought about suddenly by loss of one's family as a result of addictive drinking. An addictive drinker has become dependent on alcohol, but if he is married, he has usually also become terribly dependent on his spouse as well. When I left home, six months after my last drink, I was still fighting hard to overcome *that* awful dependence (alcohol), and the sudden discovery that I now had a second dependency problem to overcome was traumatic. In addition, I had no job and only enough money to last a short time. I had felt terribly lonely and frightened long before divorce was mentioned. But the day I moved out, I was scared to death, alone for the first time in twenty-seven years. This is loneliness in spades. It comes in different ways and forms and in different degrees, but it is always dangerous, a danger which goes on for a long, long time.

Over the next year, things began to get better. I got a houseboat and moved aboard. I went to A.A. every day, and I began to get myself involved again in living—volunteer work in a detox, repair and painting on the boat, odd jobs from carpentry to movie extra, and finally Parents without Partners. P.W.P. is a national group with chapters in most large and many small cities. I recommend it strongly to any parent—separated, widowed, or divorced. It is a self-help group, a little like A.A., that offers assistance and alternatives to people who have lost their mates. The major emphasis is on helping the members and their children to make the difficult adjustments that usually accompany loss of a marriage partner. Generally there is something going on every night of the week (in the large urban centers) as an alternative to staying home, looking at four walls, and feeling miserable. There are discussion groups, often with professional speakers talking about the problems which such people usually have, and some real solutions. There are coffee and conversation meetings, where people just sit around and talk. Then there are dances, house parties, picnics, trips to interesting places, and overnight camping trips. Most of the above are for the adults, but there is a children's program, too, and another for teenagers. Holiday dinners, most outings, and many special events are for adults and children together. Since the emphasis is not on dating, one can go to any of these events just for the pleasure of getting out of the house and doing something interesting with other people with whom you have some things in common. It was a lifesaver for me. You can have additional fun in P.W.P. by becoming an advisor/leader of the teenage group, planning trips, running cake sales, doing arts and crafts, all to give you a sense of being useful again and something to look forward to. (Parents without Partners is listed in the phone book in cities where there are chapters.)

If you have known the depth of relationship with another person that is found in a good marriage, and then lost it, nothing will ever be found to equal that feeling except another such relationship, and herein lies a danger. The need to find even a part of that old trust, support, sharing, and affection seems to make any gamble worthwhile and can lead you into a marriage which is doomed from the start. Perhaps you should consider a marriage alternative during this period, at least until you have a good year of sobriety. Today it is possible to live with someone of the opposite sex, someone you care for, without committing yourself to marriage. If you are still in recovery, I believe it is fairer to both parties, especially if you don't plan to have children. At the least, trial of the relationship for a year or so before making the final formal commitment is sound insurance against the possibility of a serious and traumatic mistake.

One or both parties, who have children from a previous marriage, may reject the idea of living together, because of the fear of its effect on the children. However, if both people are honest and aboveboard about the relationship and really do care for each other, the children are capable of understanding and accepting, as long as they too receive love and caring from both people. (The teenagers in P.W.P. were in unanimous agreement on this and entirely realistic about it. They wanted their parent to be happy.)

Holiday time is a very dangerous time for lonely recovering addictive drinkers. My first Christmas alone looked bleak, and I asked a woman friend to spend it with me. She was as lonely as I was, I learned. We had a beautiful Christmas together and some months living together after that. I told her honestly where I was, that I didn't see any likelihood of marriage for us, but that I cared for her and respected her. She was a poverty-stricken artist, so I learned to paint. We spent days out in the houseboat, moored off old fishing shanties, painting them, and we were so engrossed that we didn't speak to each other for hours at a time. She could make a superb meal out of anything, and sometimes we ate like kings—with local fish and crawdads we caught ourselves and odd things we got from a butcher when he couldn't sell them before they went bad. Brains, tripe, kidneys, and free bread and pastries a day old—we did it all!

We didn't have any money, but we had wonderful days, and we were beating the system. After a while, I stopped being scared. I still got depressed fairly often. It's part of recovery, but when I did, I knew what to do about it. I got busy. One time I went through a "kite period," after my friend and I bought a kite book and made huge five-foot kites out of old fabric lengths she had and some aluminum rods we picked up at a dump. In no time we were the "kite couple" around the neighborhood, helping all the local kids with their kites. Lots of fun for nothing.

A part of recovery, of learning to accept reality, is learning gradually that some things just can't be hurried beyond a certain point. Sometimes you just have to wait and wait, no matter how frustrating the waiting is. Living through that "single again" period is in itself a lesson in facing reality. When your life has been badly damaged by alcohol, and when you consider that recovery requires you to learn and to develop whole new attitudes, it should not be surprising to find that it takes time. Repairs and improvements have to be made in so many areas sometimes that it all comes together slowly at best. Learning to be patient (not wanting everything yesterday) and to suffer hurt, when there is no practical alternative, is also one of those things. It's too bad, but that's the way it is—in the real world. That's why they speak of the "art" of living.

The answer to loneliness is involvement, and the answer to involvement is action, no matter how frightening and unattractive action may seem to you at first. If you want to recover and live again, you act. Anytime you find yourself feeling "poor me," you're going in the wrong direction.

YOUR WORK

Most people are never sufficiently motivated to go to all the effort involved in taking over real direction of their own lives; they settle for a ride on society's carousel. Addictive drinkers are fortunate indeed, because, motivated by the hell of addiction, they must learn to direct their own lives or die drunk. So we have a choice between heaven or hell, while most other people have only a trip across the misty flats.

Your job is a vital element in the direction of your life. If your present work is not fulfilling, it must be changed, whatever the cost. Also, your work must be balanced with other, equally important areas of your life, whatever the cost again. It is so easy to let your job control your life that it is perhaps the single most powerful threat to your happiness. Your work can also control you in many subtle ways. It can bore you, sap your energy, make you sick and listless, and it can keep you in a constant state of terror for fear of losing it. It can run away with you to such an extent ("workaholic") that it becomes the be-all and end-all, to the exclusion of family, relaxation, outside interests—everything, including self. What do you really want out of life? Is your present job helping you toward that purpose? Or is it a steel wall blocking all hope?

Laura is a high-powered insurance executive who has her own agency, employing fifteen top salespeople. She thinks, talks, and breathes big insurance deals twenty-four hours a day, and, in spite of A.A., keeps having "little slips," one-nighters. She has already made more money than she can hope to spend, has a house in Haiti, a beautiful apartment on the lake in Chicago, and she travels all over the Western world for business and pleasure whenever she wishes. But on vacations she is unable to stop talking about insurance and can never really unwind. Her ulcer is flaring up again, as usual.

In counseling she talks about her four marriages, which all failed her, and about her background—how she lifted herself by her bootstraps and had her own agency by the age of thirty-five. The child of working people in Chicago, she had to quit school after eighth grade to go to work when her father died. Driven to overcome her lack of education and the shabby house in which she grew up, she took night courses and strove mightily. In matters of clothing and travel she is still striving mightily to overcome her shabby background, constantly dropping the names of her dress designers and the exotic places she's been to recently.

Used to evaluating and competing with men in business, she did the same in marriage, and in each case found herself more efficient, sharper, and able to make far more money than her husband. Three marriages lasted a matter of months, as she soon found out "what he was all about." She has given up all thought of marriage, though she talks about old lovers and sex when she is not talking about her business. When you speak to Laura, you quickly realize that she has no interest in you or your life at all. You are only a sounding board for her total concern with self and a temporary fender against loneliness. Take away her business and you still have a poor young woman pressing against the display window, from the *other* side, saying, "I'm okay. In fact, I'm better than okay, better than everyone."

At some point in your life you have to achieve enough experience, self-awareness, and personal growth to be able to decide what you really want out of life, and to find the courage to go after it, regardless of the obstacles and what anyone, or society as a whole, thinks or says about it. One has to start taking responsibility for his own life and stop blaming society and parents for where he is today. When you blame parents, and then *their* parents, you can go all the way back to the apes.

It is a fact that a high proportion of addictive drinkers are miserable in their jobs at the time they begin recovery, and have been for years. There are many possible reasons for this. Most people do not know themselves well enough, at the time they start work, to choose a job that will be rewarding and fulfilling for them in nonmaterial ways. In fact, at that time in their lives, they rarely think at all of personal fulfillment as a criterion for choosing a job. Most commonly, young people take the highest-paying job they can get. Others go into lines of work that are quite inappropriate for them, because of family and social pressure to choose prestigious occupations. Many go into a family business, because it is expected and offers special advantages. The list is long, but again the influence of other people, society, and chance have played the major role.

In addition, a line of work that was very satisfying in the beginning can become a dead end. It was interesting to meet the challenges of the job for a number of years, but then you reached the end of the challenges. The work became nothing but a matter of running in place, doing the same things over and over for years and years. Or you moved up the promotion ladder for a while and then ran into a stone wall: no further promotion possible. The list of ways in which a job can go stale or end up going nowhere is long.

The point is that, if you are miserable in your work, you are spending at least eight hours a day being bored, frustrated, angry, and unhappy. We won't mention the further hours of useless suffering spent away from work thinking and worrying about it. The level of stress created by such a situation is sky-high. If you are to have any hope of recovery, something will have to be done about it. There is absolutely no alternative.

"But I can't do anything about it. I'm trapped. I'd lose my retirement pension if I left. I've build up a lot of seniority. I can't give that up. I've got a mortgage to pay and a family to support. I can't just quit." Hold on! I haven't said a thing about quitting yet. This is an inventory. What we're doing is looking closely at one aspect of your life—your job—to see if anything is wrong and, if so, to start thinking about what you might do to improve the situation. Quitting is the last option to consider.

It is a fundamental truth in recovery that many of the problems that seemed impossible to solve when you were drinking seem to solve themselves with no effort on your part at all when you begin to recover. Certain health problems, which neither you nor your doctor may have associated with your drinking, suddenly disappear. (My violent migraine headaches, which no doctor could cure for twenty years, disappeared in three months. So did my arthritis—"alcoholic arthritis," I learned later.) Your relationships with people improve markedly, and many things cease to be problems, simply because the way you feel—your health and your attitudes—have changed enough for you to see that problems you once thought of as insurmountable should never have been looked upon as problems in the first place. Therefore, it is wise to wait until you can see in what direction these changes are taking you before you start making decisions of great importance that will have long-range effects—divorce, a new marriage, or quitting your job cold, especially before finding a new one, for example.

In the first year of recovery, it is the experience of thousands that it is wise to concentrate your efforts on new personal growth, and on putting back together those elements of your old life that are worth repairing or rebuilding. At the end of a year or longer, you will be in a much better position to make a full-scale, long-range plan and consider more important and dramatic changes.

If you are miserable in your job, even if you have felt that way for a long time, it may not be the job at all; it may be you. You need the answer to that question first. Maybe you came to think of the job as miserable because you were doing it badly and felt guilty about it. Maybe your drinking, with all the fear, negative attitudes, and lack of self-confidence that goes with it, made the job look bad, because it prevented you from doing it well and blocked any chance of promotion. Once a drinking problem has really taken hold, it can turn any good job into a nightmare, by decreasing efficiency and making everything a much greater effort. Trying to work well while drinking, even if you never actually drink on the job, is like trying to run the 100-yard dash with a 60-pound pack on your back. Once the hangovers, the missed days, the terrible fears, angers, and resentments are removed, once you start getting back your old self-confidence (or getting self-confidence for the first time), you may very well find yourself doing the old job with unaccustomed pleasure. The heavy pack has been removed, and you find yourself winning for a change. Also, you can be quite sure that this much-improved you and your increasing value to the company will not go unnoticed. Self-confidence is attractive to other people, company bosses included, and recovery builds self-confidence. You may find that your newfound confidence and increased productivity justify your going after a raise or a promotion, which you could not have dreamed of while drinking. However, don't expect this to happen overnight.

Perhaps you will come to the conclusion that it's not the kind of work you do that's bad for you but only that particular job situation. Once sober and functioning well again, you are in good shape to start looking around for the same kind of work with a different employer in a different location.

Maybe you have hated your job for years, because you really wanted to be doing something else but couldn't see your way clear to it. Look at your whole situation today. Are any factors different that might make it easier to change now? Can you alter some to make it more possible? Anything is bearable when it becomes a means to achieving something you want very badly. Maybe you can start night school or extension classes, in order to prepare for the new line of work, and keep on with the old job to pay the bills until you're ready to shift into the new one. Or maybe you can get so much pleasure out of your new activities outside of work that the work itself moves more into the balance of your life and is, therefore, much more bearable, especially if you have only a short time to go to retirement. And what about early retirement? Look at all your options. There is some way to improve the situation, if you really think about it and are willing to make the effort. I can't tell you what you must do to make your work more satisfying, more rewarding. If you go at improving your situation sensibly, it is almost certain to come out better than it was, and it can turn out to be absolutely great. But whatever you do, don't just quit before you have your new direction in mind and something to go to.

If You Don't Have a Job

If you quit or lost your job, as many do because of their drinking, much of the above still applies. Since you have to find a new job anyway, now is the time to look closely at the old one. Do you want more of the same, even assuming, if you can, that it will be a lot better now that you're in recovery? Your job must be satisfying, and you must be able to see yourself going somewhere with it. If not, an alternative must be found, if you are to recover successfully and start to get some pleasure out of living. It is not only that the stress of unhappiness in the job will be a constant, serious threat to your sobriety—there is a much more important consideration. Life is short, and if you are an addictive drinker, you've had a fair share of misery already. If it was stupid while drinking, it's doubly stupid now to continue to spend eight hours a day or more doing something that makes you miserable. Nobody has to do that if he doesn't want to. Hundreds of addictive drinkers have found that changing over to a new line of work that suited them better gave them a sense of value and a purpose in life, and they were far happier, even at less pay. However, less pay, while common when the change is first made, is not, by any means, what you have to look forward to forever. Often, people find that when they change to a job they really enjoy, they soon become so good at it that, in short order, they are making more than they ever did in the old job they hated. An example of what I am saying here is found in the story of Flynn.

Flynn is a huge man with a craggy face. He had always been a mechanic working for other men. All his life he hated taking orders, sure that he could run the business better than the boss. But he drank about it instead of taking appropriate action, so he never got the capital together or the confidence to actually try. He had always had an ungovernable temper, and finally, in a drunken rage, he attacked a man as big as he with his bare hands outside a bar, and was charged with felonious assault and jailed for six months before the tire iron he claimed the other man had pulled on him was found. He got off on self-defense.

Driving him to and from A.A. meetings, I learned that he was on welfare, and I'd talk to him about getting a job. "Nope. Can't handle it yet," he'd say. "I will when I'm ready." Then one evening he said, "Well, I'm working." He had gone to a stable and offered to work as a stable hand (he knew horses) for five dollars a day, with one stipulation: "No one gives me any orders or instructions. If they do, I quit." No one did. The price was right.

Five months later he said, "Well, I'm in business for myself," and he was. He had sold his house to get capital, moved into his van, and bought a garage. In a year he had another garage and nine employees. Recently, I saw him on the street and learned that he had cleared $40,000 the previous year. Then he told me that he thought the real reason that he had quit drinking was that he just got sick and tired of having people take advantage of him.

But more money or as much money as you were making is not the most important factor. Reducing stress and being happy with what you are doing are far more important.

I found this out for myself the hard way. During my first year in recovery, I was too mixed up in my mind about a great many things to be able to get or keep a job that paid anything like what I had been earning. I spent that year doing all kinds of odd jobs—on unemployment compensation and finally on welfare part of the time—but in the process I learned that not only could I live on a very small fraction of what I had previously believed to be the rock-bottom minimum, but I could do so and be far happier than I had been before, with much more money and material possessions. Several times I didn't have a dime and no money coming in. It was pretty scary, since I had never lived like that before, but I soon learned that something always happens. Sometimes it seemed pretty miraculous, but I never missed a meal, although I ate a lot of beans and spaghetti. I also had a backup, in case the beans and spaghetti ran out—duck! Every evening at dusk a fleet of some ten harbor ducks came swimming by my houseboat for a handout, and they could always count on me for some bread, entirely unaware that my silent spear gun was ready for the day I ran out of food. The silence of the gun (and the dusk) was important because everyone in the harbor, including me, loved the ducks, but hunger changes priorities, and backups reduce fear and the stress that results. Fortunately for the ducks, the beans and spaghetti never ran out.

You don't have to just sit by and "hang in there," either. You can reduce stress and increase your self-esteem by *choosing* to make your poverty worse—by spitting in the face of reality, as it were. One time, when I had only twenty-eight dollars and no job or income, I saw a bargain advertised: six concerts, including opera and ballet, for twenty-one bucks. So I bought the season ticket and went off to my first opera in two years, dressed in my best. As I knew (by then) it would, the whole experience made me feel just great. This may have been a milestone in my recovery, because from that moment on, I knew I was going to make it: I could dare to live my own life in spite of my fears.

I am not recommending poverty as a way of life. What I am saying is that, in the early stages of recovery, especially if you are in bad shape, unemployed, and trying to change careers, as I was, going through a long period of relative poverty may be unavoidable. If you do, you do, but it is not nearly so bad as you might expect, and it is entirely possible to have some very pleasant times along the way. How? Build big kites and fly them, go fishing, go to the beach, etc.

There is only one *real* danger when you're living below the poverty line, can't get a decent job because you're overqualified for everything you think you can emotionally handle at the moment, and frequently don't know where the next meal is coming from: it's easy to think at such times that *everything* is black and retreat into "poor me" feelings. But you know that it doesn't take much of that to put you back on your old pseudo-friend booze and the old slippery slide to real misery. So take action instead. Neither men nor fate can keep a good man or woman down forever.

About Retirement

Many people retire and start addictive drinking soon afterward. If this is you, I believe there are specific reasons for this, which you must deal with now if you are to recover.

While working on my boat up and down the east coast of Florida, I talked with hundreds of retired people, and a curious fact emerged. The vast majority of these people were successful enough in their work to be able to retire to Florida, but were failures at retirement—or so I saw them, beers in hand, sitting all day in the parks, in the shopping malls, on the waterfront, watching life go by. Talking with them, you begin to understand why.

When they were working, someone was paying them for what they were doing, so they knew they were producing value for others and had a sense of being valuable themselves. I believe that this sense of value to others is essential to happiness, and so are goals. We spend most of our lives pursuing goals, and as each is reached, we move on to pursue new ones. Retirement is a big goal in life, but it is different from other goals such as a new car or a dream house. They satisfy real desires but do not take away from your sense of personal worth or from your work toward future goals. Retirement does, unless you have planned for it very carefully.

If the reality of your retirement is that you no longer have a sense of value, no purpose except to play, and no more goals to strive for except to stay alive a while longer, it is no wonder that you, like so many retirees, including those discharged after a career in the services, feel bored, useless, and miserable—"poor me." Nor is it any wonder that such people in large numbers speed up their social drinking and move across the line into addictive drinking, as they live more and more in the past, and look into a future spelled d-i-s-s-o-l-u-t-i-o-n and d-e-a-t-h. A disproportionate number die not of disease or old age but because they no longer have any purpose or will to live.

As I see it, retirement means one thing: freedom to do exactly what you want. This is the time to go to college or art school, start a new business, write that book, teach or coach, design a better mousetrap of some kind, do consulting in your field. You have a lifetime of experience to apply in old or new ways and should be in a better position to produce something of worth than at any time in your life. The past is dead and gone. If that's all you have to talk and think about, you might as well be dead and gone, too.

There's a lot in a question the young people are asking each other nowadays instead of saying hello: "What's happenin', man?" You will notice that it is in the present tense and asks, What are you doing that's new and exciting? When people around you start asking you in other words, "what's happenin,' man," you'll know you're alive again, and you'll also see that others are interested in living, exciting people, not in dying, dull ones. That applies to your interest in yourself as well. Action is the game, even more so if you're retired, unless you choose to retire from living. If that's your choice, keep drinking. It's one of the most efficient ways to do it there is.

YOUR MARRIAGE

It is a paradox, but it is also a fact: a high percentage of the divorces that occur between addictive drinkers and their mates occur *after* the addictive drinker is on the road to recovery. It seems quite illogical that a husband or wife would put up with long years of steadily increasing misery, fear, financial loss, and even physical abuse, always hoping against hope for recovery, and then, once the long-awaited miracle is occurring, decide on divorce. It seems quite illogical, too, that many addictive drinkers themselves choose divorce after they are well into recovery. Ironically, this happens at a time when the couple should be on the verge of sharing the greatest happiness they have ever known together.

I have given what I am about to say a great deal of thought and have decided that I have no alternative but to break a generally accepted rule for counseling the spouses of addictive drinkers. It is usually felt that it is unwise to tell husbands or wives the real facts about the effects of the drinking problem on *them*. Counselors fear that to do so will so shock and frighten them that they will reject the idea as preposterous and react in the opposite way from the one that experience has proven will serve their own best interests and those of the addicted spouse. A counselor tries to handle things so that the drinker's spouse can be led very slowly and gently to the truth; that is, that he, too, has a real illness and needs to work toward personal recovery as well. The counselor achieves this by playing a game. He gets the spouse into a counseling program or Alanon in order "to learn how he or she can *help the addictive drinker*." In reality, it is also for the purpose of getting the spouse to learn about his or her own need for help and recovery by degrees. However, even the best counselors frequently fail in this stratagem. In this book I have only one chance. Therefore, I believe it is better to start with the truth.

Elaborate psychological studies and the observations of

every counselor in the field over many years have clearly shown that throughout the entire course of development of an addictive drinking problem *the spouse of the addictive drinker suffers as much personality damage as the person doing the drinking, or more*. If you are such a spouse who never even considered such a possibility, this undoubtedly comes as a shock. The natural reaction is to reject it out of hand as clearly not true in your case.

Since the problems of the male addictive drinker have been much more widely described and documented in the literature, I shall discuss this problem from the point of view of the husband whose wife is addicted. However, it should be understood that while the typical male and female roles in society are often different in a variety of ways, the reactions and feelings of the non-addicted spouse are essentially the same, and so is the developing psychological illness they suffer as a result. (There is one outstanding difference, however, which has nothing to do with the illness itself but more to do with the traditional economic dependence of females—homemakers especially. Statistically, husbands divorce addicted wives much earlier and more often than the other way around.)

For years—many years in most cases—the husband has seen his beloved wife "choose" to drink and get drunk, more and more often as time rolled by. At first she did *choose* to take a drink, sometimes drinking too much, but neither he nor she thought anything of it, until it had already become a very serious problem. This is so because of denial, which affects *both* parties powerfully. Neither one can accept the idea that she is an "alcoholic." Stigma makes that impossible for a long time. During this time, neither knows anything about the true facts of addictive drinking. From his point of view and that of everyone else around, she simply "chooses" to drink too much. How could it be otherwise, since she is sober when she starts? As the illness progresses, the awful embarrassments become more frequent. The first suggestions to be careful soon become desperate pleadings, and then escalate into violent arguments, fights, bottles poured down the sink, and all the rest of the sorry, sordid business.

In the process two people who used to love each other and share everything become mutual antagonists, playing vicious games against each other. Hiding and finding bottles is one of the most common. I am reminded of one woman whose husband became infallible at finding her stashes, no matter how clever the hiding place, until, at last, she won the game. She found the ultimate hiding place, and it drove her husband almost out of his mind. All day long—for months—she was drinking, even when he was at home, but he couldn't figure out how. It was only after her recovery that she finally told him her secret. She was sipping vodka from a new douche bag she had brought home and placed on the back of the bathroom door, exactly where the old one had been, the one place he had never thought to look.

Money is wasted, thrown away in stupid spending, lost in accidents (his money!), and "she chooses to keep on behaving this way!" "Doesn't she care for me at all, or for the children?" "Is she insane?" "How can a charming, attractive, normally smart woman (*my* wife) behave so irresponsibly?" I don't need to go on describing the feelings to you. You know them all too well.

What is the invariable result of these feelings? For the spouse it is an increasing sense of insecurity, constant fear of what will happen next time, worry about what it will do to the children, and on and on it builds. The result of all this is a deep, stomach-grinding bitterness and resentment. Did you (the spouse) ever get so frantic that you yourself did crazy things? After reading Part One of this book, do any of these feelings sound familiar? How much abnormal stress have you been living under for years? You probably don't drink to relieve it, although many do and become addictive drinkers themselves. No, you handled it in other ways, but can you suppose that that amount of abnormal stress chewing and grinding at you for years has no psychological effect? That you could even possibly have remained a perfectly normal, well-adjusted person? Impossible for any human being. It is an incontrovertible fact of life.

We have talked about negative attitudes that develop in the addictive drinker—about loss of self-confidence, guilt feelings, terrible fear, damage to self-image, desperate loneliness, etc. Do any of these feelings apply to you, the spouse—or all of them? They do in most cases. In spite of all that you have read in this book, however much you may have come to understand the illness in your own mind, if you are absolutely honest with yourself, don't you still have a deep-down feeling that somehow it was mostly her fault, that you did everything a human being could do to help her, and she rejected your help and still went right on, as though she didn't care a damn? If you don't have such a feeling, it would be very strange. All those terrible emotions and desperate thoughts you have suffered, over all that time, have created in you a host of negative attitudes toward life and toward your wife that simple intellectual understanding and her beginning recovery do not erase. The truth is that you are in as serious need of a recovery program for yourself as she is, and it is also vital for her and her recovery (and your marriage) if she still loves you, as she probably does.

By the time an addictive drinker asks for help, she knows that something is very wrong with her drinking, is full of guilt and fear and self-loathing. She often has real physical symptoms as well. (Both men and women often have flushed cheeks and broken blood vessels, creating a reddish-purple blush, and a variety of other alcohol-induced signs and ailments. She knows she's sick all right, at least physically.) Therefore, it is possible in most cases to convince an addictive drinker finally, in spite of denial, to seek help of some kind. As we have seen, it is exceedingly difficult to convince her of the true seriousness of her problem and to get her to accept enough help to guarantee recovery, but at least she knows she *has* a problem. Her husband is in a very different position.

There is a common pattern for his role in the slow development of the illness. As her drinking increases in amount and frequency, the addictive drinker begins to allow many of her normal responsibilities to fall more and more into the hands of her husband. This comes about as a result of guilt feelings, her absence from the scene, physically or mentally, at times when decisions have to be made, her increasing sense that she has more on her hands than she can handle anyway, and the general eroding of her old sense of responsibility for the family. Before long, her husband is doing both his and her share of the housework, the shopping, the laundry, the maintenance of the property, the paying of the bills, the preparation of the meals, and taking nearly all the responsibility for the care and discipline of the children. This, in addition to all his other responsibilities, which usually include an eight-hour-a-day job. If she is employed as well, he is often calling her employer to say she won't be in for work, with some cover-up excuse, because she's drunk or too hungover to go to work. If she is a housewife, he is often departing for work after getting the children off to school and leaving a breakfast prepared for her, along with some departing word about what there is for her lunch in the refrigerator. As each new responsibility is added to all the rest, somehow he manages to cope in the effort to hold his family together and keep them as safe and sane as he can. There is no doubt that husbands often achieve the heroic in these efforts, even to making the Halloween costumes and washing and hanging the curtains, and they usually feel considerable pride in their achievements, as well they might. Members of the family and friends recognize what he is doing and praise him for it, too. What is the result? He feels that he is coping better than ever before in his life with all the family's problems, but cannot avoid deep feelings of bitterness and resentment at the necessity for him to have to handle everything, including her when she's been drinking. He is truly playing the martyr's role, and he may know it. Of course, love and respect for his wife go down in direct proportion to the severity of the drinking problem, and this process goes on and on and on, often for years. How is a counselor, then, to convince this truly heroic person, who has been carrying the whole load of family responsibility for years, that there is anything wrong with him? That's why it is so difficult. But there is something very wrong. Let's look at what we see this perfectly well-adjusted hero and paragon doing.

His wife gets into A.A. and finds that she can actually stay dry just by going to a meeting every night or at least almost every night. He sees her going. He sees that she is not drinking and acts terribly pleased. Then, after a few weeks, he starts feeling hurt and lonely: "She stops drinking, and now she's gone every night with her new A.A. friends," leaving him all alone at home to do the dishes. His bitterness and resentment return. Soon he starts making nasty remarks, complaining about little things, and balances that with long periods of silence whenever he is at home. The atmosphere becomes worse daily. During this same period, she, realizing the tremendous load of work and responsibility he has been carrying for so long, and feeling terribly guilty about it, begins to resume some of her old duties—helping with the children's homework and the like, taking over more of her share of the housework, shopping, etc. This doesn't help. Consciously or unconsciously, he resents it. He has become so used to having all the responsibility and supporting himself with thoughts of how nobly he is carrying all the burdens that *he resents having them taken away*, resents the children laughing again with their mother and giving *her* the attention that is rightfully his (after all he's done for them). He is no longer the brave, persevering knight to himself and all their friends. He now becomes more confused and bitter, and the atmosphere gets even worse.

Meantime, his wife is indoctrinated with the fact that it is essential, especially in the early days of recovery, to remove herself from any situation where she feels very uncomfortable (stress), and that she must do "*whatever* is necessary to stay sober." Since her home is now a very uncomfortable place, where her husband's negative attitudes constantly make her feel guilty and frustrated in her attempts to reestablish the old love and comfortable relationship, she leaves home more and more, to escape the misery and the pressure. Her husband, seeing this, is convinced that she doesn't love him anymore, becomes more bitter and resentful, and so the spiral goes—down, down, down. This is the way it happens; similar scenarios are being repeated in homes all over the world. Divorce often follows, in due course, initiated by either party.

I do not mean to imply in the above that the wife is pure and blameless in all this. Staying dry at this stage is miserable much of the time, with compulsion nearly always present to some degree and frequently rising close to the unbearable level. She is terribly tense much of the time and far from the easiest person in the world to live with. Also, she is worried that she may drink again, and is only just becoming more aware of the problems her drinking has created over the years, and she is often hanging on by a thread. As she regains self-confidence and gets a vague idea that she is in charge of her own life, finding her own direction, that she does not *have* to do anything she does not choose to do, that she does not even have to feel guilty for saying no, she is more and more coming across as "independent," and charges of "women's-lib crap" are often heard.

In short, it should be obvious to everyone that this is a period of difficult adjustment, with a notable lack of rational communication, for both husband and wife. Both have been blaming the other in words and thought for years, the husband for her drinking and all the problems it created; the wife, in deep denial, for making her so miserable or angry that she had to drink. You do not change habits of thought (attitudes) that have been in operation for years in a week or a month. When the woman stops drinking, she can *begin* to start changing her negative attitudes, but this takes many months, as we have seen. When the woman stops drinking, her husband can start changing his negative attitudes, too. Unfortunately, most husbands do not even think of trying. Most are completely unaware of the fact that they even have any negative attitudes to change. So all the basic elements for the tragedy are in place. The question of who asks for the divorce is unimportant.

Of course, it doesn't have to be this way. Neither party is to blame for anything. The wife has fought truly heroically for years against a force which she did not understand, a force which she could only overcome finally with understanding and considerable outside help. The husband, too, has fought, just as heroically, a battle that it was impossible for him to win without understanding and considerable outside help. Neither had any hope of winning by himself. If there was ever a time in a marriage for both partners to make a supreme effort to forget themselves and dedicate themselves each to the other, this is it. If there was ever a time for two people to realize that the only possible hope for them both to recover from this terrible scourge—with their marriage intact—lies in pulling together, in showing the greatest possible consideration for each other, it is now. Blame, false pride, denial, and guilt feelings are the greatest enemies of marriage and recovery. You have both hurt each other terribly, and the absurd paradox is that neither of you meant to, wanted to, or can be blamed for it. It is all a part of a desperately grim illness, nothing more.

Now let's look at what it can be like.

Recovery is a matter of making intelligent choices, particularly to change your behavior and attitudes from the old ones to new ways of doing and thinking—consciously changing them, so that, in time, the new ways will become new habits, which operate automatically and unconsciously. So the couple starts by sitting down together to discuss and decide on how they will proceed *as a team* to overcome the problem, as they have undoubtedly done many times before with lesser problems. It might be useful to think of the whole "long night of addictive drinking" as a family fight to end all family fights. Reconciliation logically begins with both parties admitting how wrong, stupid, and frightened they were. It is hard at first, but once you get going, it is a tremendous relief, as you must know from previous experiences. Don't worry if you still feel nagging feelings of guilt, blame, and self-justification, which make it difficult to feel that you are being completely honest in what you are saying. That is the old, automatic, gut-feeling negative attitudes and false pride talking. That's the old sick stuff you've been programming your internal computer with for years. That's the proof that you, too, have a serious problem. That's what you're out to change by conscious reprogramming. Disregard those feelings. Force them down. At some stage in this process, and you'll know when, it is an excellent idea to go to bed, to hold one another, to cuddle and to caress one another as you continue to share the feelings you've had and the repairs to be made, and to make love together again. Maybe it's been a long time. Nothing like it for reconciliations.

Now we're looking at the problem that has to be solved as a double problem. It's not a matter of the husband sitting around in magnificent purity, waiting for his wife to do all the work to get well, to straighten up and fly right, the way he wants her to fly. Both will need to reassess their own flying and to blend it so they can fly united again, yet never quite the same way as before—better. Both need to work together—as a team. Recovery is for both, and remember, recovery is only the short-term goal in your program of personal growth toward a new kind of real happiness. It is this factor—personal growth—that functions as the double whammy to destroy or to make a marriage.

If the husband does sit around waiting for his guilty wife to start flying right for a change, the following is what usually happens: To get well, she has worked through a process dedicated to helping her grow in a great variety of positive ways, while he is just there, doing nothing but treading water as far as personal growth is concerned, still with all the negative attitudes and false pride developed during her illness. If this situation goes on long, she will wake up one day and realize that she has grown to a point at which her goals, attitudes, and whole approach to life are so different that the two of them no longer have anything in common, not even hate, at least on her side, because she has come to realize that it wasn't his fault, either—while he still thinks it was all hers. When that happens, divorce often follows, initiated by her. That's what I meant when I mentioned this possibility at the beginning of this section.

But it doesn't have to be that way. If the two of you can see that it was the illness that was to blame, not either of you, then you can begin to clear out the deadly negative feelings from your relationship and start to join together for the incredible experience of joint recovery, the goal of which is mutual self-mastery, understanding of a great many things that were entirely unknown to you both before, and real happiness. If that's not a goal worth working for, I don't know what is. If she is going to A.A., he can go to open meetings to share and learn with her. When she is at closed meetings, he can go to Alanon* meetings, often held in the same building and at the same time as the A.A. meeting, or he can visit with an Alanon friend. The two organizations are based on similar philosophies. Or they can attend other kinds of growth-therapy groups together and share in a variety of activities to help them both get back into the world of living and out of themselves. So now, instead of the husband sitting at home feeling negative, neglected, and lonely, he and his wife are getting out together for common purposes, and after the activities can share their reactions, feelings, and thoughts. Isn't that what marriage is supposed to be all about: sharing? Of course, A.A., Alanon, and personal growth are not everything, by a long shot. One of the major points of this book is that there is a great variety of valuable experience available to you, and all of it can be shared, so that in addition to working toward recovery and happiness, you are also working toward more sharing of everything than you have probably known for years. Thus, you are simultaneously putting your marriage back together and building it on a more solid foundation than it ever had be-

---

*Alanon is a worldwide independent organization, which exists to assist those who love the addictive drinker and want to help themselves. See Part Five, "To Those Who Love Them," page 284.

fore. The old saw about it being necessary to work at a marriage is not just an old saw, and it is probable that both of you, in that sense, have been out of work for a long time. It's not much good to feel pure, right, and divorced, when you can feel human, honestly fallible like other people, and happily married. Recovery for both parties is a matter of facing reality and making intelligent choices.

SOBER ISN'T SEXY—AT FIRST

As the country-Western song has it, "The girls all get prettier at closing time." (Reference is to a bar.) To put it another way: "Candy is dandy but liquor is quicker." In a culture that still reflects powerful puritanical and Victorian taboos against sexual activity and knowledge or open discussion about it, in spite of the present flood of pornographic literature, super-explicit girlie magazines, and serious sex books, inhibitions against relaxed enjoyment of sex, even in marriage, are widespread among us. While the convivial atmosphere of social drinking and the whole mystique we associate with it make it a perfectly natural thing to do as a prelude to lovemaking, it is certain that a large proportion of people in our country carry so many deep antisex inhibitions into adulthood that the sex act is almost impossible, and surely far less enjoyable, for these people without the inhibition-relaxing effects of at least a bottle of wine or a couple of martinis. (In many cases, it takes much more than that.) A large proportion of addictive drinkers are members of this group.

The resulting problems, for anyone coming off the booze, created by the just-dry state and the necessity of maintaining the dry state at all costs, thus can be serious indeed, especially if the addictive drinker and his sexual partner do not understand the problem or its solution.

We will consider the man's problem first. Without the alcoholic relaxation of his deep inhibitions, he frequently finds himself entirely incapable of erection; or if that is easily possible, he finds he loses it "automatically" every time he attempts entry into the vagina—as though an evil genie had suddenly taken possession of his body, after years of relatively active and successful sexual performance. (We do not count here the impotency which accompanies very heavy drinking. While most male addictive drinkers have suffered this frustrating and embarrassing experience, most of them have quickly recognized the cause and discovered that fewer drinks will solve the problem.)

Getting rid of inhibitions that are the result of outmoded codes of conduct is one of the basic problems in recovery, and sex inhibitions are usually high on the list, even if they do not result in impotency, since they can also reduce the enjoyment of both parties in a variety of ways. They are often the basic cause of infrequent lovemaking, which then leads to resentment on the part of one partner and deep guilt feelings on the part of the other. The potential seriousness of these problems can be imagined, when one considers that most male-female relationships have already been seriously strained by an addictive drinking problem, often to or almost to the breaking point. (See Part Five, "To Those Who Love Them."

The misunderstandings which often occur in this much-longed-for dry state are legion and destructive. Suddenly there is a noticeable restraint, if not impotency, on the part of the male ex-drinker, and this may be interpreted in many negative and unfortunate ways by his partner: "I guess I've become so unattractive to him when he's sober that he has to be half drunk to make love to me." "He must still blame me for all the things I did to get him to stop drinking." "I thought it would be beautiful when he wasn't slobbering and half stupefied, but it's worse." "He could get it up if he loved me. He just doesn't care. Well, the hell with it. I certainly did my part. At least now I know." And so it goes. Often these first doubts and fears lead to violent exchanges and insults, which strike deep and almost guarantee a worse failure the next time, if there is a next time. We mentioned the disproportionately high number of divorces that occur after the drinker begins to recover. We did not mention this problem at the time, but it is clearly a vital element, since the male's reluctance to make love or his impotence is often considered proof that the relationship is over.

The problem of erection failure is certainly the most frustrating, the most infuriating, and the most misunderstood by both parties. It was so important to me that I seriously considered drinking again—only before lovemaking, of course; but I knew what would happen then, so I didn't. Even when the man understands it, as he may from his talks with other addictive drinkers or therapists, it often happens that his painfully shy or logical explanations are not believed and are taken as poor excuses by his partner.

The fact is that erection is not a matter of conscious effort on the man's part. It's the reverse—you have to relax. The harder he tries to think "erection," the less likely he is to achieve it. (It's not like thinking "success.") It is like the acts of urination and defecation. While both probably appear to require conscious effort on your part, what actually happens is that the conscious effort is to relax to overcome the unconscious inhibition of the appropriate sphincter muscle, which you learned in early toilet training to control.

Now that we have said that erection is not a matter of conscious effort, we must say that erection is entirely a matter of the mind. If this sounds like nonsense, it is not. Consider the fact that erections occur in so-called wet dreams and in morning erections, when there is neither physical stimulation of the penis nor conscious thought involved. Dreaming is quite enough. Erection occurs *automatically* when a man's mind is stimulated by sexual thoughts and/or images. Tactile sensations are not required.

Erection is effectively inhibited from occurring when the man concentrates on its achievement, when he consciously believes that he will fail to achieve it, and when he is repelled in any way—by the thought of the sex act or by what he may be expected to do, if he has been programmed with inhibitions against it. The problem, then, is not in the penis, which is one of the most remarkable organs in the human body. The problem is 100 percent in the mind of the owner of the penis. Since we are dealing with a problem of the mind, no amount of physical stimulation will do any significant good.

When one is dealing with mental problems, the possible complexities that can result are considerable in number and may be subtle in the extreme. For example, imagine the following: A man, newly dry and in a highly nervous state most of the day because of compulsion, starts to have sex with his wife. He still loves her dearly, in spite of past problems, and she him. There is enough of the old familiarity to make foreplay enjoyable, and erection occurs as usual. Then, at the moment of entry, the erection disappears, as if by magic, in a matter of two or three seconds. At first he doesn't even know what has happened, because he felt no change. It comes as a complete surprise. Immediate direct stimulation is tried, to no avail. They go back to foreplay. Erection occurs again, but the outcome is the same.

Assuming that both partners thoroughly understand the problem (this is rarely the case), and the wife is kind and understanding, they both achieve satisfaction and relief of the sexual tension created by the foreplay by either individual or mutual masturbation. They then go to sleep, resigned to repeat the process as many times as necessary to overcome the inhibitions involved. If they are wise, they probably also agree not even to try intercourse again until the man feels relaxed and reasonably confident about it. This is the ideal approach to the problem.

Even so, the man's problem is instantly worse than it was when they began, because now, in addition to the inhibition that caused the problem in the first place, he has received a blow to his concept of himself as a man. This is a traumatic emotional experience so deep that he cannot forget it, no matter how he tries in his conscious mind. He fears that it will almost certainly happen the next time. Worse, even, and too terrible to contemplate, but he does because he can't help it, is his fear that maybe it will be permanent. These fears create stress of major proportions, and they are so vital to his self-image and to what he imagines must be going on in his wife's mind that he is often totally immobilized sexually, as far as erection, as well as penetration, are concerned. (Masters and Johnson have done extensive work in this field, and reference to their books on the subject is strongly recommended, if you have such a problem. Also, sexual therapy centers based on the work of Masters and Johnson have now been established in some of the major urban centers.)

Remember that the above case was described as occurring under ideal conditions of mutual love and understanding of the problem. Imagine, then, the degree of trauma that occurs when there is no understanding and the wife mistakenly assumes that it is the conscious fault of her husband, who could easily perform if he wanted to. The resulting recriminations, resentment, and lasting hurt can only be imagined. I have spoken at some length of how vital is the part of the non-addicted spouse in the recovery of her mate, whatever their marital status. It should be obvious that her role of total understanding support, even in the face of such a frustrating situation as the above, is absolutely crucial, not only to his recovery, but to the success or failure of the relationship.

The problem of the woman addictive drinker in the just-dry period may take the form of total disinterest in intimacy, or at least something considerably less than enthusiasm. And there may be sexual dysfunction as well. As anyone in the 1980s knows, the female is just as capable of turning on and getting off on sex as a man and does not have to be the passive partner the old literature (and institutions) made her out to be. But what has *not* changed is the degree to which women need to feel attractive, desired, and loved by their partners. (Men need this, too, but let's follow the woman here.)

The female addictive drinker, who has been drunk on numerous occasions, knows that she was, by any civilized standards and especially her own, repeatedly disgusting, stupid, irrational, bitchy, and vicious. Now dry, this woman still suffers the tortures of the damned, especially because she accepts society's double standard about drunkenness: a female drunk is far worse than a male drunk. ("If there's anything I hate to see it's a drunk woman—") She is feeling at this time that there is no way her husband or lover could really love her, despite what he says. Her self-esteem is so low that she herself believes she is *un*lovable.

Added to this is the amorphous picture of what "attractive" is, coming as it has, primarily, from the screen and press and from the current fads of the neighborhood, mixed with a sort of axiom for women—"Be everything to all people"—thrown in. As a result, you have a person who has almost no image of self—unique self—at all.

Further, you have a person who is just learning to *choose* her own day, to dream her own dreams—maybe for the first time. She is, in fact, a female who is learning to become a person first and a female second, if, indeed, an aspect of her problem was that she has been a female role player up to now: wife, mother, girlfriend, hostess, and "bunny." If she has also been holding her own in a race to be successful in a man's job, boozing it up with male colleagues or clients over lunch, playing the tough, no-nonsense, business-person role, she is now in the process of working out (also for the first time perhaps) "her way," instead of running along "their way" in matters of lunch conferences, her demeanor on the job, etc. Often a large number of negative attitudes toward men develop during this self-emancipation process, because she still has difficulty accepting the rightness of that emancipation while her own self-confidence remains shaky. It's a tough row to hoe when you have been conditioned for years to play "a woman's role."

Her partner will be able to break through all this confusion and low self-image with his love and support only if he can share enough of her recovery so that his "courtship" of her is through the day and not just at bedtime. She will believe that he loves her over a period of time as he continues to remind her of some aspect of her special attractiveness to him, such as getting herself cranked up again to go to an A.A. meeting after a difficult day at home or at her job, her perseverence in the face of serious problems despite her highly nervous state, and all the attractive changes in her attitudes and behavior which he truly sees. (She will know when he is sincere and natural in his appraisals, and she will know when he is talking "with something else on his mind.")

When he further supports her in how she spends her time (away from slippery places, with new friends, even if they are all A.A. at first) and in whatever steps she feels are necessary to her own recovery, and helps to lighten her job load in the home until she can emotionally handle a fuller load, she will begin to feel again that she is not alone, that she really is attractive, that she is of much worth to her mate. Working with her to support her choices toward a better life for herself, as she sees that life to be, whether it involves moving or a change of life-style or whatever, will advance rapport to the point of team planning and team feeling. When her own desires and goals in life are considered above all else, not just for the purposes of recovery from drinking to not drinking but for her own fulfillment as a person, she will know she is truly loved. And the more she stakes out her role in life, the more she will realize her own unique self; as she makes and carries out her choices in recovery, that self-mastery will increase her self-esteem further. She will, as a consequence, be far more capable of loving than she has ever been, and so more loving.

If the addictive woman has always used liquor for foreplay and sexual release, it may be that her inhibitions against all sex will need the expertise of professional therapy, but I have found that is rarely necessary. It is crucial that the frustration of both parties, no matter who is in recovery for a drinking problem, be relieved easily and effectively every time foreplay occurs. While it is entirely possible to break off all sexual activity—even after one or both parties have reached concert pitch—without blowing apart at the seams or falling into a screaming emotional frenzy, the tension created by doing so is damaging to both parties and to the relationship, and it seriously threatens the likelihood of a reasonably prompt resolution of the problem.

I mentioned above that both parties, in the ideal situation, simply relieved the resulting tension by individual or mutual masturbation. It is possible that one or both of you look upon the very idea of masturbation as dirty, improper, and disgusting. If you have a problem in this area, I probably can't help you, but I do recommend most strongly that you see a therapist who has the necessary expertise to resolve the problem.

If both parties are normally healthy, and have the knowledge and understanding love to treat each other with respect and kindness through such a difficult time, there is little reason to fear that ultimate success will not be achieved. That very understanding and kind consideration are the granite base of any worthwhile love relationship and in recovery can make the whole experience more tender, beautiful, and meaningful for you both than it ever was before. I can think of no more loving and giving way to bind up old wounds and start rebuilding the marriage to levels of joy and happiness never achieved, even during the salad days when you were young and carefree, long before the horror that is addictive drinking appeared on your horizon. Sober may not be sexy at first, but sex while sober can be fantastic beyond your dreams, at last. I wish you all of love, the ocean deeps of true caring. The choice, as always, is yours, and this one is particularly difficult and subtle.

RICH OR POOR?

In all of this inventory taking your answers to two questions are basic to your selection of where and how you want to go from here in these basic areas of living.

First, do you really need all the material things you have or have been working to get? Is the price of some of them too high? If that price is keeping you in a job you hate and from a job you would love, it is too high. If the big, beautiful house or expensive life-style is too much for your income, and the resultant stress of constant financial worry is driving you to drink, it is too high. Perhaps the question should be: "What sort of life-style, what material level of living do I really want and can I afford?"

Most people assume that there is only one way to solve financial problems—make more money. But there is a much easier and more effective way to do it: reduce expenses. The second question: If I reassess my real needs and wants, can I make basic changes in my way of living that will get rid of high expenses I really don't need or want, in exchange for cheaper, more exciting, more satisfying ways?

One thing I have found: when you step out of the standard ways of living in any respect, your costs plummet. Move to a trailer, drive a secondhand pickup truck, get turned on to cooking all kinds of low-cost, exotic dishes from around the world, raise vegetables in your yard instead of flowers and shrubs—anything unusual—and you can save money in big chunks. The funny thing is that you will find people respecting you, often envying you for doing it. Why? Because they can see that it's far cheaper and probably more fun, but they don't dare do it themselves, because "it isn't done."

I live on a boat, and people who have ten times as much money as I are constantly telling me how they wish they could do that. They even say they envy me. But they say they can't afford it. The truth is that they could easily afford it—with money to spare. The problem is that they don't dare. Boats sink in storms and people drown. Terrifying! All your eggs in one basket. But statistically you're far safer sailing from Newfoundland to Haiti, as I have just done, through some of the roughest waters in the world, than you are driving every day on the freeway. Besides, even if the odds were even, I'd still go this way, because I'm proud as I can be about making that voyage in safety. It makes me feel heroic. I dared to pit my puny skill against the mighty sea and won.

That's heady stuff for anyone and does wonders for the self-esteem. That, and buying the boat in Newfoundland, where nobody goes to buy a boat. And fixing her up myself; I got a $50,000, one-of-a-kind classic boat out of the last century—for $12,000. That makes me feel good, too. I'm always looking for things that *aren't* "done." That's where the fun and the savings are. I knew a kid who bought a secondhand Cadillac hearse cheap, because he couldn't afford a car—and had a ball. You may say, "Well, he was just a kid and could get away with it." No, sir! If you need the cheapest heavy-duty station wagon there is and have the courage to be a little nonconformist, you might be wise to look into the secondhand hearse market. It's really all just a matter of self-confidence and self-image. If it makes good sense for you, you can have fun driving a hearse. After all, it's a Cadillac, isn't it? And hearses are seldom ruined by high-speed driving. When gas cost too much during my early recovery, I traded my car for a "big Honda" motorcycle and fulfilled a dream I'd had for years. Riding a big bike is a special kind of thrill, and the price-of-gas problem was solved. Daring a little can be very therapeutic.

YOUR RELIGION

Everyone needs to know who he is, why he is here, and how and why he should behave ethically and morally. The vast majority of people also feel a need to discuss these questions together, to search for better answers, and to look up to and worship something in communion with their fellows. These needs are normally filled, at least in large part, by organized religions, of which there is a selection so large as to offer something that will suit almost anyone. If you have lost or fallen away from your faith, or never found one at all, it is important to your recovery to search for something to satisfy these fundamental needs. The lack of a sense of spiritual direction leaves one feeling rootless, purposeless, and lost, wandering alone in the wilderness—a stressful way to be.

Organized religions tend to be dogmatic. The most rigid and absolutist of these can only be described as totalitarian. Human nature being what it is, it is not surprising that a great many people brought up in one of these absolutist, superdemanding, inflexible faiths find themselves unable to live up to the rigid requirements, fall from grace, become terribly guilt-ridden, and either drop out altogether or continue only the façade of faith, only the forms and rituals. In both cases, having lost the anchor of true faith, they are blown wherever the vagrant winds take them. And so frequently end on the rocks of addiction, suicide, or insanity. Such people need to look elsewhere for a new anchor. There are many makes and models to choose from, across the whole spectrum, from rock-hard fundamentalism to Unitarian-Universalist churches, which are concerned with the search for universal truths found in all religions and philosophies, are many-prophet-centered (modern as well as ancient), and have no dogma at all.

Then there are the Eastern religions, the guru religions, and the endless number of groups who believe in all sorts of interesting things, including devil worship.

If you have no faith at present, you can't be worse off. Ask around; shop for the right one for you. Many people do, and finally find it; and when they do, it is not uncommon for their addiction problem to be greatly reduced, even to disappear, and their lives to improve tremendously. Don't sell religion short. However, let me hasten to add that finding faith and *sudden* apparent miraculous complete remission of compulsion and addiction is not common. Usually the individual finds his new faith of great help in his efforts to recover, but also finds it necessary to continue other avenues of recovery effort, such as we have already discussed.

If you have shopped around and still not found a religion, you are then left with a final alternative, a search for your own truth, your own reason for being, your own explanation of things; and in so doing you join an illustrious group of men and women who have done just that throughout history. The real point is to believe in something. Any system or organized religion is a collection of other people's beliefs. If you cannot accept any of those systems, you will be happier with your own, and you may find it a relief not to feel that you must keep trying to accept what you cannot accept.

TAKING INVENTORY AND MAKING CHOICES

For any kind of life planning you must find out what it is that you really need to fulfill yourself, and you do not do that by just sitting down and asking yourself, "What do I want?" The result would be useless, because you can't have all the things you want, anyway. On the other hand, if you are an addictive drinker, it is safe to say that at the moment you are probably quite unaware of how very possible some of your wants (dreams) actually may be. Coming to this realization and achieving some of your wildest dreams is what makes true sobriety so exciting, what pushes up your happiness quotient so much higher than it ever was in the past. This is reality we're talking about, seeing the real limitations and also the real possibilities. That means finding out, first, what you really *need*, and then, of all the things you *want*, which might make sense to think about and go after. It's all a matter of setting up sensible priorities. You can decide that you *want* a large home and a 50-foot yacht, but it would probably be unrealistic to set out to have both, not so much because it would be impossible, but because you would have to work so hard and so long to get and maintain them that you wouldn't have the time or energy to enjoy them once you got them. Learning to set realistic priorities is vital if you want to be happy, and stress drinkers are often very poor at that until the importance of it comes sharply to their attention. Money is by no means the only factor in setting priorities, either. It wouldn't make much sense to rush out to buy a 50-foot yacht until you had learned to sail and navigate something a little smaller and more manageable first, for example.

Your Immediate Situation

As an addictive drinker, I know that you will do as you damn well please. I did, and still do, a good part of the time. However, I suggest that your inventory will be far more productive if you consider each of the areas of living discussed on the preceding pages and write down an Immediate Situation Inventory plan first; that is, making choices in your situation which will help you to *stay* dry. Just that. I have added a Situation Inventory form at the end of this section to help you do that (page 208).

Addictive drinkers are famous for an approach to problems known as when-all-else-fails-read-the-directions, and it "kills" us to have to go at anything methodically. We almost never study the problem before diving in. It is for this reason that I have included after the inventory form Five Steps to Making a Good Decision (page 212) and urge you this once to be very methodical, in order to give yourself every advantage in the hope of working out a really good inventory of your situation and a mature plan of action based on it.

After you have used these Five Steps to help you determine what is best for you in each area of living (your job, etc.), and after you have written your choices down on paper, you will have a concrete sense of plan—your immediate plan—to follow, a clear road out of chaos, for the next several months. Your paper as a whole should present a picture of reduced stress, interesting change, and more fun.

And remember, just because you make a plan, that doesn't mean you can't change it as you go along or make another one whenever new factors come into your life or when your direction becomes clearer. After all, you are running your own store now. Having that paper available to refer to now and then will help to keep you on the track. So go over it once a month to see how you're getting on and make any necessary changes or adjustments.

Your Grand Goal Situation

After you have read the rest of this book (there's one more river to cross if you're to understand the Real Problem completely), you can make a preliminary effort at your longer-term or "grand goal situation" plan, using the same "Situation Inventory" form you used before. By "grand goal situation" I mean just that—the best, most ideal, total situation (circumstances) you can think of in your work, your marriage, your housing, etc., to help you to achieve your major purpose for living, the focus of your life, that which you feel will bring you the most sense of fulfillment and happiness. In order to put all these eggs (job, etc.) into the one package best organized to help you get where you want to go with your life, you must remember that it is direction, not results, that you are planning, and you'll have to figure that out first.

If you don't know what your purpose or focus is, I suggest that you do the dreaming I spoke of earlier. Then write down everything you would like to achieve with the rest of your life, assuming that you could achieve anything you chose to. Everything—no matter how fantastic. Certainly include all the things you may have fantasized yourself doing. This is not the time to be practical.

If you have never had a sense of real purpose in life, a sense that you were going somewhere or could be, study your list. There you have the things you deeply believe should be done, the things which are really important to you. Somewhere in there you can find your purpose in life. Perhaps you can't hope right now to achieve any one of those things you've written down, because they're too fantastic. Now look at them again. Could a really able person, who really had his shit together, as they say, hope to achieve a significant part of some of those dreams if he just started with step 1 and went a step at a time? If you can find one such thing where you can visualize the possible steps, you have a beginning. If you can find more than one, you're off and running. Write these dreams down at the top of your "Grand Goal Situation Inventory" paper.

Did you write any down, or did you say to yourself, "This is useless. I couldn't do any of those things"? If you thought that, you're wrong. You can get your shit together; that's what this whole book is all about. You can change yourself to be capable of achieving dreams. As to special skills that may be needed, you can learn them or find someone who has them already to do the technical part for you. There is always a way for a determined person who has himself together, knows how to look for and grasp opportunity, and stays with it.

How can you know *beforehand* that a dream really is possible? You can't. Maybe it isn't possible, but if you're facing reality now and you think it might be, it probably is. Maybe it will turn out that you don't have enough years left. Maybe you'll die tomorrow. Maybe you'll start drinking and just keep on. But if you have found one or more really worthwhile things to shoot for in the life you have left, you have at least your best chance at the brass ring. And you will have found not only purpose but challenge and excitement along the way. In fact, regardless of the final result, you will have gotten as much of the *real* brass ring of living as you can ever hope to get, because the fun and fulfillment come in the doing of it; the result, if finally achieved, is only icing on the cake.

After your purpose is stated on your paper, you can look at the specifics of your housing, marriage, etc., with *that in mind.* Now make any readjustments that seem appropriate, so that it will all fit in terms of the direction you are going, the purpose you wrote down. Then keep improving your situation as you go, looking for new opportunities that fit into your general plan. Every chance you get, move into what looks better for you, clarifying options as to how you can get from "here" to "there" next.

If you are married, you may want to ask your mate to complete a separate inventory, as suggested in Part Five, "To Those Who Love Them" (page 281), especially if you are making recovery a team operation. Then you will have a good basis for comparing your own plans and direction with your spouse's, to make the final readjustments necessary to blend the two into your joint plan of attack. This may sound cumbersome and difficult, but it is often easier than it looks. And it can be a lot of fun—planning dreams.

SITUATION INVENTORY

1. HOUSING
   Where will I live? Can I afford it on my income? Can I handle maintenance myself? If not, who will help with the maintenance? On what basis? Is the location good for me? Are the emotional associations good or bad? Where have I dreamed of living? Maybe I could form a partnership with one or more others for housing, reducing cost and effort?
   My plan:____
   ____

2. LONELINESS AND INVOLVEMENT
   What specific actions will I take to become more involved in life and have some fun? (Before you answer this, you might want to make a list under the two headings "Old Activities I Once Enjoyed" and "New Activities I Might Enjoy" and consider the following under each heading: sports, hobbies, clubs [P.W.P., "Y," etc.], community

services, church, travel, education, and research. Be specific.)
My plan:____

3. WORK
Is my present work fulfilling? Do I want the same work but with a different employer? Do I want to stay where I am for a while to see if it gets better? Should I improve my position by getting special training? What training? How? Where? Do I want to switch to another line of work? What? (Make list.) Maybe early retirement? Can I afford to quit now to pursue my new purpose full-time? Should I look for part-time or temporary jobs until I'm well enough to take on a really good job? Am I eligible for unemployment insurance payments? Should I try to get welfare to help me until I'm well enough to find and keep work? Should I look for on-the-job training? Can I make and sell some product myself? Should I create my own service job, door to door, ad in paper, etc.? Should I join a commune, the Peace Corps, or other volunteer activity where food and housing are provided (National Friends Service Committee, e.g.)? (See text for other suggestions or dream your own.)
My plan:____

4. MARRIAGE AND FAMILY
Is everything entirely satisfactory? Must I work to put my marriage back together while waiting for sobriety to help? Should I encourage my spouse to get into a recovery program? Should I suggest joint counseling? Should I suggest joint A.A.–Alanon attendance? How can we best share growing together? (Ask spouse and list ways.) Should I ask my spouse and older children to read this book to understand our problem better? What special activities can I do with my spouse? When? With my children? When? What will I do for my spouse (children,

whole family), to show my love? I have tried everything and marriage is hopeless for us, so I might get a divorce for my own sanity and future (after six months of sobriety, after a year, approximately when)? (Keep it simple and be as specific as possible here.)

My plan:______________________________

____

SINGLE

I will continue single for at least a year until my judgment is more dependable? I will consider living with someone of the opposite sex I can care for and respect during this time to reduce loneliness and have someone with whom I can share? I will look for a friend or roommate of my own sex to reduce loneliness? I will join P.W.P. or other singles groups? I will take a singles cruise or a trip? I will look for a new mate in clubs, church, or other activity groups I am interested in?

My plan:______________________________

____

5. SEX LIFE

Is it perfectly satisfactory? Should I get professional counseling for myself? My partner? Both of us? Should I get books on the subject to learn about our problems and what specifically we can do? (See or call a counselor specializing in sex problems to recommend such books.) I will talk things over with my spouse to gain better understanding and cooperation? I will work at reprogramming my own computer, as shown in Part Four, to overcome my known inhibitions? Should I ask a counselor for group therapy meetings for this? I will check with the county health department to see if a clinic is available locally which uses the Masters and Johnson sex therapy techniques? Should I arrange for an interview by myself or with my partner?

My plan:______________________________

____

6. RICH OR POOR

What do I need in money, things? Would I be happier living more simply? How can I go about doing that? I will make a list of my basic needs? If I (we) must have more money, how can more be saved by making changes in the way we live so that we can still have fun out of life? How can we make more money? Both work? Better job part-time in addition to regular work? Garage sale to get rid of unwanted items? To simplify?

My plan:____

____

7. RELIGION

Am I completely happy with my present church affiliation? I believe in God and want to continue to grow in my faith—how will I do this? I do not believe in God but want to, so what action will I take to find a belief in God? I like organized religion? I don't like organized religion? What action will I take to develop my own religion or philosophy of life (since I cannot accept any organized religion)?

My plan:____

____

NOTE: Your inventory sheet may not look like this. You may prefer to work on the basis of "Next Step" or "List of Steps" or a generalized "Try to Accomplish before (*date*)" when you are dealing with specific items such as retraining for work, garage sales, or appointments with counselors, etc. However, putting a date on a goal is potentially stressful. Use a date to spur you on if you choose to, but don't let a date ruin your sobriety and your life. Dates can always be changed, and must be if they threaten you in any way. One day at a time. Your plan should work *for* you, not against you. It's your store now, but only you can keep it that way.

FIVE STEPS TO MAKING A GOOD DECISION

The example used in the Five Steps here is not some aspect of "Housing," "Your Work," etc., so that I won't influence your choice of pros and cons in evaluating your situation in those areas of living. I have taken "My Drinking" as the example here, just to show you how logical step-by-step thinking is needed for problem-solving, especially by addictive drinkers, who, in my observation, make snap judgments all too often.

Step 1. *What are the factors involved?*

Put down the important factors in two columns, under the headings "Good" and "Bad."

My Drinking

Good	*Bad*
It relaxes me when nothing else will.	The things I do and say while drunk embarrass me terribly.
It allows me to move into a fantasy world, where things don't look so bad, even beautiful sometimes, and I can feel good for a change.	It costs too much money. It is threatening my marriage. It may cost me my job.
Etc.	Etc.

Step 2. *Evaluation of the factors*

Step 2 involves a balanced evaluation of the above factors to see whether you wish to change the situation or leave it as it is. At this point, your opinion as to the feasibility of making a change is of no importance. Would you change it if you could? Or are you satisfied with the present situation? If you reach the latter decision, you stop here and move on to another subject; if the former, you go to Step 3.

It may be helpful here to ask yourself, "What is the total

long-term effect on me in this area of my life?" Use a scale of 1 to 5. The total effect is:

1. Very bad.
2. Makes me unhappy much of the time.
3. Is neither good nor bad. It balances out.
4. It's usually good, but sometimes not so good.
5. It is good and makes me feel good most of the time.

Your score gives you a good measure of the total stress effect of that area of your life. This tells you how important it is to do something about it, or that nothing needs to be done. A score of 1 or 2 demands change, probably radical change. A score of 3 or 4 suggests the need for change within the existing framework to improve the situation, but look also at the radical alternatives for a possibly better answer. A score of 5 clearly says that you are in good shape in that department and no further action is needed.

Step 3. *What are the possible alternatives?*

Here you put down all the alternatives, every one, however far-out they may appear at first. Again, feasibility is not important at this stage. Assuming that you could do anything you wanted, without adverse consequences, what would you really like to do? This is the fun part, the time to dream, to let your imagination go. Dreams are far from impossible to achieve under the right circumstances, and you can control or change many circumstances that you may have thought uncontrollable or immutable in the past.

Common Alternatives	*Dream Alternatives*
I'll join A.A. I'll see a psychiatrist. I'll go on the wagon for a while. I'll join Synanon. I'll go to a recovery home. Etc.	I will find the strength to limit my drinking to social drinking. I'll go back to church and find a sudden religious awakening that will solve my drinking problem. Etc.

Step 4. *Evaluation of the alternatives*

First, look at the Dream Alternatives and do some more dreaming, practical dreaming. Is there any way at all I could really do that? Consider this question seriously. A lot of people do find ways to make Dream Alternatives come true. I have several times. That's how I managed to arrange things to live full-time on a 50-foot schooner of my own, and it makes sound, practical sense for me, although I still find it a little hard to believe it's all real. Remember that, to recover, you're going to change quite a lot of things, and those changes may make a big difference in what is possible for you now, as opposed to what was possible before.

If the Dream Alternatives still aren't possible, at least for now, consider the list of Common Alternatives, one by one, to see which makes the best sense for you.

To help you make a good evaluation of each alternative, I suggest you use the following scale:

1. Impossible, at least for now.
2. Possible, but very unattractive.
3. Possible and acceptable.
4. Looks good.
5. Clearly better than the other alternatives.

Step 5. *Final check and consideration*

Do not take the chosen action until you have completed the inventory and have come to preliminary decisions for action in each important area of your life, because now you need to list all the actions you have chosen, so that you can analyze them as a group to see if any of them conflict. If they do, adjustments or changes will be necessary to make all your actions dovetail for achievement of maximal results. Timing, too, is important, so figure that as well in putting together your final list of actions, according to priority of importance and the order in which they should be carried out.

Remember, too, especially if you are still in very bad shape, that you shouldn't take on more than you can realistically expect to handle. It's more important to win at what you do right now than it is to perform miracles. As the Seabees used to say in World War II: The very difficult we do immediately; the impossible takes a little longer.

Part Four

Choosing Your Own Self, The Ultimate Goal

WHERE IT ALL BEGAN AND STILL IS

As we have seen, alcohol is not the Real Problem, only a symptom. Behind the addictive drinking, superbly concealed much of the time, lies the ocean of abnormal stress—physical, mental, and emotional, rising and falling as surely as the mighty tide in the Bay of Fundy. Looking deeper still, we saw that this sea of abnormal stress was the direct result of fears that were constantly building and compounding. These fears drive us closer and closer to the brink of insanity, and more and more often to the only source of relief we know from the exquisite torture and terror—booze, drugs, or other aberrant behaviors. These fears arise in large part from the steadily growing, desperate sense of defeat, frustration, and final total impasse in our long, exhausting battle to find some real satisfaction in our lives, some true sense of fulfillment, some degree of valid purpose and worth. But even after digging down to this level, we are still faced with one more unanswered question: What is it that drives us so: what is it that *I* am searching for to fulfill *me*?

I had been searching for the answer to this question for some time when, quite by chance, it fell in my lap from a completely unexpected direction, a book, *The Denial of Death* by Ernest Becker, for which he received the Pulitzer Prize. In his second paragraph he strikes at the heart of the matter:

the need to feel heroic in some meaningful way. It's another one of those simple truths, so simple we have been walking over and around it without ever looking at it in the field of addiction treatment. "Yet the popular mind always knew how important it was," says Becker, and also philosophers of all ages.

I have always vividly remembered and frequently joked about what I now realize must have been a remarkably clear insight into myself, which occurred when I was sixteen. I was walking up the hill to school one morning, wondering what I wanted to do with my life, and suddenly it came to me. "I know what I want, a crusade." It sounded a little silly to me at the time, but somehow I felt that it was true.

"In man, a working level of Narcissism* is inseparable from self-esteem, from a basic sense of self-worth." Becker adds, "We have learned, mostly from Alfred Adler, that what man needs most is to feel secure in his self-esteem." He also reminds us that we speak casually about "sibling rivalry," as though it were just a part of growing up, but it is much more than that. It expresses the heart of each of us, the desire to stand out. When we add our basic desire for self-esteem to our natural narcissism, we come to the core need of each of us, as Becker describes it: each person needs to justify himself as an object of primary value, to be a hero in some way, to make the biggest possible contribution he can, to show that he *counts.*

We have all shown this openly as children. It goes deep in our evolutionary and organismic constitution, but, as the author shows us, "In our culture anyway, especially in modern times, the heroic seems too big for us, or we too small for it. Tell a young man that he is entitled to be a hero and he will blush. We disguise our struggle by piling up figures in a bank book to reflect privately our sense of heroic worth. Or by having only a little better home in the neighborhood, a bigger car, brighter children." Does this ring a bell some-

*Narcissism here means that "we are hopelessly absorbed with ourselves. If we care about anyone, it is usually ourselves first of all."

where with you? Does this seem to explain the apparently silly business of keeping up with the Joneses, of the driving executive, sacrificing his family time and his health to get to the top, the perfectionist drive we addictive drinkers so often recognize in ourselves and talk about in A.A.?

We learn further from this interesting book that each system (political-cultural) establishes roles for performances of various levels of heroism: from the public heroism of a Churchill, a Mao, or a Gandhi to the private heroism of the local coal miner, the country priest, the plain, everyday, earthy heroism of the dirt farmer slaving from dawn to dusk to feed and clothe his family.

People earn this feeling of primary value, of unshakable meaning, by achieving that which is of lasting worth, whether it be a skyscraper or a totem pole, or a family that spans three generations. Lasting quality, not quantity, is the key idea here. To become conscious of what one is doing to earn his feeling of heroism is the main self-analytic problem of life, as Becker says, and most frequently there is an underlying terror of admitting what one is doing to earn self-esteem. As a result, you have a "blind drivenness" seen today (in this age) as a sort of screaming for glory ("an uncritical glory and reflexive as the howling of a dog") or seen in the more passive masses wearing the "standard uniforms—but allowing themselves to stick out, but ever so little and so safely, with the little ribbon or a red boutonniere, but not with head and shoulders."

What is the central idea of all great literature, movies, theater, and television plays but the exhibition of the efforts of people, great and small, to achieve the heroic? It is the central idea because it is the one thing that all people admire most, and just as we scorn and despise in others the faults that we see or sense in ourselves, we admire in others the one quality we respect most and would most like to see in ourselves, the heroic.

I am convinced that the drive to achieve the heroic, as perceived by Becker, is not only universal in all people but is truly the core factor in all addiction and most other human behavioral aberrations. That being so, it is also the foundation stone upon which recovery and our hopes for fulfillment and a transcendent level of life experience must be based. At long last, we have the key to understanding what it is that has been driving us unmercifully for all these long years; and now that we have that understanding, we can see how many of the puzzle pieces of our lives have fitted together to frustrate and block our fundamental drive toward our own individual heroic destiny.

I said that it was my opinion that every addictive drinker who wins his battle against booze is a real hero. A.A. doesn't do it, God doesn't do it, and neither does one's spouse, transactional analysis, psychoanalysis, gestalt therapy, reality therapy, or anything else. All are only tools to help. No matter how many tools you use, no matter how good they may be, you are the one who stays away from the first drink when body and mind are screaming for it. You are the one who makes yourself go to A.A. meetings and other therapy, who makes the effort to learn new techniques to change your attitudes to be more in keeping with reality and to gain control over your emotions. You are the one who works through your inventory to plan your own situation better, so that you can have a reasonable expectation of achieving your heroic goal. When you consider a commonly stated statistic that only one out of some thirty-five addictive drinkers ever gets well again, I think it entirely reasonable to say that those who do are heroes. If you agree, then you can look upon your whole recovery effort as your *first true total commitment to achieving a heroic goal.* And it is comforting to know that you have man's most basic drive going for you.

I am reminded of an incident that occurred some years ago when my family and I were cruising the Maine coast. Our poodle had gone ashore and then swum over to my wife, who was on her way back to our boat in the dinghy. She couldn't lift him into the boat, so she had our young son tow him by the collar. As she rowed on, a lobster boat pulled alongside and the fisherman said in the unique accents of "down Maine," "Mawnin'. You doin' that cause ya wanta or cause ya havta?" If you really want to recover from an addictive drinking problem, not just feel you have to (because of whatever outside pressure), you have a good chance to be that "one in thirty-five." And if you are also willing to do "anything, whatever is necessary," you will be guaranteeing yourself a better chance of success. Anything less than such total commitment puts the whole project in jeopardy.

And it is this same formula which we have to apply to life—beyond recovery. We have to dream and to decide what it is that we really want to do to fulfill ourselves heroically. And then we have to be willing to shoot the whole wad, "whatever is necessary," for the best chance of success, knowing full well that we may lose. You must be willing to gamble all the way with your life, reputation, and worldly goods whenever it is necessary to do so to keep yourself on the road to your heroic destiny (whatever you conceive that to be), if you are to live life to the fullest possible extent and be a real human being, a hero. To hoard life like a miser and spend a lifetime in trembling search of false security, tranquilized by the trivial, selling yourself short because of a thousand fears, is to play at penny ante. Only the high rollers win against the absurdity of the world, against life, and against the Grim Reaper himself. No one else is even in the game. That's the Real Problem. You're not a drunk. You just have the most basic problem there is—fear of life, fear of taking the big tiger by the tail, *and now we know how to solve that problem.*

FROM NEGATIVE TO POSITIVE

There are two kinds of heroism—what we might call negative-defeatist heroism and positive–self-directed heroism. The chances are that you have been living heroically for a long time. You haven't seen it, because the negative-defeatist kind of heroism you have been living produces negative-defeatist results, which look like the result of anything but heroic living. If you have felt trapped in a job you hate or in a marriage that has been without love or in a lifestyle completely inappropriate for you, and yet stayed with it for years, trying to fulfill your responsibilities as best you could, because you saw no alternatives, then you have been living a life of negative-defeatist heroism. The fact that you have been drinking more and more, in order to find relief from the tremendous strain (stress) of doing that is only a measure of the heroic effort such living demands.

As an ambulance driver at the front in World War II, I became convinced that they gave the medals for heroism to the wrong people. In the heat of battle, men often do things that we have been taught to think of as heroic, and often they are, but they are not so remarkable nor so hard to do as they appear when you read about them. When a soldier is scared to death, furious at seeing his best friends dying around him, frustrated by the inability of his unit to get close enough to the enemy machine gun to put it out of action, and when his body and mind are in the primitive state of total preparedness for violent effort to achieve successful fight or flight, under these conditions it is not unusual that such a man will single-handedly attack the machine-gun nest, exposing himself to almost certain death. It happens often in war, and the fact that many such actions result in posthumous medals for valor, in failure to take the position, in the loss of a valuable soldier, and possibly in the reduced likelihood of winning the battle as a result of his exposing himself against stupid odds, is not considered. The all-controlling fact is that each of us admires such a "heroic act" so much that it makes no difference whether it was successful or not. In literature, when the hero wins out in the end, we call it a romantic novel. When he loses, we call it a tragedy, but we love both protagonists, because both are heroic; the final ending is not important in comparison to the heroic splendor of the act.

Now consider a very different kind of heroism—one that goes unnoticed and undecorated. Picture a man torn apart by grenade fragments, crudely bandaged, the initial pain-dulling effect of shock now gone, his body lying on a stretcher in an ambulance rolling over a road surface filled with potholes. This man is suffering pain so excruciating that it is hard to imagine, and he does not cry out, because to do so would make it harder for the other wounded men in the ambulance. This is the quiet heroism over the long haul, when there often appears to be little or no hope. This is the high heroism you have shown while drinking, never recognized by others or even by the drinker himself, but heroism nevertheless, because it is in the face of apparent total defeat. The heroism exhibited during recovery is similar, in that it, too, is needed over a long haul, always in the face of possible defeat, with, at first, only superficial indications of possible final victory. But it is self-directed and positive, and it can lead to a better life. If you have shown the one, you can show the other.

Now let's look at the ways in which people of all kinds are unconsciously and innocently programmed for a life of negative-defeatist heroism, which, more often than not, builds and builds—oh, so subtly—to create an unconscious conflict of such massive proportions that the individual experiences a constantly rising abnormal stress level, which can only result in final escape into insanity, addictive drinking, or other stress-relieving behavioral aberration.

In a recovery home for "indigent alcoholics," I met Bill, a man with no skill or trade above the level of swinging a pick or lifting and carrying hods of bricks or heavy timbers. He was a giant of a man. To hear him talk, there were only two goals in his life: to get blind drunk as often as possible—"have a blast"—and to take the prettiest woman home with him when the bar closed. He was very popular in the recovery home, almost a legend of the hell-bent he-man, slamming his way through life with gusto and complete abandon. However, when you looked closer, Bill was not quite the image of the hero in life that he tried so hard to portray. First, he was obviously a compulsive drunk, who ended an evening as often in the local drunk tank as in bed being the sexual athlete. While pulling down substantial construction wages, he lived alone in a rented room, with few clothes, a broken-down pickup truck, and nothing in his pocket except on payday.

He was a poker player and so was I. We became friends at the table, and then we began to talk to and understand each other. One time I asked him if he had ever thought of learning a trade, so that he could make more money. "Oh, no, none of that school shit for me. I'm not bullshitting you; I tried that once, heavy-equipment school and then auto mechanics—auto mechanics, for chrissake! Can you see a horse like me taking a whole engine apart and getting it back together right? No way! Look, let's face it, I'm stupid. I figured that out a long time ago, so now I swing a pick or any other shit that they want swung, and then I get a few drinks, pick up the prettiest dolly in the bar, and have a ball."

"What convinced you you were stupid?" I asked. "Nothin' special. I've always known it—since I was a little kid. Ya know? Even my old man knew it, used to tell me—as far back as I can remember. He was right. When I went to school, I was always the dumbest kid in the class. They passed me along. Ya know? To get rid of me. Well, I got sick of that, so I quit after eighth grade. Education, training—it's all the same if you're stupid. Shit! That's all it is."

Another time I asked him what he would really like to have, if he could live just the way he wanted to. "Well, a good job, of course, a nice car, a house maybe— But what I really want— You won't laugh? A nice woman—a woman I could love—and take care of. But I'll never get that. A woman like that, she won't even look at a bum like me. But, ya know, I think about it sometimes. Maybe it's stupid, but I don't want much—I mean for myself. I mean, shit, what do I need? But, well, it's funny. I'd work like hell to get stuff for a person I loved—I guess I'm crazy as well as stupid, but I'd sure like to be able to give a whole lot to somebody somehow. Ya know?"

Bill isn't stupid. He has a terrific sense of humor, crude as hell, yes, but really funny, because he can see common things from funny angles. I've never known anybody with a good sense of humor who was stupid. Tests we gave him proved it, but if you tell a little boy that he's stupid, over and over, and you're his father, he's going to believe it. So in school he expects to fail, and does, of course. It's called a "self-fulfilling prophecy."

Bill stayed at the recovery home for four months, had no compulsion to drink after the first few weeks, and left for a special program we found for him where he could learn heavy-equipment operation in an on-the-job situation. This would minimize the "in school" feeling. In his first weekend visits back to the recovery home—to stay in touch with his friends and reinforce his resolve to stay off the sauce—he told everyone he had never had it so good, and he clearly showed more self-confidence and a generally positive attitude.

Then suddenly Bill failed to make his weekend visits a couple of times, and the next we heard of him was from a staff member who had seen him in court. It turned out that Bill was apparently so confident about his recovery that he let his attendance at A.A. meetings run down to nothing over a several week period, stopped his Antabuse, and five days later got so drunk after work that he had had a serious fight. The staff member reported that he was willing to talk, but was very tense, blamed his drinking on the strain of "that bullshit fancy-Dan job." The last thing he said was, "I told you bastards I was stupid, and ya wouldn't believe me. You even had *me* fooled for a while. Now, you take your fancy educated ass out of my business and let me run my life the way I goddamn well want to."

Maybe he'll come back to try again, now that he knows help is available, but he's got to do some time first.

I would like to offer a whole gamut of examples of how we are "programmed to negative-defeatist attitudes," so that I could be reasonably sure of including one with which you could identify directly and personally, as was done in the book *Alcoholics Anonymous*, from which the name of the organization was taken, but there are too many other things that need to be said for the purpose of this book to allow the space. But there is this one, with which many female addictive drinkers may identify.

Patty came from a socially prominent and well-to-do family. She had a happy childhood and graduated in the upper quarter of her class at one of the East's prestigious women's colleges, where she was active in student politics. When she married Henry, a man from one of the "best families," people were not surprised. They would have been surprised if it had not worked out that way. In due time they had two fine, healthy boys. (That, too, was expected.)

After fifteen years Henry was sent to Nigeria as a Foreign Service officer, and there their social drinking increased, because Henry's position "required" it. With servants to do almost everything and the boys in the States in private school, there were large pieces of the day that had to be filled with something, and everyone in the foreign colony drank off and on all day as a matter of course—during swimming and tennis parties, at women's club activities, and while just tanning. As time went on, Henry became more and more in demand for conferences, and his time at home was eventually reduced to a weekend or a few days out of a month. More and more often he came home too tired to make love, and once he left after three days without ever having made love at all.

At first Patty didn't notice how much she was drinking, because everyone seemed to be drinking just as much all around her, but finally it began to become obvious even to her. Two friends had delicately suggested that perhaps she should "cut back a little, just to be on the safe side." Then came the time Henry arrived unexpectedly and found her out cold on the dining-room floor. How furious he had been! At last, Patty knew she was hooked, but she didn't know what to do about it. She couldn't go to one of the doctors, all of whom she knew socially, and say, "Frank, I think I am an alcoholic." He'd think she was crazy or something, and it would be just too embarrassing for anybody to actually *do*.

Six months later Henry came home to find her drunk again, and arrangements were made for her to fly to the States to a renowned medical recovery facility—the best in the country.

I met Patty at a recovery facility, not the one referred to above, but the third one since then. The marriage was over; her husband had filed for divorce at the time she went to the recovery home where I was talking with her. She said that he had been wonderful when she returned from her first recovery home, while they were still in Nigeria, but that it did not last long; and soon he was away again on business as often as ever. She had started drinking again soon afterward.

Patty was in and out of several recovery homes after I met her, and it was not until she could separate herself emotionally from what she had lost—her husband and her children (who had grown up during these years)—and get down to the reality of her situation, doing "for me," and applying all she was learning to that "me," that she was able to make progress in a recovery program. According to the last letter I had from her, she had taken a course in alcoholism counseling three evenings a week for a year and had gone to New York City, where she was working as a counselor in an outpatient facility for addictive drinkers. The last lines of her letter were: "I have found a place in the world for me at last. I feel useful as I have not for years, and wonder of wonders, I'm happy again."

Despite Patty's education and training, she was in kindergarten when it came to making choices in her own life. She had been programmed for her role in life, a sort of nebulous American Dream for Women: find a husband, get married, have children, and dedicate your life to making a happy home. She had never even considered that she might have a choice in the matter. So she followed along and found it all enjoyable and fulfilling until the dream stopped. Her most fundamental reason for being had been swept away with an absentee husband, absentee and growing up (and away) children, and no work at home to do. It never occurred to her to take stock, to make choices, to choose her company, her day, her purpose, her direction. So she lapsed into a kind of generalized "poor me," as if some of her appendages had been cut off and she didn't know where to find them.

Negative programming can be done with great ease and entirely unconsciously by parents, by society, or even by oneself. "I'm shy." "I'm not a good business person." "I can't do chemistry." "I'm not good with my hands, not mechanical." Each such idea about yourself is the final result of a series of thoughts which have been put into your conscious mind by other people or have occurred there as a result of your own personal experiences. Bill's experience buttressed his original belief, and he was so thoroughly convinced that twenty years later, a grown man, he continued to fail every time he saw himself in any kind of learning situation. However, in most people the problem of negative conditioning is far more complex, and the total result can be even worse. I have heard many addictive drinkers say, in one way or another, "There's no hope for me. I'm a loser. I've never been able to do anything right in my life. How can you expect me to get sober?" Such a person has become programmed to believe not only that he can't learn but that he can't do anything well. In both cases, the belief is absurd, because it simply isn't so. There is nobody alive, who can speak his native language and move normally with the usual complement of arms, legs, and muscles, who can't find lots of things he can do well, if he starts going at life positively and with some self-confidence.

In the following sections we will get down to the specifics of how one goes about overcoming all sorts of negative programming, while simultaneously reprogramming his mental computer positively. It's the guts of recovery and fundamental to preparing yourself to play a satisfying heroic role in life for a change.

WHAT DO YOU THINK OF YOURSELF?

This is a vital question for your inventory taking, because some very important things depend directly upon your answer: such things as your self-confidence, your ability to dare, many of your basic attitudes, and your ability to love others.

It has been my experience that *all* addictive drinkers think badly of themselves in certain areas of their lives, not only while they are drinking, but for long periods afterward. In fact, if I was to try to answer the question "How can I judge the quality of a person's sobriety?" I would say that the quality of anyone's sobriety is proportional to his honest opinion of himself, assuming that he is capable of being honest with himself, because true sobriety means true maturity. It means healthy, realistic self-confidence and self-respect. It means that a person is so comfortable with himself as a person in work, play, and all social situations that he is capable of loving others, giving of himself to them in a thousand ways, with no thought of what he may or *should* get in return. He can do this, because his own cup of confidence and contentment with himself is already full. Therefore, he needs nothing from anyone else to fill it. He is like a multimillionaire who has so much money that he can give it away with no thought of ever running short himself, because his investments are bringing in more faster than he can give it away. The only difference is that the coin we are talking about is love not money. This is the ideal, which is probably never achieved completely, but the degree of that achievement is the measure of a mature person. It follows, therefore, that the addictive drinker who wants to recover must find ways and means, and must consciously work to improve his own opinion of himself as the cornerstone of recovery. So how does a person with a self-confidence problem, who may even hate himself, go about doing that? The following suggestions are based on the practical experience of thousands of ex-addictive drinkers, including my own.

Act As If

You think it's yourself you hate, because you think your behavior is a reflection of your weak, indecisive, flabby self; and you hate your behavior, because it is in direct, violent conflict with your ideal of the way your ideal self should act. Since you know what kind of behavior is ideal, the only trick you need to learn is how to get yourself to act that way, and like most of the fundamental things in living, the trick is not very hard to learn: "Act as if—"

The common mistake here is to try to change everything at once. When you attempt to do that, you set yourself up to fail, and you do. Then, having tried and failed, you assume you can't do it and settle for being a bum. If you buy an old, beat-up, classic car to restore (that's you at the moment), you don't expect to knock out all the dents, replace the upholstery, find all the missing parts, fix the broken windows, and complete a multilayer, superior-quality paint job in one day. With a step-by-step approach ("a day at a time"), you put planning and decision-making into it, and you learn the good things about yourself as you go along. The key is to start with *one behavior* that you know you can change easily, and concentrate on that *until it's done.* Then move on to the next thing.

If you've been putting off doing fifty minor repair jobs around the house for a long, long time, you can decide to do one or two a day for a while. *Act as if* you were your ideal self. *Act as if* you were a nice person who likes to do jobs around the place, because it makes your spouse's work easier, and makes the house nicer, so that the whole family can enjoy it and take more pride in it. It doesn't have to be something that really needs doing. Bake some of those fantastic pies you used to make, or wax and polish the car. Do what you choose to do as a present to the family, preferably when nobody's home. Then say nothing about it. Let them find out for themselves that the back door doesn't stick anymore, that the hedge has been trimmed for the first time in six months, that the cookie jar is filled with homemade goodies. It won't take them long to figure it out, and you'll have fun doing it, thinking about the reaction you'll get from them.

Addictive drinking is a self-centered illness. If you look at the jobs around the house as dirty duties you have to do, and then think about a list of fifty such dirty duties to be done, you won't get anything done and you'll feel guilty into the bargain. Your wife's or husband's constant complaints about your never doing anything around the house add fuel to the flames, and you end up miserable, with that old "poor me" feeling, which usually leads to a drink. To turn a situation like this around is not easy. You start with *acting as if* you loved your spouse. Slip out of bed some morning, fix breakfast for you both, and bring it up to bed as a surprise. Why not a flower in a small vase on the tray, whatever you imagine a loving person would do. If things have been bad between you for a long time, don't be surprised if the response you get is, "Okay, what have you done wrong now?" or some other biting comment. (That sort of response will pass.) There has never been a man or woman who didn't like a sign of appreciation from time to time. So just keep at it without arguing back or getting hurt and mad. Whether you are *acting as if* with your family or anyone else, they'll come around when they find out the new you is for real. The old love may return as well. If it does, you won't be *acting as if* anymore. If it doesn't, you know you did your best and don't have to feel guilty about it.

If doing jobs around the house is the behavior you have chosen to change, you will find that if you accomplish one or two a day, it won't take long before all fifty have disappeared like magic. And remember, in recovery you have all that old drinking time to fill with other activity. But, most of all, taking on what used to be dirty duties and making them enjoyable (not dirty or a duty) will give you a sense that you are getting on top of things for a change, on top of yourself. You have really altered your actions to coincide with your image of good behavior and can begin to think of yourself as being more of the person you think you should be. You've got one fender with all the dents out, ready for painting.

Now you're ready for another fender. So choose a different behavior—going places with your husband or wife, for example. Take your wife dancing and act as if you wanted to. She might enjoy it so much that you will, too. Act as if you would like to go again soon. Buy two tickets to the hockey game and take your husband. Act as if you enjoy it. Act as if you want to get to know the players, the rules, the play. Act as if the hot dogs he brings you are delicious. Act as if you'd like to go again. Maybe you'll become a hockey fan or win a dance contest; maybe not. But you will, at least, be acting as if you want to go places with your spouse. In time you will be going out together just as you used to, or have always wanted to, and you will no longer be acting as if. Now you're ready to start on the engine or the upholstery or to take some more dents out. Just choose a behavior, any behavior; act as if you were the kind of person you want to be in any area whatsoever. And in due time you will be.

Become Involved in the Creation of Value or Beauty for Other People

If you're in A.A., ask about getting into the H&I (Hospitals and Institutions) group. This is usually a small group of people—men and women—who go to hospitals and prisons on a regular basis to run A.A. meetings. Here is a unique opportunity to help people who are in far worse circumstances than you are, by showing them that someone from outside cares about them and by carrying the message of A.A. to them, so that they, too, can begin to hope for a new and better life. As a relatively new member, you may be just the person with whom one (or more) of the inmates can identify, making it possible for you to become the key figure in getting the A.A. program across to him, and perhaps in convincing him that he can straighten out his life when he gets out, with the help of A.A. and concerned A.A. friends. H&I work is always interesting and always good for your sobriety. Addictive drinkers in A.A. help other addictive drinkers, because it has been proven over and over again that in doing so, they help themselves more than the people they are trying to help. Sound paradoxical? It works this way:

It is hard to think of yourself as no good for anything when you know that several people, trapped in a prison (or hospital) day after day with few or no friends, are looking forward all week to seeing you when you come to the meeting because you have become a real friend to them when they had become convinced that everyone who was straight on the outside was a sanctimonious, hypocritical jerk. When you know you are helping people find hope, victory over their addiction, which has been ruining their lives for years, and a chance for happiness, is it possible for you to feel that your life has no purpose? Can you imagine doing this sort of thing without feeling a whole lot better about yourself? And don't hesitate to ask about getting into the group on the assumption that those guys wouldn't want a newcomer. A.A. is very much like all other voluntary organizations around the world. Five percent of the members do 95 percent of the real work of the organization. The rest are there more for what they can get than for what they can give. That's life. You see the paradox, of course. The H&I people are giving more of themselves, and so, of course, they are having a far more interesting time and getting back far more than they give—in happiness, an increased sense of personal worth, and constantly strengthening sobriety. The selfish ones are getting far less. Always short-handed, the H&I people will welcome you with open arms. They might have a local rule requiring a bit more dry time than you have, but you will not have to wait more than six weeks or so.

If you don't want to join H&I, you can find the same kind of opportunity to help others less fortunate than yourself by working as a volunteer in a detox, doing Twelfth Step work* in company with older, more experienced members. In fact, any kind of volunteer service will bring the same rewards—coaching kids, teaching something, visiting shut-ins, whatever interests you.

There is one more advantage for you in this kind of work. When you are constantly working with people who are worse off than you, it is hard to start experiencing that "poor me" feeling. It's hard, because it is so obviously absurd by direct comparison. Besides, what would the people you're trying to help do if they saw you feeling sorry for yourself? They'd laugh at you for a fool. "Poor me" just doesn't work under these circumstances.

You will find that, once you begin altering your behavior in small ways and changing your ways of thinking and feeling (attitudes) about those things you used to hate or never did at all before, it becomes easier and easier to change your behavior in other important ways. The reason is simple. With the changes already made, your attitudes about a lot of things have begun to be more positive than negative, and you feel a lot better about yourself. All that gives you more self-confidence to move "onward and upward" to bigger and better things. You will have lots of negative, depressed times, too, during this period. Don't let me lull you into an Alice in Wonderland idea of this stage of early recovery. It ain't easy, Charlie; but once you see it working for you, you begin to believe you're really going to make it after all, and that will carry you through a lot. Also, the fact that you are proving to yourself that you can hurt without drinking, that you *can* change yourself, even though it is tough at times, justifies you in feeling considerable pride in your achievements to date. Please note that I am talking about real pride here, not the false pride of the drinking days. That's a very

*Twelfth Step work: answering calls for help from desperate addictive drinkers and getting them to their first few meetings. This is the last step in A.A.'s program of "Twelve Steps."

different thing. "When we give ourselves to others, we never lose our self-respect" (Maxwell Maltz, M.D., *Five Minutes to Happiness*).

Reprogram Your Computer

We have mentioned how, since birth, your automatic mental computer has been programmed with negative ideas and attitudes. You know what they say: "Garbage in, garbage out!" In recovery one of the most important things you should be doing is consciously reprogramming that computer yourself and arranging for others to help you in that reprogramming. It's easy. By removing yourself from bars and any other place that feeds you constant negative programming, because the people there are negatively programmed themselves, and putting yourself in positive environments, where positive ideas and people surround you—A.A. meetings, new friends, other therapies, and all other positive activities with positive people—you are arranging for positive reprogramming of yourself. Then you can add your own specific and sharply focused personal reprogramming. That's not hard, either.

Using your conscious mind to reprogram your unconscious, automatic mental computer may very well sound like a far-out idea to you, and there are plenty of far-out ideas going around today. However, this idea is not far-out at all. In fact, you have been doing it negatively for much of your life without being aware of it. A specific example of this process may be helpful.

Remember when you were learning to drive a car. You used your conscious mind to learn to perform a series of rather complicated and closely coordinated actions necessary to the acts of starting and driving the car. At first you had to think hard to do it at all, and the result was full of sudden jerks, stalls, and mistakes. Yet six months later you were performing all those complicated, closely coordinated actions smoothly and effortlessly *without even thinking about it.* Your conscious mind had succeeded in programming your unconscious, automatic mental computer so well that it was carrying out the functions better than the conscious mind. This is what I mean by conscious self-programming of your automatic mental computer. It works just as well for attitude change.

Every time you were embarrassed at making a mistake in a social situation when you were young, and thought, "Oh, how could I have been so dumb?" you were programming yourself negatively for the next social situation; and if you did it often enough, this became an automatic expectation and a conscious conviction about yourself as a shy and socially inept person. Being highly nervous and under a good deal of stress in any social situation as a result, you were more likely than ever to make mistakes, and to overcompensate for your shyness by being too loud or too forward, thus turning off people, causing them to reject you, which, in turn, made you more miserable, shy, and insecure. *Negative programming always spirals from bad to worse. On the other hand, positive programming always spirals from bad to better.*

The fact that positive programming always spirals from bad to better reflects the positive and very *fortunate* side of this programming business. *The negative programming you have suffered from happened by chance—all of it.* Some positive programming also happened by chance, too, when you functioned successfully in a social situation, for example, and you thought to yourself, "Hey, I conquered my fear and asked that boy to dance, and he accepted and really seemed to enjoy it. Now we're friends. I pulled it off that time." If you have ended the chance-programming process with strong negative opinions of yourself in a variety of areas, after years of chance positive-and-negative programming, it only means that you thought or heard or felt many more negative things than positive ones, so the negative side of the scale dominated and became the basis of your opinion of yourself. I used the word "fortunate" above in reference to the kind of positive programming or reprogramming I am talking about for the following reason:

Learning anything by chance is an inefficient way to learn, because it takes a long time. It is also inefficient because, when you learn something by chance, you seldom learn the best way of doing it. As a rifle-team coach, I found out very early that it was far easier to teach a person to shoot well who had never shot a gun in his life than one who had been potting away with a .22 for years. I first had to teach the latter not to jerk the trigger as he had been programmed by long practice to do, before I could teach him the proper way to squeeze it. When you know how to consciously reprogram yourself positively, chance and the bad habits of a lifetime are easily canceled out, and the process is far more efficient and occurs in far less time than it took to program you negatively. In fact, in a great variety of vital areas, you can succeed in reprogramming your computer *in a matter of days or weeks.*

How do you do that? Effective self-programming is simply a matter of getting hold of basic information about your problem, analyzing it in the light of that information, setting up an action plan (game plan), and then talking to yourself about what you are going to do, how you are going to feel, and why you should do it that way and feel that way. In this way, you set yourself up for positive experiences, which will convince you that your plan works.

One day I heard the operator of a marina complaining that for insurance reasons a new law forced him to hire a contractor to clean his rest rooms, and the prices quoted were exorbitant. I was broke, and so I offered to fulfill the requirements of the contractor and do the job for somewhat less. He said he'd let me know later in the week. When I had time to think about what I had just offered to do, actually cleaning public johns, I knew I couldn't do it. I thought of myself as much too fine a person to clean toilets, and yet I needed the money desperately. So I started consciously to program myself positively, since it was only my negative attitude about people who clean toilets and my false pride that was standing in my way.

First, I decided that as "president of the Vaughan Sanitation Contracting 'Company,' " I was already several cuts above a common garden-variety toilet cleaner—a businessman. The fact that I was the only employee made no difference, because a businessman often has to do all the dirty work to get the business started. Second, I decided that it would be fun, someday when I was successful again, to tell people that I had taken a job like that, to show what a remarkable guy I was. (My real pride wasn't that strong yet, and I was grasping at anything to build it up.) So I decided, with my old perfectionism showing, that my rest rooms were going to be the cleanest, most glistening, in the state. Thus, I could feel that I was, in fact, doing a better job than the average john cleaner, and that would be good for my real pride. By this time, I also had myself convinced that humbling myself like this was heroic in a way; I'd be working on getting rid of one more aspect of my false pride, because, let's face it, somebody has to clean the johns in a smooth-running society. I worked all this out in my mind over the next few days, as well as actually working in the details of how, as well as why, I should clean johns, so that I was ready for the "sanitation business" and accepted the job with pleasure when it was offered to me.

The talking-to-yourself part is to reprogram your computer in advance, so that you will be able to act and to feel the way you want to when the situation for which you have been preparing arises. Talk to yourself as described every day for ten or fifteen minutes, for a maximum of five days, before the event. (This is particularly applicable to the sections on anger, resentment, etc., which follow.) If you can do it more often, you will be buying more insurance that it will work. I cannot emphasize too much the importance of this exercise. This reprogramming process has been by far the most powerful single technique I have found in changing my own attitudes and replacing my old negative programming with its positive counterpart. It has, thus, been the most powerful single weapon in my battle for recovery.

If you don't manage to improve your self-image, you won't recover. That is a fundamental truth. You know the old line, "What do I say after I say I'm sorry?" I say, "I'm sorry you're scared and miserable, but if you don't want to be that way anymore, get off your duff and start doing something intelligent about it." In this book I am talking about all kinds of tools you can use to get well, but the key phrase is "you can use." All the help available can do only about 10 percent of it *for you.* The other 90 percent *you do* for yourself. It's hard to change yourself, and it's slow. That's why most people never do. That's why it's unusual and heroic if you do.

ANGER

Addictive drinkers are angry people who do not know how to deal with anger. As a result, the anger smolders inside, creating resentments, which are among the most stressogenic factors known. Most addictive drinkers are specialists at resentment! Living in their should-be world, they resent deeply any remark or behavior that seems unfair or in any sense a threat to them. Since virtually all have a poor self-image, they suffer great insecurity and have become very self-centered by the time the illness has reached the serious stage. The stress drinker at this time can only be described as a paranoid. When two people are whispering or talking across the room out of earshot, they are probably talking about him, and what they are saying is almost certainly bad. When a person says or does something that can possibly be taken as a slur or rejection of him, he automatically assumes that was the intent. He is also angry and deeply resentful toward any other aspect of reality that thwarts or frustrates him. He feels isolated, misunderstood, constantly on the defensive; no matter how valiantly he tries to please, and he does try valiantly, everyone is against him. It all seems terribly unfair, and he feels fully justified in being very, very angry about it. If you told him that anger is *not* something that just happens to him, that it is possible to remove anger from his life almost entirely if he chooses to do so, he would say in his usual fashion, "That's a crock," "You're nuts," "Psychological bullshit."

Anger and resentment were two of my most serious problems. I would get angry, then go drink. I would build up a resentment while I was drinking and then drink some more. Just drinking and stewing, stewing and drinking. I was trying desperately hard to design better schools, to write better textbooks, and to improve education in general. At every step of the way stupid people were doing everything they could to stop me or slow me down, I thought. I was furious most of the day on the job and drinking most of the time when I was home.

I had been taught from early childhood by my mother—a Victorian New England woman, raised by a puritanical Baptist minister—that "a gentleman never loses control or shows anger." When I was angered, and I usually went from calm to seething rage in seconds, I always jammed it inside and stayed apparently calm and polite on the surface. (Willpower alone.) Then, within hours, that bottled rage ballooned into a resentment that I could hardly contain (unbearable stress), and I would drink, and scheme wonderful forms of revenge, until I passed out. I drank that way against one man for three solid years. At last, someone in A.A. pointed out to me that I had not, thereby, hurt him in any way, but I had been killing myself physically and mentally and making myself wretched. So I came to the conclusion that *nothing anyone could do to me was as bad for me as my letting myself get angry.* Since I was trying to stay dry, I could no longer afford that.

What was I to do the next time I became furious? I knew I had to have a script of what to say and do, because I'd usually get so angry I could not think. So I set up this game plan for the next time, the script to begin the *second I started* getting angry.

1. Say: "I'm getting angry, I'll get back to you." Do: Walk away.
2. Talk to myself at home about it, look at it from all angles, etc.
3. Get back to him the next day and resolve it somehow. (Otherwise, the old resentment will build as in the past.)
4. If I can't resolve it (he's defensive, won't try, etc.), then I have done my best, and it's not my problem any longer. It's his, so I don't have to worry about it.
5. I'll try to communicate with him again, but if the problem persists, I'll just have to dodge contact with him until I am better able to handle this sort of thing.

The first time I tried this plan of action, everything went according to the script, until I got back to him. I never had a chance to give my opening speech. He said, "Hey, I've been thinking about what you said about being angry. At first I didn't know what it was all about. Did you think I meant . . . I didn't mean that at all, I meant . . ." I had, indeed, misunderstood because of my assumption of the worst (my negative attitudes), my paranoia.

The second time I used that game plan, the very same thing happened when I went back. I learned soon enough that I was perceiving insults and threats in the statements of others that were made with no such intent at all. I would indeed have to watch out for my own negative attitudes, stop the paranoic "poor me" bit.

The third time I walked out of a getting-angry situation, I knew the problem was not my own paranoia. *He* was feeling hard-done-by. But I wouldn't hurt a flea, doesn't he know that? What's he afraid of? I began to see that *anger is caused by fear.* I came up with four questions to be used whenever I talked to myself at home:

1. What am I afraid of?
2. How is this person threatening me?
3. What is he afraid of?
4. How am I threatening him?

The next time I started getting angry, I found that I didn't have to follow my script, didn't have to go away and cool off, because I wasn't suddenly furious anymore, just coolly standing there asking myself those four questions (and also, "Does he mean what I think he means?"). I found myself saying, "Now wait a minute. There's something wrong here. I'm not trying to cause you any trouble. Let's talk about it. I'm getting upset and so are you. Let's work it out. How do you see it, again?" Then we talked some more. As it turned out, he had misinterpreted something I said. I apologized for putting it badly, and we went on from there.

As soon as I started asking myself these four (or five) reasonable questions (thinking!), I found that I was able to discuss coolly anything in the world I chose to discuss—without ever getting angry. I learned that *nobody could make me angry unless I let him.*

I learned also that I could have the best intentions in the world of resolving a problem, but that there are people who are so defensive that they cannot admit the fault is theirs even if they want to, have no idea of their own fear behind their anger, and have no idea that they are letting themselves be threatened. Having understood what anger is and how it works, I finally realized that, if my motives were good, I had neither done nor said anything purposely to make that person angry, and had tried my best to get him to reason with me, then I didn't have to accept any responsibility for his anger if it continued—no more guilt feelings.

In two weeks I learned how to deal with anger that had been making me miserable, defeating my plans, losing me my friends, and getting me regularly drunk for twenty years. What a thrill! I was able to drop the four-questions game plan altogether eventually, because more and more as my self-confidence grew I started responding with reason and common sense automatically. It makes all the difference.

It sounds silly to me today to say that I used to become unhinged in traffic jams, but it is quite true. They drove me up the wall with frustration, which is nothing but a childish emotional reaction that occurs when you don't get just what you want when you want it. Very alcoholic! Traffic jams shot my stress gauge up to Blow every time, and as soon as I got out of one, I headed for the nearest bar to unwind. "Anger again. Can't afford it. What game plan can I use?" (1) "Music hath charms to soothe the savage breast—" Okay. I punch the classical-music button on the car radio, that should help. (2) I know that it gives me no real advantage to be gutsy and squeeze in ahead of ten cars or a hundred. Once I'm out of the jam at fifty-five miles an hour, what difference will a hundred feet or two—or a thousand—gained in the jam make in time saved? But it does tear hell out of my nerves every time I squeeze one out, wondering if I'll succeed or blow it. For a change I'm going to be the coolest, most intelligent person in the jam. I'll rise above it all, let others go ahead of me with a friendly wave, smile, and feel superior as hell.

I went through this thought process probably five or six times, adding refinements along the way. When the next jam occurred, it happened just as I planned. Don't ask me why, but I had a ball playing "supernice guy." I suspect part of it was that I'd always wanted to be a supernice guy, so I enjoyed being the real me for a change, and more importantly, I had licked my anger again. There is real joy in self-conquest. It's not all hard work and "stiff upper lip, old boy." (If this idea interests you, there are two excellent books on it.*)

Today I can honestly say that for the last several years, I have not allowed myself to be angry for more than a very few minutes. I learned how to meet anger head-on, deal

---

*Muriel Larsori, *You Are What You Think* and Adelaide Bry, *How to Get Angry without Feeling Guilty.*

with it quickly, and destroy it—or use it positively to motivate me to find another solution to the problem (whatever my desire was when anger got in the way). Anyone with most of his marbles can do the same thing. It takes some time, some thought, and the decision to act, but it's not terribly hard. In fact, I found it ridiculously easy, once I understood that anger is a reaction to fear. You reach a point at which you can manage your own emotional climate as well as the thermostatic machinery that keeps the temperature constant in a room or office. It's early to mention that, but try a few simple action plans and you may say it, too. At least I am not saying in this book, "Having a wonderful time. Wish you were here." I am trying to give you specifics. However, you can't get "here," unless you get off your duff and start moving, setting up and carrying out some action plans of your own.

FRUSTRATION

Frustration, any sort of roadblock in a person's path toward achieving his goals, is a serious problem for most addictive drinkers because it occurs so frequently, creates so much unnecessary stress and anger, and decreases efficiency very effectively. The added stress factor alone would place learning to deal with frustration high on any recovering drinker's list, but the resulting anger and loss of efficiency are of equal importance. We can't afford to allow frustration to get in our way if we are serious about recovery. It's a killer, too.

When I was drinking, I thought I was being efficient when I carefully planned the exact length of time it would take me to get to an appointment; and as a perfectionist and one who had been thoroughly programmed to believe in the absolute necessity of being places on time, I prided myself on nearly always making it, in spite of all obstacles. What I did not realize was that I was thereby setting myself up for frequent doses of heavy additional stress, frustration, and inefficiency.

With no margin for error for unforeseen delays, every trip to an important appointment was a tense affair. Even when nothing happened, I was constantly wondering and worrying whether or not I had figured the time right and looking out for any possible delay coming at me from all directions. As insurance I naturally drove faster than I would have otherwise. Fast driving creates stress, since it requires total concentration and a high level of readiness to take instant action in the event of any emergency, and the faster you drive, the more frequently emergencies occur. That was when there were no delays.

The reader may recall my earlier general reference to the following situation. One day I went out to the car to go to a vital speaking engagement eighty miles away, found a flat tire, and then ran into a traffic jam, with several hundred people expecting me at the other end. I did the last sixty miles between 90 and 110 in the best Grand Prix style and sprinted the final hundred yards in what I'm sure was very respectable time. I arrived on the podium as I was being introduced and made my speech reasonably well, in spite of being a nervous wreck and so badly out of breath from my sprint that I had to make a joke of it.

Like most addictive drinkers, I pulled it off. Contrary to common belief, we can be superb under pressure and the most difficult of circumstances, by applying fantastic willpower and calling up reserves of strength most people would not believe possible. But the point is that the whole thing is dumb, destructive of ourselves, and inefficient, not to say extremely dangerous. My Sterling Moss driving that day could easily have killed me and others.

Reality is loaded with unexpected delaying factors. It is stupid to drive between 90 and 110 at any time, and one cannot come close to his best performance in speechmaking or any other activity involving complex thinking when he is in a state of emotional and physical exhaustion. I think of myself as being reasonably intelligent, and I wonder today how I could have been so stupid so often. Yet I was, and most stress drinkers are in the same boat. I have concluded that we are not, in fact, stupid people. It must be that we are so focused on and intense about achieving our goals that we don't even think about such details, as I have described; we are too ready to pay any price in terms of expending ourselves to achieve the goal.

Today I always allow a healthy margin for error or delay in my timing for *anything*. That is my stress-anger-efficiency insurance policy. Now I can drive normally and safely, enjoy the scenery or my companions on the trip, and arrive in good time, taking a book with me to read if I arrive too early. Just knowing that, since I am calm and relaxed, I am ready and able to function at my best works wonders with my efficiency at the other end. Further, I am even more relaxed and pleased with myself because I know that I have planned this small segment of my life well. I know how to cope and do it intelligently, when before I thought I was coping and was a fool. You can see, I am sure, how each stress-creating element in the original situation has been reversed and turned into a positive antistress factor.

If I forget the book, or some unexpected delay suddenly hands me waiting time along the route, I have also learned to look around for something interesting to do or see or think about to fill the time positively. Sitting around fuming and getting angry at something you can't do a damned thing to change is stupid and makes you uncomfortable. We don't need unnecessary discomfort, and we don't like to feel stupid.

In A.A. they strongly recommend the Serenity Prayer, often closing meetings with it. It goes like this:

God grant me the serenity
To accept the things I cannot change,
Courage to change the things I can,
And wisdom to know the difference.

It is an excellent reminder (reprogramming device), and a stress drinker should use it frequently. If the word "God" bothers you, just change it to read, "Let me find the serenity," etc. The key, of course, is in the last line. A major purpose of this book is to make the point that a person can change a great many more things than he thinks he can, especially himself. The courage part comes with the personal growth we are talking so much about. When you find yourself functioning better and better in all departments of life, and feeling better and better about yourself as an effective, good person, you gain the confidence to dare, which is what courage and heroism are all about, I think.

Dealing with frustration requires a lot of conscious reprogramming of yourself, "acting as if," and selling yourself the bill of goods you want to buy, until the antifrustration attitudes become automatic. As usual, you start by preparing to deal with it before it occurs. You talk it all over with yourself, to let your automatic computer get the idea as to what readout you expect it to come up with when someone or something pushes your frustration button. Something like this: "Frustration. I don't want it, don't need it, and can't afford it. To let myself become frustrated and angry is stupid, dangerous, and inefficient. Frustrating people and events are an unavoidable part of reality. Therefore, I can face it, like any other problem in life, whenever it occurs, and deal with it as intelligently and effectively as possible, or I can be stupid and let it control and damage me. The choice is mine. I will allow myself extra time for unexpected, frustrating delays; if it is not enough, I can always phone ahead or explain. If I have allowed extra time, phoned if possible, and explained when necessary, I have done all that any reasonable person could be expected to do, and I will accept no further responsibility for the result. Other people know about unexpected delays and the frustrating roadblocks that occur in life. If I have taken all reasonable precautions, and still things didn't go right, they should understand. If they don't, 'it's their red wagon,' not mine, and I don't have to feel guilty about it." (You can word it any way you choose. The important thing is to plug the principles into your computer repeatedly.)

When events start to frustrate me, my first reaction is to say to myself if necessary, but out loud if possible, and with considerable vehemence, "Quote, shit, unquote!" It's dumb, but it expresses my instant emotional response with great precision and releases the instant emotional pressure that the event triggered. My second response is, "Oh, well, whatever," which is my shortened version of the Serenity Prayer. Another shortened version, used by a friend of mine, is, "Oh, what the hell!" Use whatever works for you. We're really quite simple animals at heart, especially when we're emotionally upset, and we may as well face that, too.

After my childish, but helpful, verbal exercise, I then analyze the best course to go around, under, or through the obstacle, and then get on with whatever action seems indicated. Again, the conscious knowledge that I am dealing with the problem as intelligently as possible under the circumstances helps me to keep cool and use my energy for the solution, rather than wasting it by letting myself become angry, frustrated, and uncomfortable, which only compounds the problem.

When a person becomes a roadblock, I take the same basic approach, sometimes including my "shit" release mechanism, but not out loud. Then I usually use my biggest gun, throwing myself helplessly on his mercy and subtly challenging him to find a way to help me. Instead of getting mad and telling him what a dumb bastard he is, especially when he *is* being a dumb bastard, I say, "This is terribly important to me, and I know you'd help if you could. Isn't there some way you can help me get around this [problem]?" When you get mad and say or clearly imply by your emotional reaction that you think the person is a dumb bastard, you attack him and his pride. His natural reaction is to be hurt, to go on the defensive, and to put up a steel wall of self-justification and refusal to budge, in order to thwart your desire and get even. The key in all this is that you are the one who wants something, and he is blocking you. It's stupid to make him your enemy as well. That only defeats your purpose further. Remember the old saw "You get more flies with honey than vinegar." Finally, if the problem turns out to be one of the "things I cannot change," the only thing to do is to stop wasting time and energy fuming about it, accept it, and get on with your life.

And then there's another way to look at it. The things we are trying to accomplish often become too important in our own minds, and we always want them achieved instantly (or sooner, if we can make it sooner), regardless of consequences. Yet when you stop to think about it, how really important is anything you may want or achieve? I'm not saying these things are unimportant, only that it is very important to keep things in reasonable perspective. It helped me to realize, finally, that if I were to achieve all of my wildest dreams for making the world a better place, that is, more the way *I* think it should be, it really wouldn't make very much difference in the history of the world; whatever I did could be wiped out at any time by what others chose to do. Then I realized that what I tried so hard to do for mankind I was really only doing to please myself. Therefore, it was not very clever of me to make myself miserable while trying to make myself happy. Wouldn't it be more sensible to go a little slower, enjoying life along the way, and not be driving, driving, driving anymore?

The housewife suffers a very special and refined kind of frustration, expressed partially in the saying "Man may work from sun to sun, but woman's work is never done." In addition, housework is mostly the job of redoing thousands of times the same dull, menial jobs (ones from which there is nothing more to learn). If I had been a housewife, I know I would have joined the growing ranks of housewife addictive drinkers. When you've been doing nonchallenging, repetitive jobs all day, with no adult company to lessen the boredom, and you have to keep on with cooking supper, washing dishes, and finishing up whatever else needs doing until bedtime, while the rest of the family lounges around, relaxing, it is only reasonable to feel deeply wronged, thoroughly frustrated, and very much "poor me." If that's your problem, correct it. Call a family conference; tell them that you are being exploited, that you resent it, and that you need some help. Be gentle but firm. If they don't respond, strike. Quit at 5:00 p.m., when they do, and relax. They'll soon get the message and realize how important your contributions are. You don't have to complain or cry "poor me" or get angry. Lay out the problem, ask for help, and if you don't get it, strike with a smile. Your children may even come to appreciate you more and pick up some valuable experience when they have to learn to do the laundry and wash their filthy football jerseys by hand (so they won't shrink). But beware. The standard male response is to do a lousy job, with the justification that they don't know how to do it right. This is really to take advantage of your perfectionist leanings, so that you will conclude that it is better to do it yourself. Don't be a sucker.

Be imaginative. Take turns with your spouse, one reading aloud while the other cooks and/or cleans up after supper. Or get the family together—doing dishes, folding laundry, preparing school lunches, sorting out a kitchen drawer—every family member to a task, while one member reads from a famous biography or historical saga. If that won't do, try a book of comic strips, such as *Peanuts,* the reader giving a voice to each character. Spend one hour as a family each night, getting supper together and/or clearing away, making chores into a fun time. Play Twenty Questions, whatever—while small children shine shoes in the corner . . .

As someone pointed out to me, there is only one acceptable way to get money, and that is to get someone to give it to you. If you don't want money and refuse it when offered, you won't get any. The same is true of anger and frustration. People and situations may offer them to you frequently in large doses, but you don't have to accept those feelings. You can simply *choose* not to. Try it. It's downright amazing.

Finally, it is useful to remember, from time to time, that there is more than one way to skin a cat. If you are allowing yourself to feel frustrated because people refused to do something "your way," it is sometimes very useful to take a close look at the way *they* want to do it. Could it be done effectively that way? Could it even be done more efficiently that way? Is it better for you to give in and do it their way, if only to get it done at all? Even the "best" way isn't much good if the thing never gets done because the other people wouldn't accept the "best" way. It's far less stressful that way, and we do whatever is necessary to stay sober. That's why I say "whatever," after I say "shit."

I would feel silly making such a point of all of the above if I did not see people in counseling being just as stupid as I was about frustrating things, which are as much a part of the reality of living as anything else. But as I said, it's not because we are stupid. It's because we tend to focus all our attention on reaching the brass ring, not noticing that how to sit the carousel horse and hold on with the other hand has a lot to do with reaching the brass ring. It doesn't help to fall off the horse in the process of trying. Frustration is a bummer, but it's a part of reality, and learning to cope with reality is the name of the game we're playing.

THOSE GUILT FEELINGS

Guilt feelings are about as useful to a person as thirteen teats on a boar hog, as the country expression goes. If there is one gift to us from our Judeo-Christian tradition that we don't need any more of, it is the concept of guilt (sin). I suspect that guilt is and always has been a tool used by people to control other people, and it often works like stink. The question is, "Do you need it?" Is it useful to you—*you*, not the person or group who is trying to control you. Your employer? Your mate? Society?

Whether it is a thing or an idea, there is only one final test of the value of anything. Can you use it to make your life better? If not, it makes sense to get rid of it. We usually do that with other things, but not with guilt feelings. I suppose that we do not because we have been programmed to believe that there is something good about guilt feelings, that they do help to make us better people; that's why we hang on to them. I don't believe it. When I drank too much, which was most of the time, I felt guilty as hell, but it didn't stop me from drinking too much the next time. When I did things I knew I shouldn't do, I always felt guilty, even long before I started drinking, but feeling guilty didn't stop me. If it had, I wouldn't have felt guilty. So guilt feelings don't seem to have been very useful to me. On the other hand, they made me feel terrible about myself over and over; and as we have seen, that's the best way in the world to program yourself into a negative self-image.

It's improper behavior, improper in your own mind, that makes you feel guilty. So it follows that if you change your behavior to make it coincide with what you think of as proper behavior, you will stop feeling guilty. If it is also true that developing a good self-image, pride in yourself, is vital to changing your own behavior—and guilt feelings tend to prevent that—then you have got to get rid of guilt feelings. Let's see how you might go about that.

One of the things you have been feeling most guilty about is, of course, your drinking and the things you did when drinking. As you have probably discovered, there isn't very much you can do about the past, aside from a few efforts to make amends. The past is past. However, "today is the first day of the rest of your life." Today you can start to stop drinking and doing the things you used to do. How better to make amends for the mistakes of the past than by living a decent life from now on? Will guilt feelings help you to do that? No way! They will make you feel that you're too worthless to do it in the first place. They'll sap what little confidence you've got and make you feel terrible about yourself, just the reverse of what you need to get well.

Once you realize that you were not responsible for the things you did (or didn't do) while drinking and start feeling grateful for the fact that you're not doing insane things anymore and are getting well again, you can stop feeling guilty and start looking forward to better things. Yes, I said "insane things." Every addictive drinker has done a lot of insane, stupid things that he would never have done had he not become ill. It is only our absurd false pride that makes us pretend to ourselves that we did not do insane things and were not, at least at times, temporarily insane. Think about it. Is it better to be prideful and pretend that you were sane when you did those things (which is slightly insane itself) or to realize that you had an illness (that is now over) that made you temporarily insane? Guilt creates heavy stress and has to be eliminated before you can recover. You were either insane or stupid. Take your choice. *If you can accept the idea of temporary insanity, you are home free as far as guilt is concerned.*

It's very interesting. I find that recovered addictive drinkers don't have guilt feelings. Sure, they're sorry about the things they did while drinking, but they don't brood about it. It does no good. They spend their time working on good things, happy, positive things that they can be proud of and take real pleasure in. They're just damned thankful they never did some of the horrible things they hear at A.A. meetings and elsewhere that others did. They realize that if they had lived the lives of the other people, just the way they did, they'd probably have done the same horrible things, not because they were evil people, but because they were scared, confused people who didn't know what else to do under the circumstances. Consequently, they have become far less judgmental of themselves and others than they used to be, and so will you.

Ask yourself this question, "If I had been sober, would I have done the things I am so ashamed of having done drunk?" I'm sure the answer is no. It was for me. I was frightened inside, terribly frustrated, and furious at people and a world that had treated me badly, and it all came out when I drank. The crazy thing was that I knew perfectly well that I was a good person inside. I never wanted to hurt or cheat other people. Quite the reverse. All I wanted was a chance to be nice to people and to help them as a teacher, that and to be left alone to live my life with my family. In fact, it was knowing this about myself that made me doubly furious when everyone seemed to be trying his best to block, frustrate, and hurt me. It was naked fear, total frustration, and what I thought of as perfectly justified fury that made me do crazy things, not any sort of basic evil nature. I have known people worse off—murderers, vicious fighters, wife beaters, child abusers—who are today the kindest, most gentle, caring people anyone would ever hope to know, simply because in learning how to get sober, they learned how to get rid of their fears, which made them do those insane things, especially when under the inhibition-release and blackout of alcohol.

When you stop drinking and start learning to reduce stress in your life (your fears), you automatically stop doing those crazy things and start being the decent, caring, good person everyone wants to be—and guilt feelings have nothing to do with it, unless you let them prevent you from getting well. Talk to yourself every day to reprogram your computer to feel guilty no longer and to accept no more guilt in the future. Guilt feelings make you miserable, block your effort to recover, and furnish some of the finest reasons to drink again that man has ever devised. If you insist on hanging on to them, then you don't really want to quit drinking and you enjoy feeling miserable. If that's the case, stop playing games with yourself and get drunk, because you're certainly not ready to get sober.

SHYNESS

In a sense I believe that everyone alive feels shy; that is, insecure, lacking confidence in certain social situations. However, the shyness I am discussing here, the shyness that almost every addictive drinker will admit to in confidence, is much more than the normal shyness felt by "everybody." It is a much bigger thing than that, a shyness that is at least exaggerated, certainly abnormally intense, and often of a degree of seriousness that can only be described as pathologic.

Many addictive drinkers who suffer from this kind of painful shyness would never be described by any of their friends as shy, because they have concentrated so hard on hiding this feeling that they have become apparent extroverts, exuding social confidence and a sense of complete ease at all times—on the surface. Often these people have become so good at this game and gradually so out of touch with themselves that they succeed in fooling even themselves, believing with everyone else that they are not shy at all.

Be completely honest with yourself for a few minutes. Remember what you felt growing up and how you have felt since and feel now. Maybe you know you can do a lot of social things well and put on a great show, but underneath it all, are you still really very shy, wondering what people are thinking of you—and worrying about it?

In hundreds of A.A. meetings, I have heard people say over and over that they were doormats for other people to step on for years. I have heard this so often, always with a sense of unanimous agreement from the others hearing it, that the feeling has to be a common denominator of addictive drinkers, and I am certain that it is a direct reflection of the basic insecurity and lack of social self-confidence referred to above. We want so badly to be accepted, liked, respected by others that we will pay any price, do anything to achieve it, and we often go to such absurd lengths in the desperate search for social acceptance and confidence that we become "people pleasers."

When I had gained some self-confidence and became convinced that it was vital for me to start being my own man, I decided not to be a "people pleaser" any longer. If I disagreed, or didn't want to do it, I said so. If I was uncomfortable in a social situation, I made a polite excuse and left, instead of suffering through, as I used to do. And an amazing thing happened: I found that people liked me better and respected me more.

I went to a Christmas Eve party at this time at the home of a friend. There were about ten people there, and somehow the evening became an endless exchange of dirty jokes, fed especially by two of the people present. Having lost my family only months before and loving Christmas as I always have, I had looked forward to carol singing around a piano and a general Christmas-spirit sort of feeling among friends. Dirty jokes were all wrong for me that evening, and I found myself getting angry and uncomfortable. As soon as I realized this, I made some remark about getting some Christmas spirit going with a carol or two—but no soap. The jokes continued. I then told my date how I felt and suggested leaving. She agreed, and we stood up to go with some excuse. Since it was still very early, someone didn't buy our excuse and asked for the real reason we were leaving. At that point my new-won confidence and decision to be myself came to the fore, and I told them that we had come expecting a more traditional sort of Christmas Eve. That, as a result, we were not enjoying the jokes and were planning to spend the evening doing what we wanted to do. Then we left. Over the next week two of the people who had been there told me, in one way or another, that they had felt as I did, had hated it, but had felt they just had to put up with it. And both expressed respect for my *courage* in doing and saying what I had. Note that these people were not addictive drinkers. Lots of other people are shy, too—to their own cost.

If exaggerated shyness is a part of your problem, if you are a "people pleaser," a doormat, this is proof positive that your self-image (self-esteem) needs work. To change oneself, to improve one's self-image, one's self-esteem, takes considerable courage. One must decide on new ways of behaving and find the courage to start behaving that way when he is still shy and insecure. Only by daring to change can he hope to do so. There is no magic involved. You do it yourself, or you don't. Neither God nor A.A. will or can do it for you. As Dostoevsky said, "Taking a new step, uttering a new word, is what people fear most." And according to Thomas

Carlyle, "The courage we desire and prize [*esteem*] is not the courage to die decently, but to live manfully." And Helen Keller: "Security is mostly a superstition. It does not exist in nature, nor do the children of man as a whole experience it. Avoiding danger is no safer in the long run than outright exposure. Life is either a daring adventure, or nothing." Boris Pasternak: "Man is born to live and not to prepare to live." Emerson: "The virtue most in request is conformity. Self-reliance is its aversion."

So here we have the fundamental paradox: Everyone around us says, "Conform, please me, and I will like and respect you." But if you are to get well, be really liked and respected, be happy, then the person whose liking and respect is most important of all is you. The absurdity of it is that when you find the courage to be yourself, to be self-reliant, to dare in the face of all evidence to the contrary, you gain it all. If you don't want to be shy, a "people pleaser," a doormat any longer, if you want people to like and respect you, if you want to like and respect yourself—dare to be yourself. It's scary, but it's living, not a "reasonable facsimile" of it, and it's great!

To get you started, here are some action steps you may wish to take:

*A Bill of Assertive Rights**

I: You have the right to judge your own behavior, thoughts, and emotions, and to take the responsibility for their initiation and consequences upon yourself.

II: You have the right to offer no reasons or excuses for justifying your behavior.

III: You have the right to judge if you are responsible for finding solutions to other people's problems.

*From *When I Say No, I Feel Guilty* by Manuel J. Smith, Ph.D.

IV: You have the right to change your mind.
V: You have the right to make mistakes—and be responsible for them.
VI: You have the right to say, "I don't know."
VII: You have the right to be independent of the goodwill of others before coping with them.
VIII: You have the right to be illogical in making decisions.
IX: You have the right to say, "I don't understand."
X: You have the right to say, "I don't care."

YOU HAVE THE RIGHT TO SAY NO, WITHOUT FEELING GUILTY.

DO YOU NEED GROUP HELP FOR SPECIFIC PROBLEMS?

I mentioned earlier that it is vital, when a person stops drinking, to fill up the time previously spent drinking with constructive, interesting, *fun* activities. In the section "Alcoholics Anonymous" (page 80), I mentioned that the more you do to overcome your problem, the more comfortable you will feel and the more confident of success. Getting into a growth group, whatever kind appeals to you, is a perfect solution to using this time effectively, and the groups are both interesting and fun. These groups are applicable as soon as you have developed enough self-awareness to be able to pick out some of your specific needs, things which you want to change in yourself.

Women will find Women for Sobriety groups excellent as an alternative or in addition to A.A. These are small conversations-in-the-round with a quite different but highly successful program, at no charge, the emphasis being on consciousness-raising and concerns particular to women (WFS, P.O. Box 618, Quakertown, PA 18951).

There are many kinds of groups, some specifically for addictive drinkers and many more for people with other kinds of problems. For example, if you are shy in social situations, if you feel henpecked or like a doormat, if you can't speak up for yourself in public or in situations where someone is making fun of you or putting you down in other ways, you can find groups to help you become more assertive. It's really no different from learning to handle a canoe paddle or to do algebra. Some groups are dedicated to developing more self-awareness, but almost *any* kind of self-improvement group will help you gain awareness and improve your self-image as well. A transactional-analysis group, especially one for addictive drinkers, will do the job nicely, and at the same time will help you to understand a great deal more about how people communicate (or fail to) with one another. To find out which groups are available in your area, contact the nearest office of the National Council on Alcoholism or your county or city mental health department. The latter often has special facilities and groups for addictive drinkers that are free or on an ability-to-pay basis. Many colleges and universities have such free or inexpensive groups, and they are usually quite good, since the leaders are in training and motivated to do a good job, as well as being under the close supervision of instructors.

It is a basic idea behind every group that what is said during the sessions is never carried outside the meeting. Normally, all members get to know one another quickly because of the nature of the discussions. As trust develops, you have a grandstand seat to observe and learn from other people about their personal problems and to see how the group leader and group suggestions help them to find solutions. It's almost like a soap opera sometimes, as a person decides to change his behavior in a specific way to solve a problem and then reports back next session as to what happened. Nor is it all deadly serious, since some of the situations people talk about are quite incredible and sometimes very funny, especially after the problem has been solved. Once you get into it and see yourself actually becoming the kind of person you want to be, it's one of the most exciting experiences you can have. That's why they become fun. Don't knock the groups, not if you want to make love instead of just fooling around with sobriety. They work.

A.A. will do most of the things I have mentioned here, if you give it a real chance over a period of years. But if you can find a group which specializes in your particular weakness or problem, you'll get from here to there an awful lot faster by joining that group—in addition to A.A.

DO YOU NEED SELF-HELP BOOKS?

Lots of people pooh-pooh self-help books, believing that they are all empty promises or psychological bullshit. Some of them are, but most are not. The good ones were written by knowledgeable people, many of whom found the basic truths about which they write through their own suffering or through professional observation of the deep suffering of others. Whether any seriously written book will be useful to the reader depends upon his attitude and his ability to discriminate. The main thing is: does it make sense to *you*? Can it do something for you, such as helping you to obtain enough self-awareness to decide what kind of group therapy you need?

Some of these books can give you completely new insights and specific techniques (game plans) that can change your whole life in days or weeks, if you really listen and take the trouble to try the techniques. A prime example of one such all-powerful reading for me was *How to Get Angry without Feeling Guilty* by Adelaide Bry. I developed my ideas for overcoming anger from this book.

Reading these books is also an excellent way to go about reprogramming your computer from negative attitudes to positive ones. Each author says many things that others say, but in different words, so you are hearing over and over in different ways many of the basic truths about how to live more successfully and happily. They are often saying the same things, because the fundamental truths about living are universal and have been discovered time and again throughout the ages. "A day at a time" is the A.A. wording, but the Bible says, "Sufficient unto the day is the evil thereof." Modern writers keep saying that you must find the courage to make your own decisions about how you will live and stop being a "people pleaser." Yet someone a very, very long time ago said, "To thine own self be true."

In general these books express the authors' conviction that it is possible to change one's whole life and outlook in positive, exciting ways. Hope is the first prescription for recovery, and positive attitudes are the basic building blocks. Such reading even has a high-falutin' name. It's called "bibliotherapy," and high-falutin' term or not, it is sound therapy that can make your spare hours far more interesting and valuable than TV—or a B&B.

WHAT AM I AFRAID OF?

We have talked about anger, frustration, guilt feelings, shyness, and some of the advantages of getting into growth groups and using self-help books in order to find help in overcoming specific problems. However, there is a common principle behind all these things. It is *the* fundamental principle that can be used to identify and reduce or remove *every* kind of emotional stress—great or small. And like most fundamental principles, it is simple to understand, but often not so easy to carry out.

All you have to do is ask yourself two questions whenever you are worried, upset, uneasy, unhappy, angry, frustrated, feeling guilty, or unsure of yourself (shy). The first question is: "What am I afraid of?" As soon as you answer that question, you will have identified the problem specifically. The feeling of discomfort is still there, but it is no longer a shapeless, fearsome something. It is fear of losing your job, fear of making that speech on Saturday, fear that that lump in your breast is cancer, fear that someone doesn't like you (or won't like you), fear that the evening coming up will be a crashing bore, etc. Specific fears can be dealt with; generalized fear cannot.

The second question is the zinger: "What action *must* I take to reduce or remove that fear?" Throughout this book I have been stressing the need for action as the key to recovery, action based on intelligent choice, after careful consideration of the options available. If the answer to the first question is an honest "My God, I'm afraid I'll drink at any moment, I'm afraid my wife will divorce me, I'm afraid my kids won't listen to me, I'm afraid my job is hanging by a thread, I'm afraid I can't pay the bills—"don't panic. Panic is fear magnified into emotional terror. It makes any form of sensible, intelligent choice about what to do impossible and pushes your stress level through the roof. If your whole life is a mess right now, and it was at some point in recovery for most of us, this principle still applies.

START IN A CORNER

So what do you do? You simply use the garage-cleaning approach. Just start in one corner, it doesn't make much difference which one, and work out from there. When the garage is so full of accumulated junk that you can't even move around, cleaning it out and organizing all that stuff looks impossible, but it isn't. It's exactly the same in the garage of your life. If it's an impossible mess, pick a corner, any corner, and start working. You will feel better almost at once. Then, once you've cleared a space, move to another corner and do the same. You'll find yourself feeling better and better all the time.

And if you've racked your brains and can't figure out what

to do in any area, for God's sake, ask for advice, don't just hang there spinning in the wind.

There is no problem that thousands haven't had before you, and there are solutions to all of them. If you can't pay your bills, an officer in any reputable financial institution or a lawyer can tell you how to proceed. You may not like the answers, but the result will be far less painful and expensive than doing nothing, worrying yourself to death, and drinking. To get your life on an even keel again, to find more peace and fulfillment, you're going to have to pay a price, maybe a high one, maybe an unfair one, but that's reality. Reality is a demanding and unforgiving mistress. She will not and cannot be disregarded.

Intelligent action applied to any corner will lessen your stress, reduce the problem, and make you feel better, even a little heroic. Inaction, when action is so clearly required, makes you feel worse and worse and worse.

Identify the fears and do something, anything sensible, to reduce them. That is the real principle behind recovery. It works across the board.

FROM THE ROAD BACK TO THE HIGH ROAD

In the first part of this book we saw the steps down, the "slippery slide," which shows the progressive nature of addictive drinking—if one keeps on drinking. In this section are listed the steps up, "the road back," to show the progressive nature of recovery—if one follows the principles discussed in this book. The recovery steps listed here should be helpful to your assessment of how you are coming along. Also described in this section is "the high road," what lies beyond recovery if you choose to shoot for the ultimate goal, "self-actualized, almost totally independent living."

The Road Back

STAGE ONE

—Denial system finally breaks down; sees self as completely helpless, beaten, and desperate
—Has an honest desire for help and is willing to ask for it
—Learns addictive drinking is an illness, not a character weakness or sign of insanity
—Learns that illness can be arrested
—Meets former addictive drinkers who are obviously both sober and happy
—Finds acceptance and understanding in therapy group; begins to lose old feelings of rejection and difference from other people
—Identifies with recovering addictive drinkers; believes they can help and begins to hope
—Stops drinking and gets back to regular meals and enough regular rest
—Accepts group and/or professional therapy and counseling
—Begins to learn about addictive drinking and practical ways people are going about getting well
—Develops interest in personal cleanliness and appearance
—Makes friends among stable recovering addictive drinkers
—Begins to learn how to reduce stress in many ways
—Gets complete physical checkup and follows doctor's recommendations for improved physical health
—Begins to feel markedly better physically and mentally

STAGE TWO

—Gains first real confidence in recovery
—Self-esteem increases and learns actions to take to increase it further
—Learns difference between real and false pride

—Begins to have more concern for others while becoming less self-centered
—Develops old and/or new interests to enjoy when sober
—Begins to solve problems that previously appeared insoluble
—Family and friends show appreciation of efforts, and all personal relationships improve
—Compulsion to drink lessens appreciably
—Begins to accept or take back some responsibility
—Does complete personal inventory and begins practical, realistic life planning

STAGE THREE

—Finds indefinable fears disappearing and real pride, self-esteem, and confidence increasing
—Achieves increasing objectivity and honesty in self-evaluation
—Begins to rid self of guilt feelings about past and fears of future
—Compulsion to drink becomes rare
—Begins to accept more and more responsibility in all areas of life
—Faces fact that recovery is slow, but has made enough progress to move ahead with confidence
—Begins to face world as it is and find happiness
—Refines personal inventory and life planning
—Develops a new, more realistic and fulfilling value system; rebirth of ideals
—Economic situation improves markedly; regains confidence of employer and fellow workers
—Economic control steadily increases as result of development of increasingly positive, realistic attitudes toward life
—Begins to relax much more and to truly enjoy sobriety
—Achieves reasonably stable, relatively happy and productive life-style

ULTIMATE GOAL

—SELF-ACTUALIZED, ALMOST TOTALLY INDEPENDENT LIVING

The addictive drinker can get off the slippery slide at any stage and start up the recovery ladder, so if he gets off the slide early he won't have to pass through the lower stages of recovery. The situation of each individual is different, so that the recovery steps will be taken by each person in a somewhat different order than listed here. Looking at a cluster of steps, though, should let you know where you are.

Many of these steps are not reached by intellectual understanding alone. They are specific signposts of personal growth, achieved by changes of attitude and feeling, that operate automatically *once they have been achieved.* You can look backward to the way you used to be and note the changes, in order to tick off some of these steps as achieved. Only concentrated thought and effort toward these goals, using some of the methods described in the book and the help of your support group or groups, will get you there.

There is a Personal Inventory form at the end of this part of the book to help you formulate action steps as regards your game plans for resolving anger, guilt feelings, etc. That is the intellectual part. At some time after practicing these game plans, you will begin to function automatically in more and more of the steps listed, each time at a higher, more satisfactory level—and it feels great, because each time it happens you know you're getting there—one step more attained. When you have achieved "a reasonably stable, relatively happy and productive life-style" entirely free from booze—the final step in recovery—I suggest that you are "recovered."

Recovering vs. Recovered

A large proportion of people in A.A. will be upset by my use of the term "recovered." They feel that the only appropriate word is "recovering," since it is possible only to arrest the illness, not to cure it. In their minds, "once an alcoholic, always an alcoholic." That is, the individual can never drink socially again, without returning to addictive drinking—if not with the first drink, then soon thereafter. This being so, they feel that such a person can only be thought of as recover-*ing* for the rest of his life.

Certainly, once addicted, a person would be a fool to try to return to social drinking, especially when there is no point in being a social drinker if one now finds social situations much more fun and interesting without booze—that is, if he has really gotten well. To say that one has "recovered" is not to say that he will never drink again. Maybe he will play the fool. Maybe he is not completely well and doesn't know it. As they say in A.A., "Some people are sicker than others!"

Perhaps it is only a question of semantics, but I don't think so. The word "recovered" in this context means to me that a person, having reached a certain level of personal growth and effectiveness, lost ground in both respects for a period of time as a result of his addictive drinking, and then, by dint of considerable effort, stopped the drinking and climbed the road back to his original level of grace or development. That's recovery. If he then proceeds *beyond* that point in personal growth and effectiveness, he is, it seems to me, no longer "recovering." Thus, a "recovered" addictive drinker is different from a "recovering" one in that he has moved beyond his original high point.

Why bother with this discussion at all? This difference is very significant to me, as a counselor in the field of alcohol addiction, because the matter of the individual's self-image is a most important factor in getting well, *completely* well. To think of oneself as only recovering forever—always still sick, so to speak—is neither realistic nor rewarding. Since I want to feel as good about myself as I possibly can, while still being completely realistic and honest with myself, I think it's better for me to think of myself as "recovered" and somewhere beyond that into levels of maturity I've never known before. That's my choice.

The High Road

The concept of continuing the growth process beyond recovery toward "self-actualized, almost totally independent living" was never in the earlier Jellinek and Glatt lists (see footnote, page 8) and has never been considered in A.A., apparently because of the belief that the only goal is to stop drinking and to grow enough to find some peace and happiness in life. I want much more than that, and I believe that planned growth toward self-actualization is the answer.

To me, this is the area of personal growth that puts the capstone on the whole process. You begin by shifting your dependency from alcohol to people, your therapy group (including A.A.) or your alcohol addiction counselor. Then you are ready to move on from there. A small percentage of people, through remarkable insight and certainly much good fortune, has always been able to achieve virtually total freedom from dependence on a person or support group of any kind, but the vast majority has not. This is why most members of A.A. expect to continue regular frequent attendance at meetings for the rest of their lives, believing that this is their only protection against a return to drinking. They say they believe this after ten, fifteen, and twenty years off the sauce. And they are right, because the A.A. growth program stops at a certain point. There are no advanced levels beyond a basic recovery level, which still requires the A.A. group for constant support. After ten or twenty years in the program, the individual is still talking about "a day at a time," "keep it simple," "anger," "gratitude," etc., still having step meetings at an elementary level, and always in company with new people who need just that. In other words, having completed grammar school, he continues to attend, perhaps more in the role of teacher, but finding nothing in the program in the way of new growth and challenge for him. That's all there is, and it's a lot, but to me it is only the necessary groundwork that prepares one to grow toward almost total freedom from all dependency.

As one psychiatrist put it, "True maturity is a fine goal for any man, but for an alcoholic it is absolutely essential." He was not talking about maturity in the usual sense of that word; that is, an adult who manages to conduct his life in a reasonably responsible manner in spite of fairly frequent falls from grace in the form of emotional upsets, depressions, lost temper, and other childish responses, which are accepted in so-called mature adults as long as they are neither too frequent nor too serious. He meant, I believe, the kind of maturity that can best be described by the term "self-actualized." When a person has reached this stage of maturity, he is self-inspired, self-motivated, self-directed, and independent.

This stage frees you almost completely from dependence on any person or support group. (The fact that such a person may choose to share in an interdependence with a mate or his fellows is beside the point.) This is the stage in which a person—whether an ex-addictive drinker or not—has ceased to model his life, thought, and behavior on the standard norms of family, church, and society and has moved on to choose his own unique style of life, thought, and behavior—that combination which fulfills what is uniquely him and no one else. This is the state of maximum freedom from dependence of any kind, the ultimate freedom of the spirit.

As the addictive drinker was once motivated to learn self-awareness and the techniques for changing himself in the whole growth continuum which is "recovery," he is now superbly prepared to continue his own direction in personal growth by his own motivation. In the highest sense, he has reconstituted himself from his ashes, like the mythical phoenix, and is then ready to fly upward to the highest level of life experience and joy. Such a goal is worth getting sober for.

At this point he is ready to take over full management of all aspects of his life and all execution for his continuing growth toward becoming that which is uniquely him. All I can do is to offer a portrait of the self-actualized person as I see him—in a generalized way. Only you can flesh out such a portrait. All I can say is, don't stop now, when you've reached the launching pad. Self-actualization is only a fantasy for most people, because they don't know how to go about it and don't have the courage to become the heroes of their fantasies. You have both the knowledge and the courage if you've come this far in your recovery. Why not shoot for the whole ball of wax?

Portrait of the Self-Actualized Person

He (or she, as you read) may or may not look any different, but you sense very quickly that he is. In an uptight society he always seems relaxed and thoroughly enjoying whatever he may be doing, whether it's mowing the lawn, riding the subway, or going up in a balloon. He is interested in everything and everyone around him and is always asking questions, trying to learn more about you and anything you may have some special knowledge about. He is a wonderful listener, but he is so enthusiastic about living that, when he gets going on almost anything, his enthusiasm is apt to carry him away at times.

He is unlikely to have a television set or to watch television much, because he is a doer who has so many interests that there isn't enough time in the day for all of them, much less to watch others do while he sits. If he's sitting, he's much more likely to be thinking, reading, watching a sunset, or talking to a bum, a child, or a friend.

He will try just about anything, because he has no fear of failure. Failure means only one thing to him: a chance to learn so that he won't ever make that mistake again. Since he long ago realized that feeling down because you failed at something is a completely useless emotion, and since he knows that he and everyone else is at all times trying to do what is best for himself, if he fails at something, it's only because he didn't have enough information or enough experience, and he knows that we learn best from our own mistakes. He will simply regroup and try a new approach.

He does not worry about the future either, knowing that most of the things people worry about never happen and that circumstances change so rapidly that future planning can only be done in a very general way, so he plans his direction rather than specific results. Also, he knows that bad things do happen, whether he worries or not, but so do good things; by not getting uptight with needless worry, he will be in a better position to look objectively for solutions and to see and grasp opportunities when they appear.

A self-actualized person may seem something of an oddball, because he is so little concerned with many things that others think of the greatest importance. For example, he may seem indelicate at times. The reason why is that he hasn't time to play silly people games. If you ask him if he would like to go fishing or to a fashion show, he may just say no without explanation. That's the answer, isn't it? Perhaps he doesn't want to tell you why, because it would hurt you if he were completely honest and he doesn't believe in social lying. His dress and life-style may seem odd as well. This is because he dresses and lives to please himself and really doesn't care what others might think about it. He knows it suits him, and that is enough, because he likes *and* respects himself and does not need the acceptance and approbation of others. If he's not having a good time at a party, he will leave quietly to do something else. He will not stay on just to be polite.

He is likely to be involved in creative, challenging work of some kind, regardless of the pay, and he is especially likely to be in a line of work that involves people, because he likes them and finds them endlessly fascinating. Another reason is that he's good with people, because he always seems on top of the situation and in control of himself. No temper tantrums, grumpy days, and lengthy descriptions of his ills from him. He learned long ago to deal with his emotions, so that he could spend more time being happy, and his positive attitudes, optimistic outlook on life, and interest in the unexpected that every day brings make grumpiness highly unlikely. Illness and other unpleasant aspects of life are realities that must be accepted, insofar as they can't be avoided, but he learned long ago that moaning about them is not very interesting to others and makes things worse for the moaner by his dwelling on them. In sum, having learned that joy is in the process of doing, not in the final result, he never has to wait for happiness, since it is all around him most of the time.

Such a person, having learned to love and respect himself, is capable of really loving and giving to others—for the pleasure of it, without hope or expectation of return—but his close friends may be few, because he will find only a few who have the depth and variety of interests to justify the large expenditure of time that real friendship requires. On the other hand, he will have very few enemies, because he is not a taker, not a person who puts people down. He believes in the live-and-let-live principle, treads on few toes, and usually walks away from a fight or unfair treatment, rather than make an unpleasant issue of it. He knows that's not the way to be happy and enjoy life. Also, he laughs a lot, and his sense of humor and interest in other people make it hard for people to be his enemies.

He doesn't expect to change the world or to set it on fire, so he is never a zealot, although his ideas about government, big business, and the committee approach to doing things may be quite radical. Nor is he a joiner of groups of any kind. Rather, he tends to be an individualist who prefers to do things himself or with a few friends.

He knows who he is, and the general direction in which he is going, and has his own conception of his purpose on earth and what he believes in. It is unlikely to include any organized religion or organized anything.

He has learned long ago what the animals have always known—that our first purpose on earth is to enjoy life, so just about everything he does is dedicated to that end. He's really a very nice person. I'd like you to meet him. He can be the best friend you ever had—yourself.

When You Coast
You Have to Be Going Downhill

A warning here. As one works to grow toward self-actualized living, the conscious thought and effort toward that end take far less time and effort than you spent in the days of learning to grow for recovery. Now the major part of every day is spent in doing a great variety of things and enjoying the process of living. However, since becoming more and more self-actualized means not becoming less human but the reverse, it is easy to be so involved in enjoying the view from the high road in your new machine—fenders smooth and glistening with paint, upholstery all spruced up, the works—that you can forget about working at new growth altogether, even about maintaining the old growth. When that happens, just as when one becomes so involved in his day-to-day problems that he forgets to work at his marriage, things begin to fall apart. It is easy to let frustrations and unfairness start to bother you again, to fragment your energies and activities until your overall direction is lost, to let a goal become so large that you lose the balance you achieved in the important areas of your life.

Without ever taking that first drink, you can easily fall back into your old drinking days and crash, after learning to fly superbly. Don't rely only on your autopilot. Like any complex mechanism, your life-planning and personal-growth machinery needs regular maintenance and attention. Include a maintenance check at least once a month.

In addition, I suggest you go to A.A. once a month, just to remind yourself and to give something back, if for no other reason. Also, I suggest rereading this book from time to time. I was required to do it repeatedly in the editing process, and I found it helping me each time in different ways, because as with the repetition of discussions on the same old subjects in A.A. meetings, my head and my life were in a different place each time, and I got new thoughts and insights that I found valuable.

Whatever you do, don't coast too long. It's dangerous.

PERSONAL INVENTORY

SELF-ESTEEM

What specific things will I do to increase my self-esteem? (Join a growth group? Which kind? Do volunteer work? What kind? I'll stop being a doormat? I'll do something nice for my family every day? Etc.)

______________ ______________ ______________

______________ ______________ ______________

______________ ______________ ______________

NEGATIVE PROGRAMMING

I know that I have the following negative attitudes which I want to change to positive:

______________ ______________ ______________

______________ ______________ ______________

______________ ______________ ______________

I will work to reprogram myself in each case as follows:

______________ ______________ ______________

______________ ______________ ______________

______________ ______________ ______________

ANGER AND FRUSTRATION

I know that the following specific situations make me angry or frustrated:

______________ ______________ ______________

______________ ______________ ______________

______________ ______________ ______________

What game plan will I use to deal with each of these situations? (Write each game plan down for each situation, including words you will say, etc.)

______________ ______________ ______________

______________ ______________ ______________

______________ ______________ ______________

GUILT FEELINGS

What specific things will I do to get rid of my guilt feelings?

1. Make amends to the following people as best I can, at least verbally?

   a.   d.
   b.   e.
   c.   f.

2. Go to confession?
3. Do the following things that I have been feeling guilty about not doing:

   a.   d.
   b.   e.
   c.   f.

4. Work to program myself about guilt feelings in general?

   Every day? ____________ When? ____________

   (I recommend you talk to yourself about this for five minutes a day, every day, for two weeks. Then, later, include guilt feelings in your monthly maintenance and growth check.)

SHYNESS

Do I really have a problem with shyness? ____________

If so, I will do the following:

1. Join a group to become more assertive? ____________
2. Make a point of doing something I would normally be shy about doing at least once every day? ____________
3. Other? ____________________________________

SELF-HELP BOOKS

I will buy or order the following self-help books: (A recommended paperback reading list is included at the end of this book. You may know of others. Or look up your particular "weakness" in the library or bookstore.)

____________________   ____________________

____________________   ____________________

____________________   ____________________

Do I feel that I am communicating well with my family? ______ With others? ______ (If not, a Transactional Analysis group is strongly recommended, especially one for addictive drinkers, whether you are the drinker or the spouse.)

I want to change the behavior of the following people toward me:

a. c.
b. d.

To do that I will change my behavior toward them in the following ways:

______ ______
______ ______

SELF-AWARENESS

What will I do to gain greater self-awareness and the ability to be really honest with myself?

1. Join an awareness or consciousness-raising group? ______
2. Spend time thinking about, listing, and facing squarely in my mind all of my weaknesses and inappropriate behaviors, so that I can work to remove or reduce them? How will I go about this systematically? ______ ______ When? ______
3. Other? ______

PHYSICAL HEALTH

I will do the following to improve and maintain my physical health:

1. Get a medical checkup? (I strongly recommend an orthomolecular specialist here.) ______
2. Have a dental checkup? ______
3. Do the following as regular exercise: ______ ______
4. Change my diet as follows: (I strongly recommend no drastic diet change until well into recovery. It adds too much stress.)

______ ______
______ ______
______ ______

NOTE: In some of the above your decisions or plans may not work out for some reason, but don't feel you have failed; try another approach. Of course, if you are forced to admit that you really did fail, that the plan or decision was good, don't panic. We're all human. Get angry with yourself to motivate yourself to try harder, and try again to show yourself you can do it. Maybe you took on too much, so pigeonhole that plan until you are up to it. That's not failure. That's intelligent regrouping. No plan should ever be ironclad. It is useful only when it serves your purpose. It must be subject to change without notice when you honestly feel that the change will suit your purposes better. Use the finest scientific research method known to man—trial and error. It will work if you can be honest with yourself.

Part Five

To Those Who Love Them

The first question is usually "What can I do to get my drinker to recognize his problem and seek help?" As we have seen in this book, there should also be a parallel question, "What can I do to save my own sanity, to protect our children from being harmed, and to insure my own future if, in spite of everything, my drinker should be unable to bring himself to make the effort necessary to get well?" The latter is a distinct possibility that has to be taken into account, however unpleasant. Your own life, and probably the lives of others, are at stake here, too.

To answer these questions I recommend, first, two organizations as primary sources of help and information.

The nearest office of the National Council on Alcoholism can offer you pre-treatment counseling, as described on page 68 of this book, good information about all the services available in your community, and answers to most of the questions you may have.

ALANON

The second organization is Alanon, to which the pretreatment counselor (or A.A.) can refer you. Alanon is an independent worldwide organization, offering the same kind of help to you that A.A. offers the drinker, as described in Part Two of this book.*

We saw in the text that "bottom" occurs in different people at dramatically different stages of the illness, some being able to see the terrible handwriting on the wall so vividly that they are motivated to take the necessary action long before alcohol has caused any serious problems in their lives (high bottom); others seem to have to go all the way to skid row before they can see it (low bottom). People and circumstances certainly vary, but that is not the only reason to account for this radical difference. There are other factors that bear heavily on the final result and make all the difference between a "high bottom" and a "low bottom."

A large part of the problem is psychological denial, as we have seen, which prevents the individual from recognizing the reality of his situation. Another is the fact that many addictive drinkers honestly believe that there is no way for them to get well. This being the case, experience has shown over and over that the individual will continue drinking until circumstances make it impossible for him to deny the reality of his situation any longer, until the pain and suffering brought about by his drinking become so great that his denial system is temporarily destroyed and he can at last see the situation for what it is. It follows, then, that if the circumstances surrounding the drinker can be changed *by others* to cause him to reach his bottom sooner, at the same time letting him know that there is a way out, he can then be motivated—by desperation on the one hand and hope on the other—to seek help much sooner. This is the newest art

*Alateen offers the same kind of help for teenage members of a family, and there is a similar group for elementary-school children in the larger city and suburban areas.

in addiction counseling, and more and more counselors are specializing in it. That National Council on Alcoholism can tell you who and where they are. (See page 68.)

As someone who cares about the drinker, you may be shocked to hear that *you are almost certainly one of the major factors making it possible for your drinker to keep on drinking,* thereby preventing him from hitting bottom, but this is true in almost all cases, to such an extent that you have a title among professionals in the field. You are called the "enabler." Let's look closer at this apparent paradox. (This subject is handled well in Alanon, as it so badly needs to be.)

The typical spouse (parent, friend, etc.) of an addictive drinker usually does most of the following things, over and over again. In an effort to protect the drinker from himself, and you and your children from further drunken episodes, you hide the liquor or pour it down the sink. You do everything possible to make the drinker happy and relaxed, since you have observed that he is most likely to drink when unhappy and tense (under stress). You are more or less constantly at the drinker, cajoling, pleading, ordering, or threatening to get him to limit or stop the drinking. You argue about it and try to shame the drinker by reminding him of those embarrassing and dangerous things he did on a recent drinking occasion. You complain bitterly about the money spent on liquor or drunkenly wasted in other ways. When the drinker is too drunk or hungover to go to work or meet other social or work responsibilities, you cover up for him with an endless list of his nonexistent illnesses, medical or dental appointments, and other excuses. To ease the financial situation, you often go to work (or if employed already get a second, moonlighting job). And, of course, you take care of your drinker when he is drunk, sick, or hungover.

As time passes, you become more and more bitter and resentful, as we have seen in the text ("Your Marriage," page 183), and often end up being moralizing, patronizing, nagging, and nasty. The list goes on and on. These are all sincere efforts to get the drinker to control or to stop drinking and to try to keep the family intact. At the same time, you have taken over many of the drinker's normal responsibilities, as mentioned in the text.

How can these things make it more possible for the drinker to continue or, in fact, make the drinking much worse? Let's look at the picture from the drinker's point of view, remembering all the time that *every one of these actions was doomed to failure from the start,* because there is no way that this person can either control or stop drinking by himself.

If you had a violent headache, how would it make you feel to find that your spouse (parent, friend, etc.) had hidden your headache medicine or poured it down the sink? Would you not be furious, hurt, say nasty things, and go out to the store to get more? If you knew perfectly well what your drinking was doing to someone you cared for and felt terribly guilty about it, as drinkers do (in spite of what they say), how would you feel when that person continued to do everything possible to keep you happy and relaxed? Wouldn't that make you feel even more guilty? (The drinker would rather have you fight.) How would you respond to cajoling, pleading, ordering, and threats to get you to limit or stop doing something when there was no possible way you could comply, except for short periods using tremendous effort? How would you respond when you knew that that person was 100 percent right and there was not a damned thing you could do about it except lie and pretend that it wasn't true or that you just didn't give a damn? How would you feel if that person kept reminding you of all the embarrassing and dangerous things you do (did), to shame you, when you were already so ashamed, so frustrated, and so frightened that you were seriously wondering inside if perhaps you were not really insane? (Most addictive drinkers do wonder about this.)

How would you feel to have someone complaining bitterly all the time about the money you were spending and wasting, when there was no alternative from your point of view and you were already so worried about that that you had to keep on doing it in order to be able to forget it more and more often. What would it do to your pride to listen to someone covering for you all the time when you couldn't meet your responsibilities? How would you feel when your mate (whomever) had to take a job because of money you had lost or spent foolishly? Imagine being torn by guilt twenty times a day, and hearing beyond that guilt more comments, more nagging, to make you feel guiltier; is it not true that you would become furious with that person (persons) and blame him for causing you to drink—as the drinker usually does? What is the total effect of all these actions on the drinker? It is a degree of massive stress that would drive anyone to drink, and I do not speak facetiously. It does drive him to drink, while at the same time giving him a perfect excuse for doing it.

That you are doing your best and feel entirely justified in doing these things has nothing to do with it. The addictive drinker doesn't understand what is wrong, can't control his behavior, and believes that his problem is totally unique and incapable of solution. The drinker does not believe that his problem is more than superficially alcohol or addictive drinking. Therefore, going for help for "alcoholism" is no solution in the drinker's mind, either.

The drinker believes that he is the innocent victim of other people and a vicious, uncaring fate over which he has no control. That is reality for the drinker, and he drinks primarily to escape that reality, because it terrifies and frustrates him so. What the drinker doesn't know and needs desperately to learn is that he is *right* in believing that alcohol is not his primary problem, and that the treatment for addictive drinking is really a learning experience to help to so change attitudes, goals, and life-planning skills that he will be able to free himself from being the "innocent victim of other people and a vicious and uncaring fate," which was the problem the drinker knew he had in the first place.

This is why I said at the very beginning of the text that treatment has to be tailored to the needs of each individual. If you want to change the circumstances surrounding your addictive drinker so that he will seek help, I suggest that you begin by stopping all of the above-mentioned behaviors and starting a whole new program entirely geared to achieving that end. The only way that one person can truly change another person is by changing himself and his behavior, and by giving the other person needed information to help him change himself if he chooses to do so. Then the other person must adjust to the new circumstances. Alanon is dedicated to helping to bring these changes about.

Like A.A., Alanon is made up of autonomous groups of people whose common problem is that they have a special interest in an addictive drinker and want to learn about addiction—and how to help themselves to a better life. They have chosen Alanon, because, again like A.A., it is the single organization that has helped the largest number of such people to find *practical* solutions to their problems. The two organizations are very similar in philosophy and function, since they are both dealing with essentially the same problem. The only real difference is in point of view. Both are concerned with the art of coping with addiction to alcohol, and both offer parallel programs of support and information leading to the personal growth of the individuals involved, so that they may recover from the damage done to them by the addictive drinking, and then move on toward greater personal fulfillment and happiness in their lives.

For somewhat different reasons, you who have a special interest in an addictive drinker suffer most of the same damaging degrees of fear, frustration, shame, and anger that the addictive drinker suffers. For you, too, there is terrible loneliness, a progressive withdrawal from many of the once familiar and enjoyable social contacts that made life worthwhile, loss of self-esteem and personal confidence, and a deep sense of being the innocent victim of other people (the drinker, in particular) and a vicious, uncaring fate. There is a similar kind of vicious stigma to suffer and a similar sense of being caught in a steel trap of unique circumstances from which there seems to be no escape. In the process you have developed the same kind of negative attitudes that are destroying your drinker. And as the drinking gets worse and worse, month by month, year by year, your bitterness, anger, frustration and sense of total helplessness and desperation increase in direct proportion. We have said that addictive drinking is invariably a progressive illness. We can now add a significant sentence, "Addictive drinking is invariably a progressive illness for the addictive drinker and for those who love him or her as well." This is why addictive drinking is called "the family illness."

We have noted in the text that you (if you are the drinker's spouse) suffer psychological denial of the reality of the addictive drinking problem as does the drinker, but that the denial is not so deep for you, allowing you to see the reality much sooner than the drinker. However, you also suffer another kind of denial, denial of the seriousness of the psychological effects of the addictive drinking on yourself. The progress of your illness is every bit as gradual and as subtle as it is in the case of the drinker, and it is just as difficult for you to recognize once it has reached serious proportions as it is for the drinker. (In fact, it is my opinion, after working with hundreds of mates of addictive drinkers, that it is considerably harder for them to see than it is for the drinker.) After all, however deep the drinker's denial, he cannot avoid recognizing the fact that something is seriously wrong when he can't control his drinking—frequently having blackouts (i.e., not remembering everything during a drinking bout), being embarrassed, getting into trouble, and suffering the misery of withdrawal every time he stops drinking for any significant period of time. You probably see no sign of illness at all in your own situation. In fact, you will say, the opposite appears to be true. You have gradually assumed more and more of the drinker's responsibilities, as he becomes less and less able to handle them, while continuing to carry all of your own. As a result, you feel that you are functioning far more efficiently as a person than you ever did before.

That being the case, how can anyone suggest that you are incapacitated in any way? It seems absurd. This is why your denial of the reality of your illness is far more difficult to break through than that of the drinker himself. Ask any counselor in the field, and he or she will tell you the same thing. It is the single most difficult problem we have in the alcohol addiction treatment field, and one of the most vital, because we know from long and painful experience that if we fail here, and we do more often than not, the odds against recovery for the addictive drinker go much higher, and divorce becomes almost a certainty if he does make it, since the drinker will grow in positive ways, while the spouse remains behind, as negative and bitter as ever. This is the real cause of so many of the tragedies, so many of the failures to recover, so many of the divorces. Isn't it ironic that this should be so, that it should be you yourself who kills the best chance for your spouse's recovery and are the direct cause of the divorce, while honestly believing that it's all the fault of your drinker. It's ironic and so very, very sad.

Whether you can accept the above or not, it is quite certain that you feel terribly alone in your apparently hopeless situation, that you have racked your brain for years to find a solution, tried everything you could think of, and failed totally, that you often feel completely defeated, a failure, and so desperate that you, too, may sometimes wonder about your sanity. If you would like to do something about that, why not consider the way which has been found most successful by people like yourself?

Alanon can give you some peace of mind by relieving your sense of loneliness and desperation. It can give you some understanding of what addictive drinking is all about, and answers as to how you can do something constructive and positive about yourself and the problem. It can give you hope and a sense of direction. In Alanon you will soon see that your problems are in no way unique, as you may have thought, and will learn that they are not insoluble after all. Here you can talk openly and honestly about your feelings and problems with people who not only understand perfectly, because they have been where you are, but also can offer sound answers to your questions, answers that years of practical experience have shown to work. Here you can begin to grow as a person, so that you will be in the best possible position to help your loved one recover and grow with you, or at least to recover yourself, so that you can handle whatever is required of you to build a new life if, in spite of everything, your addictive drinker is unable to achieve recovery.

I could offer you a list of reasons why many people never go to Alanon or are turned off by it after one or more meetings, as I did in the case of A.A., but there is not really much point in doing so. The facts are essentially the same in both cases. Far more people in your situation are helped by Alanon to find peace of mind, recovery for themselves and their immediate family, and happiness than are helped to do so by all other specialist counselors and institutions added together.

Of course, there will be things about Alanon that you may not like. It is an organization of people, and people are not perfect. It can be said with equal truth to you as I said it to the addictive drinker: If you want to save your life and happiness from this terrible, life-destroying scourge, *you must be willing to do anything whatsoever to achieve that goal.* Experience has shown over and over that anything less than total commitment usually ends in failure for the spouse of the addictive drinker, too. If you were drowning, which would you choose, a bottle cork or a nice big life preserver? Alanon is the life preserver and the odds are that you will drown without it. It is really a double life preserver; your loved one may drown, too, if you don't reach out for it, so that you will learn how to change your behavior, so as not to increase your drinker's stress from now on. The choice is yours, and as we have said, recovery is a matter of making intelligent choices. That applies to everyone involved in this deadly business.

For a variety of reasons, there are many more women in Alanon than men. (This is not because there are proportionately more male addictive drinkers than female ones.) As a result, a man going to his first Alanon meeting may feel a bit uncomfortable. It is much harder for some men to open up and discuss their fears, feelings of hopelessness, and desperation. I suspect it is all tied up with the ideas we were taught in our culture that a man doesn't cry, doesn't admit to being afraid, and shows weakness when he asks for help (especially from women, of all things!). Men are the "solid rocks," or so they are conditioned to believe that they must pretend to be, the ones who always know what to do and how to do it, who must "meet any foe," however horrendous it may be. If this is a problem with you, it may be that your denial of your own vulnerability, your viewing a group of women as less than a group of persons, or your general uncomfortableness in group situations will change as you get into your own personal growth. Until that time, you can go to your first meeting prepared to be uncomfortable. Or you can seek out stag Alanon meetings (in many of the larger cities). If there isn't one in your town, there is nothing to stop you from contacting the local Alanon group for books and information as to how to go about starting a stag group. By so doing, you may solve your own problems, find some great new friends, and perform a significant service in helping a lot of other men who are too shy at this point to discuss their problem in a mixed crowd. At some point, though, I would suggest you get the benefits that are to be had by joining an Alanon group that has members with wider experience than yours.

As I have said, the first goal is recovery, which means the process of putting oneself and one's life back together to the point at which you are able to function in all areas at least as well as you did prior to the onset of the drinking problem in your life. This is true for both you and your drinker. At that point you can be said to have *recovered* the lost ground. It might seem that recovery does not apply to you, since presumably you were well before the drinking problem began to affect you. However, life is a growth process. If the drinking problem had not occurred, it is reasonable to assume that you would have continued to grow and mature in the normal way; but the drinking problem did occur, and you did not grow and mature in the normal way. Instead, you went backward, growing negatively when you should have been going forward, growing positively. Thus, recovery brings you only to the point at which you were, not the point to which you would have grown during the drinking period, had it not occurred. Therefore, since no one can "recover" that which he never had in the first place, and since both the drinker and you have been deprived of the opportunity for normal growth—for a considerable period of time, one way or another—both will profit by entering upon a program of growth designed to carry you from the first day that one or both decided to do something about the problem to the point of recovery to the original level, then on to the level of growth and maturity that you both should have achieved, and finally to higher and higher levels that are rarely achieved, even by people who have never had such a problem at all.

It comes down to this: You can change the most terrifying, soul-grinding defeat of your life into a major victory, which, at its upper limits, becomes truly transcendental. This is the ultimate victory over addictive drinking and over life itself, the highest purpose of man. This is heroic victory. I am a practical, down-to-earth human being, despite the "transcendental victory over life" talk, who was trying to build career, family, and self higher, better—just like you—and I was drinking to the point of insanity. Then I started bumbling my way back on the long, long road to recovery and well-being. I got there, finally, and then I found myself still moving on into the lower levels of higher experience, where I find myself today. It is still happening for me, as I write this, and I know it can happen for you.

BRINGING YOUR DRINKER TO SEEK HELP NOW

It is a common idea among A.A. people that there is no real way to help an addictive drinker "until he is ready." Over and over, they have seen a person come to one meeting, or even quite a few, and then go back to his old drinking life for months, years, or the rest of his life. "He just wasn't ready" is the comment. But what is "ready"? "Ready" is a state of mind, reached when the individual, in spite of his denial, is finally forced to face the reality of his situation by the circumstances surrounding him. In the past, when no one had any practical idea as to what to do to help an addictive drinker, the illness progressed until the individual had lost everything, including his self-respect and his health. Finally he died. When A.A. first began, it was believed by A.A. members that an addictive drinker could not be helped until he had reached this ultimate "bottom," which preceded death. Only then was he "ready." They accepted no one else for this reason. But as time passed, and word that A.A. could help spread, more and more people began to knock on A.A.'s door who had not quite reached the lowest levels of personal disintegration, but who sounded convincingly ready for help. One by one, a few were accepted and began to recover. It was obvious then that bottom was not necessarily the cellar. It could occur sooner in some cases. More time passed; it soon became apparent that bottom came for some people, not only just above the cellar, but at the level of the first floor, the second, the third, and in a very few cases, it occurred at the penthouse level. As a result, today in A.A. it is common to meet well-dressed, affluent, charming people who have never lost much of anything. These are the "high bottom" drunks. (Today one needs only a "desire to stop drinking" to be accepted in A.A.)

If bottom occurs so much earlier for some than for others, one would assume that there must be a reason. There is. Bottom, high or low, occurs only when, and not until, two things happen: (1) The individual, in spite of denial, is forced to face the reality of his situation when the circumstances surrounding him become so terrible and/or so clear that they can no longer be rationalized or denied. At this point, he is ready for help. (2) The individual knows or finds out that it is possible to get well, and that there are people with the necessary expertise and facilities to help him. At this point, he is "ready" to take action.

It follows that if the illness is left to run its normal course in the addictive drinker and his family, bottom will usually be a long time coming, and when it is a long time coming, it is usually low. If, however, the people around the drinker, the people who are most concerned about his welfare and most important to him, take concerted action to see that he becomes fully aware of the circumstances surrounding him, allowing him no chance to avoid or sidestep a single serious aspect of it, bottom for him will occur then or very shortly, and it will be a far higher bottom than it would have been otherwise. Of course, the bottom (personal crisis) must be brought about with skill, love, and careful planning or it will not be successful.

The people presently achieving the greatest success in orchestrating and handling this business of bringing about what might be called therapeutic personal crisis are the Industrial Alcoholism Counselors, with the help of specialized people and services. Here is a dramatic example of how some of them go about it.

Careful records are kept—records of Monday-morning absences, frequency and kinds of illness causing absence from work, accidents involving the individual, both on and off the job. Supervisors and administrators are required to keep an eye out for losses in productivity and efficiency, especially if they show a continuing pattern in a downward direction. By careful monitoring of this data, it is easy to pick out those employees—men and women—who are in trouble. Of course, the trouble may not be addictive drinking. It may be other drugs, serious family problems, real physical illness, or something else. However, the specific cause of the problem is not hard to find once attention is focused on the individual and further information is gained through discreet questioning and observation.

Once the addictive drinking has been clearly established, the second act of the play begins. Let us assume here that the drinker is male. The Industrial Alcoholism specialist, representing the company, calls upon the employee's wife or arranges a private interview with her. He explains the situation: what the company has found, what the company is willing to do to keep from losing a valued employee, and what the company hopes family and friends will be willing to do to help. Then, with the wife's help, he arranges for the other important people in the drinker's life to play their parts. Act 3 follows.

One day at work the drinker receives a call from the office to come to such and such a room. No explanation is offered. He walks into the room and finds, seated in a circle, most of the people who are closest to him: his wife, his children (if they are old enough), his best friend (who is not an addictive drinker himself), his minister, perhaps his doctor, his parents, and his boss. He is asked to sit down, and then it begins. Going around the circle, each person, having come prepared for this, tells him, with concern and love, but pulling no punches, exactly how the drinking behavior affects him, and what he has decided to do about it. Typically, the drinker hears this: his older daughter says she can no longer stand to see her father in that condition, will no longer be embarrassed by him when she brings home a friend, and has taken an apartment in town. His mother, weeping, tells him that she knows it is not his fault that he drinks, but that she will never see him again until he stops, because it is just too painful for her. His friend says that he thinks he is the greatest guy he ever met, but when drunk he is a complete bore, and no longer welcome in his home if he has had even one drink. His wife outlines what life has been like for her over the past months or years, and announces that she has filed for divorce, which she will carry out unless he gets help for his problem immediately. Finally, his boss tells him how valuable he has been to the company, but adds that, in his present condition, he is a liability and will be fired as of now unless he agrees to accept therapy. He may even specify the amount of therapy required, and make it clear that further drinking, even off the job, will be cause for instant termination.

As you can well imagine, the tremendous shock of such a sudden confrontation almost invariably results in a personal crisis, with frequent breakdown into weeping and fervent promises of immediate efforts to recover. Both are usually sincere, and the individual enters therapy. However, this is not the last act of the play, with the hero walking off bravely into the sunset of happy future sobriety. As we have seen, the moment of decision to recover is the moment when the curtain goes up for an entirely new and different play—that of recovery itself. However, we are talking about the problem of getting the drinker to the point of seeking help.

Whether or not your drinker's employer has an Industrial Alcoholism Counselor on its staff—or if your drinker is self-employed or a housewife—intervention with a counselor's advice must occur as soon as possible. (And even while you work with such a special counselor, I recommend strongly that you go to Alanon for the vital help it offers you directly.)

One thing that will relieve your drinker's mind greatly: his high compulsion will be *brought down to willpower-controllable levels within two hours of his entry into a recovery group.* (For how this works, see pages 82–84 for compulsion-reduction in A.A. and pages 260–262 for other groups.)

You begin by attending Alanon regularly, to achieve some peace of mind and a better understanding of what it is necessary to know about addictive drinking and recovery if you are to prepare yourself emotionally to carry out an intervention. During this same initial period you learn that you are not responsible for the drinking, except insofar as your efforts to stop it and your own negative attitudes caused by the drinking have had the opposite effect, quite unbeknownst to you. Thus, your guilt feelings are removed. There is more. The total effect is to give you confidence in yourself and serenity, which are essential if you are to be successful in your endeavor to bring the drinker to the point of asking for help. The actual program used to achieve this end will have to be tailored to your particular situation, but the principles are essentially the same in all cases.

First, you stop all actions of yours that have been supporting the drinking, usually after explaining what you are going to do and why to the drinker, at a time when he is sober and in as relaxed a mood as possible. At this time you tell him that you are all through trying to get him to stop drinking, that you now realize that it is his business to decide whether he drinks or not, not yours. You then go on to say that you have decided that the drinking is making your life so miserable that you are convinced that the time is not far off when you will have to leave him, since, in spite of your love for him, you cannot go on living this way much longer. You explain in some detail what you have decided to do from that moment on. You will not buy him alcohol in any form, but you will not hide or pour down the sink what he buys. You and the children will eat at the normal mealtimes, whether he is at home or not, and if he has been drinking, you will prepare no special meals for him at other times. You love and want to be with him, but not when he is or has been drinking. At such times you will leave him alone, and leave the house if he insists on your attention while under the influence. In future, if the plant or office calls when he is absent from work because of a hangover, being out drinking, or too drunk to go to work, you will no longer cover for him. You say that, from now on, if you know he is out drinking, you will tell them that when they call, and ask him what he wants you to do when he is home. Either you will tell them his condition when they call, or you will call him to the phone, whatever his condition, and let him handle it any way he wants. It's his decision. In order to convince their husband that they are absolutely determined in all of this, many wives announce, at the same time, that they have enrolled in some educational or training program to prepare them to support themselves and their children in the event that he does not decide to get help to stop drinking. Others file for divorce for the same reason, not because they necessarily want one. (However, if you do this, be ready to go through with it, or he may sense that you don't mean it.)

The details you have decided upon will vary in each case, but two things are absolutely required if you are to have any hope of success: (1) There must be no bitterness or sense that you are angry and choosing to do all these things out of spite or revenge. The whole tone must be that you love him very much and are taking these actions only because there is no longer an alternative for you, since you have learned that this is the only way in which you can hope to help him and protect your own future and that of the children. No matter how he responds, and he will usually try everything, you do not argue, and you do not get angry. Your one and only purpose in this discussion is to state the position you have chosen to take and to do everything possible to convince him that your decision is final, that nothing he can do or say will change it, and this must be so. "This is it," as they say in the war movies, for him and for you. (2) All this is very difficult for a person to do, and there is the distinct possibility that such a confrontation will trigger the drinker to physical violence. You will be able to judge the likelihood of this better than anyone else.

Whether you expect violence or not, it is often much safer and more effective to use a variety of the Industrial Confrontation described above. If the wife alone tries this confrontation, she has no support and may well fail to carry it through, because emotions run high in such a situation and the highest resolve can fail. Also, when it is the wife alone, it is much easier for the drinker to believe that she is taking these decisions out of anger, bitterness, and desire for revenge, however well she tries to remain calm and emphasize that she is doing this for love of him and for self-preservation. If possible, it is usually much wiser and more effective if the confrontation is made by a whole group of people at once, those closest to him: wife, older children, parents, brothers and sisters, best friend, business partner (if he is also a friend), etc. These others can support the wife's position, prevent physical violence, and, by their number, lend far greater importance to the seriousness of the situation and the reality and rightness of the decisions taken. After all, five or ten concerned people, all united behind a decision, are far more convincing and difficult to sway from that position than one lone woman (or man), who is, necessarily, deeply involved emotionally. Also, any effort on the drinker's part to find motives of anger, bitterness, and revenge will be more effectively discouraged and spread out over the whole group instead of being concentrated on the wife or husband alone.

There is a third alternative, described in an excellent book, *Helping Your Alcoholic Before He or She Hits Bottom*, by Roque Fajardo. In this book a much milder approach is described in detail. It is my own feeling that this is the best way to begin. I think it is also the easiest and kindest. The book contains step-by-step directions for putting steadily increasing pressure on the drinker to go for help, starting with the mildest possible approach and building gradually toward the sort of hard confrontation described above. Since it is vital for success that your drinker realize that, however you exert pressure on him, it is done out of love, beginning this way may take more time, but I think it is well worth it.

You may well have noted in all of the above that there is no talk of reasoning with the drinker. We are talking about coercion tactics pure and simple. Can a person be coerced into seeking help and working hard to achieve recovery? The answer is not only yes. It is, "Yes, there is no other way." Addictive drinkers, because of denial, cannot see the reality of their situation until the denial is smashed at a time of personal crisis. It makes no difference whether the crisis is finally brought about more or less by chance as a result of the steadily worsening circumstances that accompany the inevitable progress of illness, by his vivid imagination, which shows him clearly where he is going, or on purpose by those who love and are concerned for him. The factors are the same.

It is true that coercion is only effective with an addictive drinker in the rarest of cases when it is used in the form of punishment, with neither understanding nor love, as in the case of the drinker who is jailed for drunkenness.

Coercion only works when it comes in the form of the drinker's own recognition of the desperate nature of the situation he is in, however that comes about, and when he knows, in addition, that effective help is available to him from people who really care, understand, and have the necessary expertise. The difference here is that we are talking about positive coercion with love, not the old-style negative coercion involving fear and degradation. Fear is, at the same time, the basic cause of the problem and the basic motivation for recovery. However, it can function as the basic motivation for recovery only when it is combined with hope, love, and the necessary information. Anger, bitterness, and revenge, whether exhibited by wife, boss, or society, offer the kiss of death to any hope for recovery from addictive drinking. There is no question about that.

PROS AND CONS OF TEAM RECOVERY

Once your drinker has begun his recovery program, an entirely new play begins, as noted before, and it is essential that you be aware of certain things from the beginning if you are to be a part of the solution, rather than a continuing part of the problem. False pride is one key element.

False pride is always the result of ignorance or of insecurity and lack of self-confidence. In the latter case, it is a rigid assumption of one's own absolute rightness in holding to a certain position, supported by every argument at one's command, to cover up and prevent the individual from having to face an unpleasant fact about himself, or to make it unnecessary for him to face the need to do something he regards as unpleasant. It is as common a problem in the recovery of the non-addictive partner as it is in that of the drinker himself, and it is a serious problem indeed, so serious, in fact, that it can easily block you very effectively from taking some of the most vital steps in the recovery of your loved one and yourself. Let's look at a typical situation, assuming here that the drinker is a woman.

The wife has joined A.A. (or other group therapy) and asks her husband to go to open meetings with her. She also tells him that she understands that Alanon can help him to understand addictive drinking and the recovery process much better, so that he will be able to assist in her recovery. Of course, she wants him to go. The husband is against doing either of these things. He has read several books on one or more phases of the alcohol addiction problem and, perhaps, talked once or twice with a doctor, psychiatrist, or other apparent authority on the subject. As a result, he assumes that he knows all he needs to know, that it's her problem, not his, and that he has no responsibility to become an active participant in her recovery program.

In fact, his refusal to attend open meetings of A.A. or Alanon is based on factors that have nothing to do with the above. First, he cannot accept the idea that he is in any way responsible, since she was the one who chose to drink and is, therefore, the only one responsible for the results and, logically, for her own recovery. Second, he does not understand the need for changed attitudes and behavior on his part as key factors that can make the difference between success and failure in his wife's recovery efforts. Third, he is entirely unaware of, or cannot accept, the fact that the illness has affected him to such an extent that he needs a recovery program fully as much as his wife, if he is to return to a happy, productive life, whether his wife makes it or not. Finally, he has suffered so much embarrassment and shame as a result of the stigma that he and society place on the addictive drinker and anyone closely associated with her that he cannot bear the idea of being seen at meetings of either organization, of associating with ex-drunks or their husbands and wives. He doesn't want to think about the whole miserable business, let alone listen to his wife talk about it openly in front of other people, or have to do the same himself. Such is the effect of denial. Such is the effect of social stigma, and the whole sorry business can be summed up in two words: "false pride."

He is still so angry, bitter, and vengeful, so lacking in self-confidence, as a result of his total failure to force or beguile his wife into stopping drinking, so full of fears, with which he has been living as helpless victim for years, that his only defense and protection is the conviction that it was and is all her fault and responsibility, and that everything he has done and is doing is absolutely right and proper. He is as afraid to look deeply into himself to see what is really there as she is.

It is understandable that he should have false pride in abundance, and that he should be emotionally and spiritually exhausted after the long ordeal. This is one of the primary reasons for Alanon's existence, to offer him emotional and spiritual balm to ease his suffering and to give him hope and strength with which to renew the battle. And, just as the addictive drinker cannot hope to conquer her addiction alone, he, too, must find the strength and hope that only others who have been through the same fire can give.

If resentment and false pride are two of the greatest enemies of the drinker who wants to recover, they are equally deadly enemies for her mate, or anyone else in her immediate family. Winning the battle over false pride and resentment is a hard thing to do, but if you can find the courage to do it, you will have a good chance of saving your marriage, of guaranteeing your spouse's recovery, and of finding peace of mind and joy in your life again. If you cannot find that courage, the prospect is grim indeed in all three areas. If you can do it, you will have earned a feeling of real pride and self-respect.

Since you both have been seriously damaged by the illness and both need to work for each other's and your own recovery, the whole affair should be a team operation, a process of learning, sharing, and growing together out of chaos into joy. It requires tremendous effort from both and great patience, but if you are working together toward a common goal, attending open meetings of A.A. or other therapy groups together, reading the same self-help books and discussing them together, working out your joint answers to the Inventories (Situation and Personal) and the Early Recovery Plan in this book—after each has done them separately, while supporting each other every step of the way when either one is down, frightened, confused, or discouraged, you will soon find that you are communicating again and loving again—in depths you have never experienced before.

In your efforts to assist each other, there is often a tendency to try to help by removing the necessity for your spouse to make his own decision (a serious mistake); for example, by arranging ahead of time that the dry drinker will be offered only soft drinks at a party or by assuming all responsibility for solving family problems, so that your spouse need not worry. Making his own decisions is vital for everyone in recovery, as it is for you in yours. Let him do so.

When there is no effort at team recovery on the part of either husband or wife, one or both are more than likely to fail, and divorce is almost a foregone conclusion. But if you grow together, each sharing and noting the progress of the other and commenting now and then to show that recognition, you each help the other to gain hope, confidence, and self-esteem. And it gets to be more fun and less work all the way along, once it gets properly rolling. Team recovery, when both partners really work at it, is the fastest, most effective, and most rewarding kind.

AFTERWORD

I can hear you, but can you hear me? As a recovered addictive drinker and an alcohol addiction counselor, I have often described my job as being like that of the wagon-train scout who rode out ahead of the wagons to find passes through the otherwise impassable mountains. It is not that I am an authority in the accepted sense. All I can do is tell you that I wandered through many dark valleys, only to find that they led nowhere, followed promising trails that too often petered out to nothing, and finally, after endless search and suffering, found paths through the terrible, frozen mountains to the sunny slopes of California. I then rode back to the wagon train to report what I had found. This book is my report.

I have given my "report to the wagon train" to hundreds of addictive drinkers, as other recovered-addict counselors do every day, and I can report to you that, however long we have been in this work, one fact never ceases to amaze and frustrate us, to the point that many have either returned to drinking or left the profession in self-defense.

When you come to me to talk about "your little drinking problem," I listen to your story, feel the tension and fear behind your words, and hear an old, old story, told with a thousand variations, but always monotonously the same, the addictive drinker's story of denial. Yes, I hear you loud and clear. The problem is that you do not hear me, your would-be counselor. No matter how reassuring my report, no matter how carefully I choose my words to describe the wonderful trails and passes we ex-drunk counselors have found, I see a blankness behind your eyes, and I know that you are hearing my words but you are not accepting them. You know the mountains are there, and you are terrified of trying to cross them alone, as you may well have been trying to do for years, but there is something in you that keeps saying, "The trails he describes sound very rough, the passes very high. There must be a better, easier trail and a lower pass, which I will surely find if I just keep on looking," and you go away to look again for that easier trail. Perhaps you try one of my recommended trails for a little while, but soon you're off on your own again, wandering in the wilderness of bars and bottles. Then, perhaps, you come back in six months or a year to hear again about those rough trails and those high passes. This time you are much worse off from your long wandering in the wilderness, and perhaps now are willing to go a little farther along the recommended trails and passes. Some come back and back and back, and never follow them all the way to sunny California. Some do the second time or the third, and a very few do it the first time.

What will you choose to do? You can ride day and night, you can perform miracles of endurance and courage, but the killer mountains are still there, and you are a greenhorn. The only way to California for you is with the wagon train, along the rough trails and over the high passes. It's hard, but not so hard as the uncharted route which leads forever down to the final oblivion. So listen, please, and join the wagon train. California is a very nice place!

RECOMMENDED READING LIST OF SELF-HELP BOOKS

Abell, Richard G., M.D., with Corlis Wilber Abell. *Own Your Own Life.* New York: Berkley, 1979. Good on how one goes about changing oneself. Explains Transactional Analysis and Gestalt therapies well.

Alberti, Robert E., Ph.D., and Michael Emmons, Ph.D. *Stand Up, Speak Out, Talk Back!* New York: Pocket Books, 1975. How to become more assertive, less shy.

Beecher, Willard and Marguerite. *Beyond Success and Failure.* New York: Pocket Books, 1971. About dependence, people-pleasing, the desire for recognition.

Benson, Herbert, M.D., and Miriam Z. Klipper. *The Relaxation Response.* New York: Avon Books, 1976. Will help you understand better the origins of physical and psychological (emotional) stress and its relationship to other illnesses besides addictive drinking. You may also wish to practice the Relaxation Response to reduce your tension level.

Bry, Adelaide. *How to Get Angry without Feeling Guilty.* New York: New American Library, 1977. Lists at least ten specific ways of dealing with anger of different kinds.

Cammer, Leonard, M.D. *Freedom from Compulsion.* New York: Pocket Books, 1977. This psychiatrist writes in good clear English, not jargon, and offers especially useful and practical insights into the causes, kinds, and appropriate treatments for compulsive behavior, including perfectionism and other problems so common among addictive drinkers.

Dyer, Dr. Wayne W. *Your Erroneous Zones*. New York: Avon Books, 1977. Excellent. One of the best. Covers the emotional waterfront.

Fast, Julius. *Creative Coping*. New York: Harper & Row, 1977. About coping with reality more effectively in a variety of ways. Practical and down-to-earth.

Frankl, Viktor E., M.D. *Man's Search for Meaning*. New York: Pocket Books, 1975. About finding your purpose in life.

Fromm, Erich. *The Art of Loving*. New York: Harper & Row, 1974. One man's fine perception of what love is all about.

Glasser, William, M.D. *The Identity Society*. New York: Harper & Row, 1975. An excellent explanation of the causes of behavioral aberrations and how they can be removed or reduced.

———. *Reality Therapy*. New York: Harper & Row, 1965. An excellent description of his therapy.

Harris, Thomas, M.D. *I'm O.K., You're O.K.* New York: Avon Books, 1976. All about improving your self-image and more effective communication; Transactional Analysis explained and elaborated.

Lair, Jess. *I'm Not Much, Baby, but I'm All I've Got*. New York: Fawcett, 1978. How to gain more self-confidence and a better self-image.

Maltz, Maxwell, M.D. *Five Minutes to Happiness*. New York: Ace Books, 1977. How to program or reprogram your mental computer. Suggest a reading of his book *Psycho-Cybernetics* first.

———. *The Magic Power of Self-Image Psychology*. New Jersey: Prentice-Hall, 1964. Very helpful in offering specific ways to become more self-aware and improve your own self-image.

———. *Psycho-Cybernetics*. New York: Pocket Books, 1970. Explains the whole concept of the mental computer; also an explanation of a problem-solving technique that I have used with remarkable effect on numerous occasions.

Newman, Mildred, and Bernard Berkowitz. *How to Be Your Own Best Friend.* New York: Ballantine, 1974.

Ringer, Robert J. *Looking Out for No. 1.* New York: Fawcett Crest Books, 1978. Excellent help in developing a better self-image and more self-confidence.

Rogers, Carl. *On Becoming a Person.* New York: Houghton Mifflin, 1970. Fine on the subject and very readable.

Seabury, David. *The Art of Selfishness.* New York: Pocket Books, 1979. Deals with getting rid of guilt feelings and reducing stress; can help you change some basic attitudes about yourself.

Smith, Manuel J., Ph.D. *When I Say No, I Feel Guilty.* New York: Bantam Books, 1975. Another explanation of how to become more assertive, less shy.

Zimbardo, Philip C., Ph.D. *Shyness.* New York: Jove, 1978. The best I've found on shyness. You will find yourself in here.

Books Especially for Those Who Love an Addictive Drinker

Cooper, J. T., M.D., with Paul Hagan. *Doctor Cooper's Fabulous Fructose Diet.* New York: Fawcett Crest, 1979.

Fajardo, Roque. *Helping Your Alcoholic Before He or She Hits Bottom.* New York: Crown, 1976.

Maxwell, Ruth. *The Booze Battle: A Common Sense Approach That Works.* New York: Praeger, 1976.

Wegscheider, Sharon. *Another Chance.* Palo Alto, CA: Science and Behavior Books, 1981.

Woititz, Janet G. *Marriage on the Rocks: How to Live with an Alcoholic.* New York: Delacorte, 1979.

INDEX